This crisply edited volume addresses compelling questions concerning the transformation of India's economy: Why does development-induced displacement generate differing levels – and types – of political resistance? To what extent have socalled 'tribal' communities been able to realize new rights accorded to them? How have India's grassroots democratic institutions, and its diverse array of social movements, responded to the challenges posed by 'extractive' industries, particularly mining? Some chapters address contemporary cases and confine themselves to a single region; others are broader in scope, temporally or geographically. Though diverse in their perspectives and preoccupations, the authors share one indispensable trait: they probe ambiguities, rather than wishing them away.

Rob Jenkins, *Professor of Political Science, Hunter College & The Graduate Center, City University of New York (CUNY), USA*

The fast growing economy in India is somewhat of a paradox. The growth is in the service sector and in the building industry, not in manufacture, not in mineral production. Conscious of this, the Indian State and Corporate Capital now try to exploit every possible natural resource for their industrial production and exports.

For long the need for state land expropriation was beyond questioning. Now it is increasingly contested by people threatened by loss of land and forest. With education and political practicing of citizens' democratic rights, and with laws to protect forest people, people now increasingly fight back with all possible means, legal, political, non-violent or even violent. India's democracy is deepening and broadening bit by bit but not without many obstacles.

This book gives a balanced account of ground realities in many concrete case studies. It helps us to grasp the odds of a sustainable development and not just devastating destruction of human lives and of nature.

Staffan Lindberg, *Professor Emeritus of Sociology, Lund University, Sweden*

India's quest to industrialize has been a fraught one. This collection of essays by a new generation of scholarship ably captures the complicated plots and troubling narratives about popular resistance, dispossession, displacement, Special Economic Zones and the consequences of extractive industries. Industrialization, however, as the editors are keen to remind us, also announces new beginnings and debates for democracy, livelihoods and alternative imaginations over what constitutes meaningful development. Critiques and challenges are not without hope. This is a very significant contribution, refreshing, seminal, empirically rich and tells us, above all else, that environmental politics and the everyday worlds of the disempowered give us a full ring side view into how neo-liberal economic growth uncurls on the ground.

Rohan D'Souza, *Graduate School of Asian and African Area Studies, Kyoto University, Japan*. Author of *Drowned and Dammed: Colonial Capitalism and Flood Control in Eastern India* (2006)

As the slogan of 'Make in India' is amplified across the country, it sets in motion fresh waves of land alienation, cultural dispossession and ecological devastation. *Industrialising Rural India* offers a close and nuanced analysis of these processes, placing them within the nation's long engagement with capital-intensive development and its current quest for global power. Attentive to the diversity of temporal and spatial trajectories, this important collection helps us understand the complexities of state-led capitalism and appreciate all the more the resistance it encounters on the ground. Recommended reading for everyone interested in Indian political economy and ecology.

Amita Baviskar, *Professor. Institute of E   India*

Industrialising Rural India

Rapid industrialisation is promoted by many as the most feasible way of rejuvenating the Indian economy, and as a way of generating employment on a large scale. At the same time, the transfer of land from rural communities and indigenous groups for industrial parks, mining, or Special Economic Zones has emerged as perhaps the most explosive issue in India over the past decade. *Industrialising Rural India* sheds light on crucial political and social dynamics that are unfolding today as India seeks to accelerate its industrial growth.

The volume examines key aspects that are implicated in current processes of industrialisation in rural India, including the evolution of industrial and related policies; the contested role of land transfers, dispossession, and the destruction of the natural resource base more generally; and the popular resistance against industrial projects, extractive industries and Special Economic Zones. Combining the work of scholars long established in their respective fields with the refreshing approach of younger scholars, *Industrialising Rural India* seeks to chart new ways in the study of contemporary industrialisation and its associated challenges in India.

Kenneth Bo Nielsen is a Postdoctoral Research Fellow at the Department of Sociology at the University of Bergen, Norway.

Patrik Oskarsson is a Researcher at the Department of Rural and Urban Development, Swedish University of Agricultural Sciences, Uppsala, Sweden.

Routledge Studies of the Extractive Industries and Sustainable Development

African Artisanal Mining from the Inside Out
Access, norms and power in Congo's gold sector
Sarah Geenan

Mountain Movers
Mining, sustainability and the agents of change
Daniel M. Franks

Responsible Mining
Key concepts for industry integrity
Sara Bice

Mining in Latin America
Critical approaches to the new extraction
Edited by Kalowatie Deonandan and Michael L. Dougherty

Industrialising Rural India
Land, policy and resistance
Edited by Kenneth Bo Nielsen and Patrik Oskarsson

www.routledge.com/series/REISD

Industrialising Rural India

Land, policy and resistance

Edited by Kenneth Bo Nielsen and
Patrik Oskarsson

Routledge
Taylor & Francis Group

LONDON AND NEW YORK

First published 2017
by Routledge
2 Park Square, Milton Park, Abingdon, Oxon OX14 4RN

and by Routledge
711 Third Avenue, New York, NY 10017

First issued in paperback 2018

Routledge is an imprint of the Taylor & Francis Group, an informa business

British Library Cataloguing-in-Publication Data
A catalogue record for this book is available from the British Library

Library of Congress Cataloging-in-Publication Data
Names: Oskarsson, Patrik, editor. | Nielsen, Kenneth Bo, editor.
Title: Industrialising rural India : land, policy and resistance / edited by Patrik Oskarsson and Kenneth Bo Nielsen.
Description: London ; New York : Routledge, 2017. | Includes bibliographical references and index.
Identifiers: LCCN 2016016526| ISBN 9781138936713 (hbk) | ISBN 9781315676678 (ebk)
Subjects: LCSH: Rural development–India. | Industrialization–India. | Land use, Rural–India.
Classification: LCC HN690.Z9 C655327 2017 | DDC 307.1/4120954–dc23
LC record available at https://lccn.loc.gov/2016016526

ISBN 13: 978-1-138-59756-3 (pbk)
ISBN 13: 978-1-138-93671-3 (hbk)

Typeset in Goudy
by Wearset Ltd, Boldon, Tyne and Wear

Contents

viii   *Contents*

Illustrations

Figure

Tables

Contributors

Editors

Kenneth Bo Nielsen is a Postdoctoral Research Fellow at the Department of Sociology, University of Bergen, Norway.

Patrik Oskarsson is a Researcher at the Department of Rural and Urban Development, Swedish University of Agricultural Sciences, Uppsala, Sweden.

Contributing authors

Heather Plumridge Bedi is Assistant Professor at Dickinson College, Pennsylvania, US.

Stein Sundstøl Eriksen is Research Professor at the Norwegian Institute for International Affairs, Norway.

Bengt G. Karlsson is Professor of Social Anthropology at Stockholm University, Sweden.

Kuntala Lahiri-Dutt is a Senior Fellow, Resource Environment and Development Program, Crawford School of Public Policy, ANU College of Asia and the Pacific at The Australian National University, Canberra, Australia.

Sarasij Majumder is Associate Professor of Anthropology and Interdisciplinary Studies, Department of Geography and Anthropology, Kennesaw State University, Atlanta, US.

Jørgen Dige Pedersen is Associate Professor, Department of Political Science, Aarhus University, Denmark.

Prakruti Ramesh is a PhD Fellow at the School of Global Studies, Aarhus University, Denmark.

Siddharth Sareen is a Postdoctoral Fellow at the M.S. Merian – R. Tagore International Centre of Advanced Studies in the Humanities and Social Sciences, New Delhi, India.

Acknowledgements

The idea for this volume has emerged out of the editors' conversations over many years on the subject of industrialisation and resistance in rural West Bengal and Andhra Pradesh in particular, but also in contemporary India more generally. In the spring of 2015 we invited a number of colleagues to reflect on these and related issues at a panel on 'Structural Transformation and Social Conflicts' in India, organised as part of the SASNET international conference on 'Structural Transformation in South Asia', held at Lund University in Sweden in May the same year. Several of the chapters in this volume were presented at this panel, and we are very grateful to both the panellists and the general audience for their comments and suggestions on how to develop our arguments further.

We would like to thank our authors for bearing with our pedantic editorial nit-picking over many months. Special thanks goes to Siddharth Sareen who joined us late in the process, and who worked hard to meet our increasingly inflexible deadlines. Kenneth would also like to thank Sarasij for accepting his invitation to co-author a chapter on Singur. Lastly, we thank Routledge UK for opening its press to us, and the entire editorial team for all their committed work.

Part I

Introduction

1 Industrialising rural India

Patrik Oskarsson and Kenneth Bo Nielsen

The challenge of industrialisation has emerged as one of the most burning issues in India today. With an agrarian crisis believed to be looming large across substantial tracts of India, and with the country's globally renowned IT and ITES sectors incapable of absorbing the large number of workers and migrants seeking a way out of a stagnating rural economy, rapid industrialisation is promoted by many as the quickest and most feasible way of 'moving people out of agriculture' while also rejuvenating an economy that has produced sluggish growth rates over the past several years. Nowhere is this as evident as in the current Indian prime minister Narendra Modi's spirited electoral campaign in the early months of 2014. Promising to transfer his 'Gujarat model' of development – enabled by an investor-friendly and pro-business regime – to the rest of India, Modi successfully captured the imagination of large sections of the Indian population, including the 'neo-middle class' (Jaffrelot 2015), who aspire for upward mobility and an improved quality of life.

At the same time, the transfer of land from marginal rural communities and indigenous groups for industrial parks, mining ventures or Special Economic Zones have undoubtedly been among the most contested issues in India over the past decade. Such contestation has been common enough to generate 'thousands of small wars against land acquisitions' (Levien 2011: 66) across India. As critics have repeatedly pointed out (Banerjee-Guha 2013; Levien 2013; Sampat 2015) the large-scale dispossession, displacement and destruction of rural livelihoods and cultures that have historically accompanied industrialisation processes around the world appear integral also to the kind of development policy currently pursued in India. What Banerjee-Guha calls a new 'multiscalar geopolitics of popular resistance' (Banerjee-Guha 2013: 167) has thus been a close companion to many recent industrial ventures across rural India, even if one takes into account the considerable inter-state variation that exists across India's federal geography.

In *Industrialising Rural India*, we aim to shed light on what we believe are some of the most crucial dynamics and contestations currently at work in present day India. The questions we explore include: How have policymakers sought to strike a balance – over time and across sectors – between the idea that industrialisation is the way ahead for the nation, and the compulsion to protect vulnerable groups unlikely to make a swift 'transition' from peasants to industrial workers? Who benefits and who loses from the current ways in which nature and resources are governed? And who gets to be heard and who is silenced in the uncertain struggles over land and social justice in the context of often top-down industrial change in rural India? In engaging these questions, we focus, first, on the making and remaking of economic and industrial policies over time, and interrogate their impact on rural lives and livelihoods; second, we analyse the consequences for land-dependent rural communities of how nature and society are governed in a context in which industrialisation is being promoted by political interests across the board; and, lastly, we engage with the myriad ways in which India's rich democratic heritage and freedom of expression allows for disagreement and active contestation in a situation in which land transfers for rural and/or extractive industries are altering rural mores and livelihoods. Empirically, we take the reader into an abandoned car factory in rural Bengal and to the coal mines of Meghalaya; to the Adivasi areas in Jharkhand and Odisha, rich in natural resources and minerals; to the scrapped Special Economic Zones in Goa; and on a tour of key policy documents of the postcolonial Indian state. While we have aimed to cover the vast field of industrial development and change in rural India in a broad sense, several chapters focus particularly on new extractive industries (of coal, bauxite, etc.). While this is a reflection of the research agendas of several of our contributors, we also believe that rural industrialisation based on the intensified exploitation of nature represents one of the most important elements of the contemporary moment and that it therefore merits particular attention.

In this introduction we contextualise the questions and cases outlined above, starting with a short overview of the shifting political economy of the Indian state and its industrial policies. We then move on to analyse why resistance to land dispossession for industrial purposes has. increased in recent years. We briefly touch upon the impact so far of the Modi government's policies on industrialisation and eminent domain, before we round off with an overview of the chapters that follow.

Industrialisation and the Indian state

As is well known, India has gradually moved away from the so-called Nehru-Mahalanobis strategy of state-led development of the early post-Independence period. From 1947 onwards, India had aimed at creating self-sufficiency and an economy free from external domination. This was to be achieved through state-led economic planning, carried out (ostensibly) in relative isolation from the partisan squabbles of politics (Chatterjee 1997). The state assumed a central role in the supply-side of the economy by actively pursuing a strategy of rapid import-substitution industrialisation that focused on the building of state-owned industries producing capital goods. This approach was not very dissimilar from what many other newly independent nations attempted throughout the 1950s and 1960s, aiming for a high degree of self-reliance as the foundation of truly independent and socially just nations (Kohli 2004). While clearly inspired by socialist and communist countries the private sector was, however, allowed to live on, even if it was often severely straight-jacketed. In India, a 'license regime' was established to regulate domestic production in accordance with the dictates of planning. For a while, as Pedersen also shows in this volume, this policy rested on solid foundations – there was a near consensus across the board, from industrialists to left-of-centre politicians and radicals, on the need for national development, poverty alleviation, progress, and an interventionist role for the state (Kothari 2005; Ray and Katzenstein 2005).

As Pedersen notes (this volume), in the period of the first three five-year plans, from 1951 to 1966, India's industry grew at a rate never to be achieved again. To a large extent this growth was based upon the establishment of large industrial and infrastructural projects funded by the state. But this accomplishment notwithstanding, the state in India oftentimes emerged more as a regulatory rather than a developmental state (Corbridge and Harriss 2000: 113). And, by the 1970s it had – in spite of respectable industrial growth – largely failed to effect any significant reduction in poverty (Ray and Katzenstein 2005: 7–8); and since poverty reduction was one of the foundations on which the legitimacy of the state-led model of development rested, it lost much of its sheen. The comparatively lacklustre performance of the Indian economy stood in marked contrast to the booming economies emerging in Southeast and East Asia around the same time, adding to the emerging critique of the state-led model of economic development. In particular, critics writing from a (neo)liberal position argued that Indian planning as it had been practised so far combined the worst features of capitalism and socialism (Das 2006), and promoted an economic system that was over-licensed, bureaucratised, inefficient and corrupt (Bhagwati 1993).

While the Indian economy had experienced liberalising economic reforms already in the 1980s, these gathered momentum in the wake of a fiscal crisis in 1991, when India was on the verge of default. Ostensibly to stabilise its economy, India opted for the implementation of a package of structural and economic reforms. Shifting towards what Kohli (2009) has called a pro-business model of development, much of India's industrial licensing system was dismantled and private sector companies allowed to trade in industries that had once been arrogated by state-owned enterprises (see Eriksen, this volume, for further details). In addition, foreign investments in many areas were welcomed in a situation where the state was actively redefining its role in the economic process from that of planner to manager (Kurien 1994: 94; Rudolph and Rudolph 2001b).

The fact that India's economic reform process is commonly referred to as 'liberalisation' often gives rise to associations to 'neoliberalism', under which the market decides on most economic matters, the public sector is privatised, and global economic actors gain influence (Williamson 2008). Yet a number of key features in the Indian reforms experience stand out and set it apart from a model of 'pure' market liberalism. International companies have attempted to invest in

India but have often not been very successful. And while we do find important cases of international investments in the field of rural industrial development – including mining and the processing of minerals – it is by and large Indian big business that has been the main beneficiary of economic reforms; and, importantly, the public sector remains strong (Kohli 2006). In fact, a key factor in the governance of industrialisation in India is the continued crucial importance of the state. Reduced state intervention in controls over export and import licenses have thus come with an increased state-presence elsewhere, including in areas such as land transfers and conversions, and environmental control procedures and clearances (Kohli 2007; Nayyar 2008) that are required to set up industries. As Eriksen shows in this volume, the Indian economy even after more than 25 years of economic reforms remains among the least 'liberal' in the world, when seen in a global, comparative perspective.

Yet although the reform process has proceeded piecemeal – with sectors such as agriculture, mining and retail remaining partially exempt for a longer period – there is little doubt that the broad thrust of the reforms has been to increase the powers of private capital. Indeed, to Chatterjee (2011) and others (Gupta 2012; Gupta and Sivaramakrishnan 2011; Kohli 2009), liberalisation signalled the decisive rise of the corporate capitalist class as *the* dominant group within the state apparatus, increasingly displacing other erstwhile dominant classes such as the rich farmers and the salariat (Bardhan 1984). Today, there is a virtual consensus among all major political parties about the need to prioritise rapid economic growth led by private investment, both domestic and foreign (Chatterjee 2008: 57), evidenced by the fact that successive waves of liberalising reforms have sought to be carried out irrespective of the combination of parties in power in New Delhi (Chandrasekhar 2011; Jenkins 1999). As a corollary of this shift in economic policy and emphasis, the very idea of 'development' has been redefined: As Chandra (2015: 50) has recently argued, business has increasingly acquired the ideological dominance to define what 'development' means in India today, reducing it to a 'shorthand for a package of vaguely defined terms including "urbanisation", "industrialisation", and "infrastructure creation", in which it is assumed that the private sector will take the lead'. Yet at the same time, business has not yet fully acquired a matching political dominance that allows it to pursue this agenda with full consent or compliance. This tension is at the heart of many current contestations over land, natural resources and industrial development in India today, and we explore it further in the next section.

Land acquisitions and resistance

We have in recent years, as noted above, seen more and more activities come to be included among activities seen as 'development', including the acquisition and allocation of land by governments in favour of profit-making, private industries (Reddy and Reddy 2007: 3325) and the setting up of Special Economic Zones (SEZ) with significant exemptions from regular legislation in a range of areas (see Bedi, this volume). A rapid increase in mining and the exploitation of natural resources such as coal, iron and bauxite on a large scale by private and public companies has also been an integral component of this shift; these are profit-making entities in their own right, but are also seen as necessary to support the wider economy. The consequence has been serious environmental degradation – air and water pollution, changing hydrological regimes, forest degradation, water scarcity and fugitive dust emissions – in and beyond the mineral-bearing areas, coupled with large profits and attendant corruption (especially for coal and iron ore) for those who are able to bend the law into approvals of mining leases. As the chapters in this volume show, land acquisitions, SEZs, mining and other extractive industries with their related forms of dispossession have been the target of considerable popular criticism, with critics sometimes labelling what they see happening around them as a 'land grab by capital' aided by 'the neoliberal and corporatised Indian state' (Kapoor 2011: 135–136).

In all of this, the role of the state remains crucial. Land transactions are impossible to carry out on the scale required for industrial use without the active intervention of governments, especially at the state level. For example, in the case of the now aborted Tata Motors factory in Singur in West Bengal that Majumder and Nielsen describe in this volume, the acquisition of around 997 acres of farmland ostensibly directly affected more than 10,000 land owners. While the intervention of the state via eminent domain ensured the acquisition of the full and contiguous area in little time, the alternative scenario where Tata Motors would have had to negotiate individual deals with so many landowners would have proven immensely cumbersome and would have likely led to a significant 'hold-out problem', the euphemism often used to designate what happens when landowners are capable of strategically navigating the land market to press for a higher price for the last remaining pieces of a planned industrial estate. To resolve land dilemmas prospective investors need the state, including judicial and administrative institutions and procedures for the orderly and lawful transfer of certain parcels of land, backed by the potential use of force and punitive measures by the police in case the 'land losers' do not agree to plans. The 'master manipulators' (Nielsen and Oskarsson 2016) of land transactions are, however, the elected politicians who, with an intimate knowledge of local social and political relations and with a firm grip on the local state machinery, work through networks of brokers and intermediaries at proposed sites to ensure that dominant interpretations of 'development' are able to embed themselves in particular parcels of increasingly valuable land (ibid.). Land transfers in this sense remain dependent on the 'patronage politics' of the state in a manner not radically different from that which prevailed under the licensing regime (Chandra 2015).

With a radically lower, liberalisation-induced level of national public investment, state governments have since the early 1980s increasingly been forced to compete for industrial investments in a completely new manner (Rudolph and Rudolph 2001a), potentially paving the way for a race to the bottom to attract industrial investments. In this context it is perhaps unsurprising that the ability of state governments to furnish land for investors has become 'the most important factor in inter-state competition for investment' (Levien 2012: 944). Land, permits and clearances thus often mediate the relationship between states and industrialists, even if this 'nexus' may be closer in some states than in others. It is in this context that land becomes a vital concern to farmers, agricultural labourers, forest-dwellers, top decision makers and industrialists alike, effectively making it the site on which diverging perspectives on, and interests in, rural industrialisation and the future political economy of India play out. And, it is a site of considerable ambivalence, ambiguity and indeterminacy, as several chapters in this volume illustrate: Farmers may be unwilling or unable to move out of agriculture, even if the prospects of industrial jobs are alluring; forest-dwellers face ongoing dispossession from rapidly expanding extractive industries, even as they are tempted with new rights that supposedly vest control of forest lands with them; decision makers rely on their ability to offer land to industrialists to attract capital, even as they seek to appease key constituents and manage political fallouts at the state level; and investors seek to see their investments carry fruit, even as they remain dependent on the goodwill of key decisions-makers to see their projects through.

While at the aggregate level this policy of transferring landed wealth and resources upwards conforms with the basic presuppositions of the Marxist notion of primitive accumulation, or accumulation by dispossession,[1] several scholars have pointed out how India's vibrant democracy simultaneously exercises a moderating effect on this process. Successive governments, it is argued, have found it necessary to strike a delicate balance between 'democracy and globalisation' (Lakha and Taneja 2009) by way of welfare policies aimed at providing livelihoods, employment, health services and affordable food for the poor through a plethora of schemes and programmes. Chatterjee (2008) famously called this balancing act an attempt at reversing the worst effects of primitive accumulation, that is, a strategy that seeks to sustain the momentum of the pro-business orientation of the overall economic policy without hurling more people into abject poverty. In Chatterjee's writings, this appears as a pre-emptive move by the state to prevent popular discontent, manifesting itself in social programmes as well as in the continued support for 'food for the poor' programmes that have by now become institutionalised to the point of being almost impossible to dismantle. In addition to social spending, a number of important pieces of rights-based legislation have been passed to the same effect during the two UPA regimes from 2004 to 2014, with some observers likening it to a 'rights revolution' (Ruparelia 2013). This rights-based legislation affects, for example, basic education, forest access, rural employment and transparency in governance. And, with new rights-based laws on land acquisition, compensation, rehabilitation and forest access, inroads are starting to be made into decision-making in core areas of the economy, including industrialisation and its attendant land matters, which have otherwise until recently remained the privilege of closed elite policy circles. Like many other legislative efforts, these legislations have been implemented with varying degrees of success in different contexts, and often the popular mobilisation of support in civil society has been crucial in terms of implementation. Yet while there are thus clear signs of a long-term trend in active citizenship in at least parts of the country, the emergence of what Polanyi would term a counter-movement against the commodification of nature and people remains extremely varied across the country (see e.g. Corbridge *et al.* 2011 and Eriksen, this volume).

Nonetheless, in the context of policy moves aimed at curbing the impact on marginal groups of rapid transfer of land and resources for industrial purposes, it needs to be kept in mind that the popular resistance which many industrial ventures have faced, almost across the country, has been an important engine in both limiting forced displacement, and in bringing about progressive changes in union and state laws governing the exercise of eminent domain, rehabilitation and resettlement (Nielsen and Nilsen 2015). In other words, it is not only pre-emptive state strategies, but popular mobilisation that has produced these results, even if these mobilisations have often been led by middle-class activists and intellectuals. Many SEZs and other industrial projects all over India have, for example, been 'stuck in land acquisition purgatory' (Levien 2013: 353) for several years because of popular resistance or litigation. As Kennedy (2014: 83) writes, there has 'in almost every part of the country where SEZ projects have been proposed … been some form of protest, and in many cases prolonged mobilisation'. Indeed, the SEZ policy from 2005 appears to have acted as somewhat of a catalyst, creating an increased focus on the adverse and socially unjust impact of state-led dispossession. To Jenkins (2011), because the implementation of the SEZ policy was so visibly and 'consistently abusive' (2011: 61), it came to mark the end of the era of 'reforms by stealth' – that is, the ability of leading politicians and decision makers to get unpopular policies of economic liberalisation implemented by shrewd and stealthy management, such as careful policy sequencing; insulating protests; blame-shifting; selectively compensating key interests; etc. – and brought questions of SEZs and rapid industrialisation into the arena of mass politics. In addition, recent popular resistance has also stalled a number non-SEZ industrial projects, including, among the most prominent, the controversial POSCO steel project in Odisha; the Tata Motors factory in Singur in West Bengal; and the several scrapped SEZs in Goa (Sampat 2015; Bedi, this volume) whose fate still remains uncertain. A number of bauxite mining projects in Eastern India have also remained stuck for decades (Oskarsson, this volume). Such 'development deadlocks' (Oskarsson and Nielsen 2014; Nielsen and Oskarsson 2016) in the context of rural industrialisation are usually the result of prolonged resistance; but they are also underwritten by institutional incapacities that prevent the effective handling of often legitimate grievances; and they are routinely fuelled by cross-cutting and opposing political interests that ensure that any decision can be challenged, appealed, worked around, or in some other way redefined. Deadlocks are in this sense cultivated as much as they are an expression of different ideas of development. Often, however, a 'deadlocked' or even seemingly 'defeated' project can soon lead to 'new' or 'reworked' proposals being submitted because top politicians remain convinced of the merits of such projects, and because industrialists are desperate to gain access to land or minerals to ensure that their already completed industrial investments – potentially worth hundreds of millions of US dollars – are not completely wasted (Oskarsson 2012). Radical policy turnarounds and possibilities to challenge earlier 'final' decisions, whether by courts, governments or other bodies, are intrinsic parts of most such long-running controversies in a highly uncertain terrain, where a multiplicity of social forces and interests clash or combine to determine the fate of specific industrial initiatives, as the chapters in this volume bring out.

The Modi regime

The current conjuncture sees a majority government in place in New Delhi that is committed to further liberalising and economically 'enabling' reforms as perhaps no other Indian government in the past has ever been. When Modi ran for prime minister in 2014, he framed his campaign around the trope of *acche din*, or 'good times', while also promising that he would do for India what he had done for Gujarat over more than a decade, namely generate high economic growth rates that would, or so it was projected, translate into 'good times' for most Indians. The stated aim was to 'expand modern infrastructure amenities and mass employment opportunities through rapid industrial growth across the country' (Ruparelia 2015: 755). The promise of transferring Modi's Gujarat model to all of India, however, was seen as a cause for grave concern by analysts more familiar with the actual ground-level realities in Gujarat under Modi. Here, economic growth has coexisted with growing inequalities; the further marginalisation of the weakest sections of society (Dalits, Adivasis, and Muslims); mediocre social indicators; comparatively low spending on education and health; social polarisation; and an intensification of the, in Gujarat, old tradition of very close cooperation between the state and the corporate sector (Jaffrelot 2015). Under Modi, businessmen in Gujarat could, for example, acquire land more quickly and at a better price, and could obtain more tax breaks than in many other states (ibid.: 837).

In the field of industrial development, two significant political moves are testimony to Modi's early efforts at transferring some elements of his Gujarat model to ease the conditions of operation of industrial investors in India: The launching of the 'Make in India' programme, and the concerted effort to undo much of the rights-based legislation of the previous UPA government – particularly those that related to land and forests required for industrial expansion. The 'Make in India' programme was launched in September 2014 as a 'powerful, galvanising call to action to India's citizens and business leaders, and an invitation to potential partners and investors around the world'. In keeping with Modi's tenet of 'minimum government, maximum governance', the programme envisioned a 'comprehensive and unprecedented overhaul of out-dated processes and policies [and] a complete change of the Government's mindset – a shift from issuing authority to business partner'.[2] The aim is, simply put, to transform India into a global design and manufacturing hub, and to increase the ratio of manufacturing to GDP from 15 to 25 per cent and to create 100 million skilled jobs by 2022 (Ruparelia 2015: 763).

Towards a similar end, Modi's government tried to dilute key provisions in the 2013 Right to Fair Compensation and Transparency in Land Acquisition, Rehabilitation and Resettlement Act so as to make the compulsory acquisition of land for private investors easier and cheaper. Indeed, making the cumbersome process of acquiring land easier was a key prerequisite for boosting industrialisation as envisioned by the 'Make in India' programme (ibid.: 767). His government similarly sought to discard a key provision in the Forest Rights Act requiring the *gram sabhas*' prior informed consent to industrial activity. This has been coupled with other policy initiatives to weaken labour protocols and environmental regulations, as well as the lifting of a moratorium on new industries in 43 critically-polluted regions, to name some (Ruparelia 2015).

At the time of writing, the 'Make in India' programme had not taken off, and the attempt to dilute the legislation on land acquisition had foundered because Modi's government lacked the required numbers in the upper house of parliament. But, to analysts such as Ruparelia (ibid.: 775), the policy trend under Modi reveals 'a clear neo-liberal vision' that has, however, been subject to contestation both inside and outside of parliament. Great uncertainty thus exists regarding which direction industrialisation in India will take next. As indicated, rapid industrialisation and economic growth remains the preferred route in top policymaking circles, and the influence of big money on elections, and the mandatory seats for private sector representatives on most policymaking committees, appear to reinforce this trend. And yet it also appears to be acknowledged that increased participation in democratic decision-making is the way ahead, if nothing else than in order to prevent increasingly assertive groups from quite conceivably obstructing plans. India will surely continue to foment its own unique mix of pluralism and institutionalised democracy, coupled with enormous inequality based on the dominance of a narrow, historical elite. Irrespective of vantage point, this state of affairs might conceivably be considered a 'poor compromise' since it appears neither capable of rapid industrialisation, nor of delivering a just sharing of resources. On the other hand, it is at the moment above all a (just about) workable approach amidst widely varying preferences, and one that allows a large and enormously varied population to move at least somewhat according to the same pace. As further pressure continues to build towards a deepening of democratic decision-making, we remain hopeful about the breaking-up of the present dominance of political, commercial and technocratic elites on vital industry and land matters.

The chapters

The chapters in *Industrialising Rural India* have, in addition to this introductory section and chapter, been divided into three broad thematic sections: *Policy evolution*; *Governing nature and society*; and *The ambiguity of resistance*. In *Policy evolution*, the authors take a longer, institutional view on how industrial policy and land relations have developed since Independence. In *Governing nature and society*, we look at how land and nature – including resources lying above or beneath its surface – are governed in the context of industrialisation, as well as their repercussions on local society. In the final section, *The ambiguity of resistance*, we present in-depth ethnographic case studies that throw light on the often deeply ambivalent ways in which different actors perceive and resist social injustices emerging from rural industrial development, as well as how they navigate the uncertainties and risks associated with advocating for change.

Policy evolution

Jørgen Dige Pedersen gives us a historical, institutionalist account of the Indian state and its approach to development via large-scale, state-directed industrialisation and infrastructure development. As we noted above, the approach to industrial development adopted by India after Independence was not unusual as many postcolonial states attempted to take control over their own destinies. Like elsewhere, industrial and infrastructural development in India had severe consequences in terms of displacement and dispossession – but as Pedersen shows, public protests and outright resistance were rare in the early post-Independence decades. This 'dog that didn't bark' – i.e. the relative lack of protest movements – stands in marked contrast to how land dispossession has in contemporary India increasingly been drawn into the arena of popular mass politics. While mapping the fascination with industrialisation among leading policymakers in the 1950s and 1960s, Pedersen also offers us a series of illuminating reflections on why issues related to land governance have suddenly emerged with force as a truly explosive political issue in India today.

The debate on the role of the state in economic development is justifiably among the major concerns in the academic literature. Stein Sundstøl Eriksen adds to this debate by tracing national policies on industry and social protection over time, to provide a comparative perspective on key recent transformations during the period of economic reform. While not denying that the Indian economy has indeed 'liberalised' significantly, Eriksen shows how, when set in a global, comparative perspective, Indian economic policies are still among the least liberal in the world. Another finding is that, in spite of the launching of a series of 'flagship' pro-poor policies during the UPA, the Indian state still spends very little on social policies – indeed, a further downward trend in social spending has been clearly visible during the first two years of the Modi government (Ruparelia 2015). What Eriksen sees in India is a state that is neoliberal in some ways, and statist in other ways, which mainly benefits the capitalist class. But, because industrial growth is limited – and because the growth that has taken place has been far from labour-intensive enough to generate sufficient employment – those dispossessed from agriculture or old industries end up in the vast informal sector, as, e.g. casual labourers, street vendors or hawkers – politically, socially and economically fragmented in ways that make political mobilisation for better social protection extremely difficult. As a result, there is no Polanyian 'double movement' at work that could potentially have, *pace* Chatterjee (2008), reversed the effects of primitive accumulation.

Sarasij Majumder and Kenneth Bo Nielsen move the analysis to the state level to reflect on the ambivalence of industrialisation among state-level policy-makers and project-affected landowners at a proposed industrial site in Singur in rural West Bengal. As testimony to the often fierce inter-state competition to attract industrial investments, Majumder and Nielsen show how a government led by the communist parties has come to accept the need for private sector-led industrialisation. In Singur itself, however, the new industry was met with a complicated mix of enthusiasm and resistance, with individual villagers some-times strongly endorsing the idea of generating more off-farm employment, while in the next breath decrying the setting up of the proposed factory in the vicinity. Majumder and Nielsen unpack this ambivalent view of the implemen-tation of industrial policies by analysing how land-based identities embody contradictory aspirations and produce a conflictual desire for land *and* for respectable off-farm employment. By looking at the ambivalence of resistance in the face of rural industrialisation, they also point towards the discussions in the book's final section.

Governing nature and society

Kuntala Lahiri-Dutt's chapter draws on several decades of extensive research in the coalfields of Eastern India. She argues that for us to understand why the nation continues its dependence on a fuel that has such dramatically negative effects on the global climate – and on local environments – we must know what the coal economy and industry is really about. Lahiri-Dutt disaggregates what is officially presented as 'publicly mined coal' by large corporations into a number of public, private and small-scale forms of mining, which she in turn terms as legal, semi-legal and illegal. Lahiri-Dutt's understanding of coal livelihoods comes to the fore in her detailing of the semi-legal and illegal forms of coal extraction that are carried out by small-scale operators, including those scaven-ging on the margins of the massive corporate operations. While branded illegal by governments, she shows how such forms of mining become necessary for the dispossessed, who have few other means of survival left once the coal mines have taken their lands and polluted their forests.

Continuing the discussion on India's extractive industries, Bengt G. Karlsson examines the ways in which governance in Meghalaya in Northeastern India has come to be closely aligned with the main natural resources that have been extracted from the state. He draws particularly on Timothy Mitchell's book *Carbon Democracy*, in which the link between democracy and coal in the nine-teenth and early twentieth century is compared and contrasted to the link between oil and authoritarianism in more recent oil economies. For Mitchell, the characteristics of coal enable effective and disruptive forms of worker mobilisation, thus paving the way for the modern welfare state. Since Meghalaya is coal-rich and coal-dependent, one may expect Mitchell's arguments to apply there as well. But what Karlsson describes from Meghalaya is far removed from a democratic welfare state. Coal workers are mainly migrants with almost no political leverage or power to push for higher salaries and improved working conditions. They are spread out across a large and difficult terrain in many small mines and unable to organise, resulting in child labour bordering on slavery being widespread, and the political elite and the coal lobby are virtually indistinguishable. In addition, the wealth generated from the coal industry is channelled mostly into buying land and property.

As several chapters in this book show, mining has come to be a key part of the many land contestations India has witnessed in recent decades. Patrik Oskarsson adds to this debate by showing how interpretations of nature itself – and they ways in which certain forms of mining interact with this nature during extractive activities – become part of decision-making as well as struggles over land. Drawing on a decade of research into bauxite mining in Eastern India, Oskarsson compares three case studies to show how bauxite hills are much more varied than what is usually understood by both officials and activists. In contrast to what is often claimed, bauxite hills are not exclusively the home of Adivasi groups; they are not all forested; and their extraction does not easily impact on larger, regional water supplies, even if the local hydrology is likely to suffer if and when mining commences. Oskarsson concludes that there is a need for a mixed and more nuanced approach to governing resource use and industrial projects, one in which the universalising tendencies of both the pro- and anti-mining advocates need to be opened up for more broad-based scrutiny on the natural and social implications of mining with improved possibilities for the inclusion of site-based social and physical specificities.

Siddharth Sareen explores resource extraction and governance in an Adivasi-dominated district of Jharkhand. Here, independent statehood and supportive policies in decentralisation were supposed to lead to a stronger grassroots democracy, with enhanced accountability and local control over nature. This, in turn, was expected to ensure that local wealth was shared to the benefit of local communities. Yet Sareen shows how local democracy has more often been characterised by chaos rather than accountability. And, at the district and local levels, the prospects for improved governance of forests and nature have been effectively negated by the mineral boom, with extractive industries – and iron ore mines in particular – being the main culprits, undermining the control of the forests by the Ho Adivasis. The picture Sareen presents of the impact of the mining industry in rural Jharkhand is thus a bleak one: Industrial mining degrades the natural resource base that local Adivasis depend on for their survival, extracting valuable resources while destroying the productive capacity of Adivasi lands. In the end, their only means of survival is short-term logging of forests.

The ambiguity of resistance

Heather Plumridge Bedi moves the discussion of governance concerns into the context of SEZs in the small state of Goa. Here, the introduction of the SEZ policy in 2006 led to a public outcry that soon gained enough momentum to force the incumbent government to scrap the SEZ policy entirely. Drawing on Ong's work on neoliberalism and zoning techniques in China, Bedi documents the widespread concern among fenceline communities that SEZs in Goa would – because of their exceptional status as 'enclaves' – undermine the capacity of the local *panchayats* to decide on matters within their own jurisdiction, including the governance and use of land. This and other governance concerns were, Bedi argues, important in fuelling widespread popular discontent with SEZs. To Bedi, the anti-SEZ movement in Goa can therefore be seen as an attempt at deepening democracy, or asserting citizenship; yet the outcome of the movement remains ambiguous as the status of the land allocated for the SEZs remains disputed to this day.

Prakruti Ramesh draws on a close reading of the recent Forest Rights Act and ethnographic evidence from Niyamgiri Hill, the site proposed for Vedanta's bauxite mine in Odisha, to analyse how the granting of community rights to forests imply both a partial continuation and a radical re-evaluation of the history of India's forests and the role of people in them. Ramesh shows that indigenous groups, in order to protect themselves from dispossession from industrial projects like bauxite mining, have to be able to both understand and make use of modern tools of governance such as legal texts, written proof, and map-making. Yet at the same time, they also have to effectively perform – and gain official recognition of – their identity as a 'traditional' community dependent on the forests for their survival. This produces a deeply ambivalent modality of resistance, in which Adivasis are, on the one hand, expected to integrate into modern government while, on the other hand, also being expected to be 'tribal' (by state classification and/or by the fact of their dependence on forests for subsistence needs). While such identity performances through ceremonies, rituals and ways of being are critical to the Adivasi encounter with the Indian legal apparatus in the context of mining and looming dispossession, they may also generate a certain unease by simultaneously pulling people towards *and* against ideas of modernity.

In combination, the ten chapters in *Industrialising Rural India* offer stimulating analyses of a complex set of issues pertaining to planning, implementing, governing, and resisting different forms of industrial production and extraction in contemporary rural India. While we have deliberately sought to cover this heterogeneous field in a broad sense, we have not aspired to offer the final say on any of these matters. Indeed, there are several crucial areas of inquiry that we have refrained from engaging, including questions of rural–urban linkages, and the role of localised class–caste–ethnicity relations, in shaping responses to rural industrialisation. We therefore hope the reader will treat the chapters that follow as an invitation to further, in-depth research across scales and contexts.

16   P. Oskarsson and K.B. Nielsen

Notes

1 We do not intend to enter the debate on how best to characterise the current wave of land transfers in India. Readers may consult Levien (2015) for an instructive overview.
2 All citations from Make in India website, online, available at: www.makeinindia.com (accessed 9 February 2016).

References

Banerjee-Guha, Swapna (2013). 'Accumulation and Dispossession: Contradictions of Growth and Development in Contemporary India'. *South Asia: Journal of South Asian Studies* 36(2): 165–179.

Bardhan, Pranab (1984). *The Political Economy of Development in India*. Oxford: Blackwell.

Bhagwati, Jagdish N. (1993). *India in Transition: Freeing the Economy*. Oxford: Oxford University Press.

Blaser, M., H.A. Feit, and G. McRae (2004). *In the Way of Development: Indigenous Peoples, Life Projects and Globalization*. London: Zed Books.

Bedi, Heather P. and Louise Tillin (2015). 'Inter-state Competition, Land Conflicts and Resistance in India'. *Oxford Development Studies* 43(2): 194–211.

Chandra, Kanchan (2015). 'The New Indian State'. *Economic and Political Weekly* 50(41): 46–58.

Chandrasekhar, C.P. (2011). 'Unusual Asset' *Frontline* 28(12). Online, available at: www.frontline.in/static/html/fl2812/stories/20110617281202600.htm (accessed 19 August 2013).

Chatterjee, Partha (ed.) (1997). *State and Politics in India*. Delhi: Oxford University Press.

Chatterjee, Partha (2008). 'Democracy and Economic Transformation in India'. *Economic and Political Weekly* 42(16): 53–62.

Chatterjee, Partha (2011). *Lineages of Political Society: Studies in Postcolonial Democracy*. New York: Columbia University Press.

Corbridge, Stuart and John Harriss. 2000. *Reinventing India: Liberalization, Hindu Nationalism, and Popular Democracy*. Cambridge: Polity.

Das, Gurcharan (2006). 'The India Model'. *Foreign Affairs* 85(4): 1–7.

Evans, Peter (1995). *Embedded Autonomy: States and Industrial Transformation*. Princeton, NJ: Princeton University Press.

Ghosh, Ashish (ed.) (1999). *Dalits and Peasants: The Emerging Caste-Class Dynamics*. Delhi: Gyan Sagar Publications.

Gupta, Akhil (2012). *Red Tape: Bureaucracy, Structural Violence, and Poverty in India*. Durham: Duke University Press.

Gupta, Akhil and K. Sivaramakrishnan (eds) (2011). *The State in India after Liberalization: Interdisciplinary Perspectives*. London: Routledge.

Jaffrelot, Christophe (2015). 'What "Gujarat Model"? – Growth without Development – And with Socio-Political Polarisation'. *South Asia* 38(4): 820–838.

Jenkins, Rob (1999). *Democratic Politics and Economic Reform in India*. Cambridge: Cambridge University Press.

Jenkins, Rob, Loraine Kennedy, and Partha Mukhopadhyay (eds) (2014). *Power, Policy, and Protest: The Politics of India's Special Economic Zones*. New Delhi: Oxford University Press.

Kapoor, Dip (2011). 'Subaltern Social Movement (SSM) Post-Mortems of Development in India: Locating Trans-Local Activism and Radicalism'. *Journal of Asian and African Studies* 46(2): 130–148.

Kennedy, Loraine (2014). *The Politics of Economic Restructuring in India*. London: Routledge.

Kohli, Atul (2004). *State-Directed Development: Political Power and Industrialization in the Global Periphery*. Cambridge: Cambridge University Press.

Kohli, Atul (2006). 'Politics of Economic Growth in India, 1980–2005: Part II – The 1990s and Beyond'. *Economic and Political Weekly* 41(14): 1361–1370.

Kohli, Atul (2007). 'State, Business, and Economic Growth in India'. *Studies in Comparative International Development* 42(1): 87–114.

Kohli, Atul (2009). *Democracy and Development in India: From Socialism to Pro-Business*. Oxford: Oxford University Press.

Kothari, Uma (2005). *A Radical History of Development Studies: Individuals, Institutions and Ideologies*. New York: Zed Books.

Kurien, C.T. (1994). *Global Capitalism and the Indian Economy*. New Delhi: Orient Longman.

Lakha, Salim and Pradeep Taneja (2009). 'Balancing Democracy and Globalisation: The Role of the State in Poverty Alleviation in India'. *South Asia: Journal of South Asian Studies* 32(3): 408–424.

Levien, Michael (2011). 'Rationalising Dispossession: The Land Acquisition and Resettlement Bills'. *Economic and Political Weekly* 46(11): 66–71.

Levien, Michael (2012). 'The Land Question: Special Economic Zones and the Political Economy of Dispossession in India'. *Journal of Peasant Studies* 39(3/4): 933–969.

Levien, Michael (2013). 'The Politics of Dispossession: Theorizing India's "Land Wars"'. *Politics and Society* 41(3): 351–394.

Levien, Michael (2015). 'Six Theses on India's Land Question'. *Economic and Political Weekly* 50(22): 146–157.

Nayyar, Deepak (2008). *Liberalization and Development*. New Delhi: Oxford University Press.

Nielsen, Kenneth Bo and Alf Gunvald Nilsen (2015). 'Law-Struggles and Hegemonic Processes in Neoliberal India: Gramscian Reflections on Land Acquisition Legislation'. *Globalizations* 12(2): 203–216.

Nielsen, Kenneth Bo and Patrik Oskarsson (2016). 'Development Deadlocks of the New Indian State'. *Economic and Political Weekly* 51(4): 67–69.

Oskarsson, Patrik (2012). 'AnRak Aluminium: Another Vedanta in the Making'. *Economic and Political Weekly* 47(52): 29–33.

Oskarsson, Patrik and Kenneth Bo Nielsen (2014). 'Development Deadlock: Aborted Industrialization and Blocked Land Restitution in West Bengal and Andhra Pradesh, India'. *Development Studies Research* 1(1): 267–278.

Ray, Raka and Mary Fainsod Katzenstein (eds) (2005). *Social Movements in India: Poverty, Power, and Politics*. New Delhi: Oxford University Press.

Reddy, V. Ratna and B. Suresh Reddy (2007). 'Land Alienation and Local Communities: Case Studies in Hyderabad-Secundarabad'. *Economic and Political Weekly* 42(31): 3233–3240.

Rudolph, Lloyd I. and Susanne H. Rudolph (2001a). 'Iconisation of Chandrababu: Sharing Sovereignty in India's Federal Market Economy'. *Economic and Political Weekly* 36(18): 1541–1552.

Rudolph, Lloyd I. and Susanne H. Rudolph (2001b). 'Redoing the Constitutional Design: From an Interventionist to a Regulatory State'. In: Atul Kohli (ed.). *The Success of India's Democracy*. Cambridge: Cambridge University Press, pp. 125–162.

Ruparelia, Sanjay (2013). 'India's New Rights Agenda: Genesis, Promises, Risks'. *Pacific Affairs* 86(3): 569–590.

Ruparelia, Sanjay (2015). '"Minimum Government, Maximum Governance": The Restructuring of Power in Modi's India'. *South Asia: Journal of South Asian Studies* 38(4): 755–775.

Sampat, Preeti (2015). 'The "Goan Impasse": Land Rights and Resistance to SEZs in Goa, India'. *Journal of Peasant Studies* 42(3/4): 765–790.

Williamson, John (2008). 'A Short History of the Washington Consensus'. In: Serra Narcís and Joseph E. Stiglitz (eds). *The Washington Consensus Reconsidered: Towards a New Global Governance*. Oxford: Oxford University Press, pp. 14–30.

Part II
Policy evolution

2 'The dog that didn't bark' (very loudly) – large-scale development projects with little protest in Nehru's India

Jørgen Dige Pedersen

India has in recent decades seen an explosive growth in public protests against the acquisition of land for purposes of industrial use, including mining and large infrastructural projects. The acquisition of land has become a hot political topic that has contributed to the toppling of state governments and to several cases of aborted investment projects, even those deemed to be of crucial interest to the future economic growth of the whole country or a specific region (Oskarsson and Nielsen 2014). For the present central government, led by prime minister Narendra Modi, a suggestion for revising the law governing land acquisitions has become a political headache because of protests both inside and outside parliament against the new and more business-friendly version of the law.

This increase in social activism and protests may easily be seen as a natural response to the increased economic activities in India over recent years, but if we look at the phenomenon through a historical lens, the new activism raises questions about how to interpret the rising protest activities. If they are natural phenomena to be expected, given the rapid economic development, how come similar protests were far less common in earlier times with high growth rates? To understand more deeply the causes and mechanisms that lie behind this increase in protest activities, we probably have to go further than just to see it as a natural, almost self-evident, companion to a renewed economic and especially industrial growth process. Overall economic growth rates may indeed have reached unprecedented levels in recent years, but industrial growth rates and infrastructure investments have previously experienced similar or even higher growth rates than today, albeit evidently from lower levels of economic activity.

In terms of social conflicts, the situation today contrasts markedly to an earlier period when India experienced perhaps the most dramatic increase in industrial investment projects. In the period of the first three five-year plans, 1951–1966, under the leadership of prime minister Jawaharlal Nehru, India's industry grew at a rate never to be achieved again. To a large extent, this growth was based upon the establishment of large industrial and infrastructural projects. Nehru had at the time termed the construction of these large-scale projects as the building of 'the temples of modern India' and this expression captures very well the optimism of the era and the uncritical embrace of the modern industrial future by practically all relevant voices in the political life of India. Even among academic observers who were highly critical of the chosen strategy for economic development it had been acknowledged that India's growth experience during this crucial early period had been 'fairly impressive indeed' (Bhagwati and Desai 1970: 4). Possibly the best picture of the mood and thinking of the leading figures of the Indian nation at the time was provided by Gunnar Myrdal in his monumental three-volume work, *Asian Drama* (Myrdal 1968). Myrdal noted specifically the spread and impact of the ideology of planning as being a part of the more encompassing 'modernisation' paradigm as an interventionist and rational approach to achieve development (ibid.: ch. 2 and 15). According to this rational planning ideology that Myrdal found to be dominant with practically no dissenting voices at the time, existing social conditions were seen as undesirably backward features that had to be reformed or changed in order for modernisation to progress.

From the perspective of today's tumultuous experiences with the promotion of rapid industrial progress, this raises the questions whether and to what extent this early period of rapid economic industrial progress had experienced similar waves of protests, how the policymakers of the time looked upon the inevitable associated processes of displacements of thousands of people all over India, and whether other socially active forces had been concerned about or had acted upon the displacements. If not, the question arises as to what may explain this significant divergence in the social response to a process of rapid industrialisation between the early period and the recent period. The purpose of this chapter is to provide a first survey of how the Indian authorities and organised social and political forces have viewed the early process of rapid industrial modernisation and whether they displayed any awareness of the 'social costs' involved. Second, some indications and examples will be provided of the limited but nevertheless existing protest movements at the time. Finally, the article will briefly discuss some of the likely explanations for the markedly different situation existing today where, as mentioned, protests are widespread and to be expected whenever new projects are initiated. It goes without saying that the explanations can only be suggestive, as what needs explaining is the (relative) lack of protest during the early period – 'the dog that didn't bark'[1] – i.e. a counterfactual phenomenon, something that did not happen.

The road to national legislation

The construction projects that have caused the displacement of the largest numbers of people are without doubt the construction of dams across India's many rivers, but the establishment of mines (coal and assorted minerals), power plants, large industrial projects and possibly many highway projects have also necessitated the removal of many poor families from their land. Unfortunately, there are no fully reliable (official, or non-official) statistics or estimates of the exact magnitude of the displacements, but there is agreement between many sources that the number of people displaced by especially the construction of large dams should be counted in the millions, from the 21 million officially recognised for the period 1951–1990 (Planning Commission 2002: 458) to perhaps 50 to 60 million people by unofficial estimates (Hemadri et al. 1999: vii; Fernandes 2007: 203).[2] These are large figures and one might have expected that in a democratic country like India these displacements would have caused considerable debate, fuelled the establishment of political movements and eventually led to changes in the policies being implemented by the political authorities, the central government or the state governments. The available information, however, indicates that it was only from around 1980 that the widespread evictions of people all over India due to the process of modernisation and industrialisation became significant political issues (Hemadri et al. 1999: xxvi ff.; Khagram 2004: 34; Menon and Nigam 2007: 69) and only in the 1990s would they slowly lead to political reactions at a national level in the form of new parliamentary legislation. In 1985, the government published a report on 'Rehabilitation of Displaced Tribals due to Development Projects', thus demonstrating awareness of the problem, and in 1993 it was decided to formulate a national policy for the rehabilitation of displaced persons (Sinha 1996). This policy was finalised in 2003, and ten years later, in 2013, a new land acquisition law with new rules for compensation, resettlement and rehabilitation for those affected by various development projects was passed by the Indian Parliament (Sathe 2015).[3] This is the law that the current government is trying to revise in a more business-friendly direction, so far without success due to considerable opposition. The widespread opposition to changes in the present law indicates that issues of land acquisition, resettlement and compensation today have become stable ingredients on the political agenda.

Despite large and small development projects having displaced people in the millions from their land over the years, it has taken more than 30 years before this process began in earnest to produce social and political opposition movements organised around the problem, and it has taken around 50 years or more before the problem has become sufficiently recognised by the central political decision makers to enter the agenda of national politics. The explanations for this long delay could be many, and we shall return to this later, but before that it seems appropriate to look into some of the key policy documents of the early period of the 1950s and 1960s in order to compose a picture of how the problem of a people-displacing development process has been perceived by the political and administrative officialdom, the top decision makers who formulated the policies that were implemented from early on in the development process. We will also provide a little more insight into the process of the displacement of local people in a few concrete and important instances, including select glimpses of the reactions of the local people experiencing this process.

In the following analysis I will begin by providing a broad survey of relevant key documents from the period indicating the viewpoints and concerns of policymakers at the time, from the making of independent India's constitution over the various five-year plan documents to the more specific documents on the strategy for industrial development. The analysis of the policy documents will be supplemented by examples from the scattered evidence available on

specific projects and the reactions to them. After that I will provide some evidence of the concerns that potentially important political actors (parties, trade
unions, etc.) have – or have not – expressed at the time. To end this chapter, I
will provide some speculations on possible explanations to the puzzle of why the
situation today has become so dramatically different from this earlier period.

The Indian Constitution and its making

In the Constituent Assembly debates, the question of the expropriation of
private property for public social or political purposes did play a significant role
and was hotly debated, especially with regard to the nature of eventual compensation and with regard to the question of whether an act of expropriation could
be challenged in the courts. The focus was, however, mainly on issues relevant
to the eventual expropriations in connection with future land reforms, abolition
of *zamindar* properties and expropriation of foreign owned property. Expropriations necessary for the establishment of large infrastructural or industrial projects were apparently not considered worthy of debate. The general rule that
became inscribed in the constitution was the principle of compensation
(presumably fair) and that any expropriation of land had to be for 'public purposes' and had to be regulated by law. The size of any monetary compensation
could not be challenged in courts, however (Government of India 1977; Austin
1966: 87–101). In more general terms, the debate could be said to involve the
rights of property owners vis-à-vis a government that was committed to pursuing progressive social and economic development. This was a battle that clearly
involved the courts, and in the decade that followed the battle was fought,
mainly over land reforms, in the states (Austin 1999: ch. 3 and 4). Nothing was
mentioned concerning large dams or other developmental constructions that
would require the taking over of land and the relocations of the land's inhabitants. The constitution did, however, make it mandatory to give special treatment to tribal people living in 'Scheduled Areas', and the general directive
principles of state policy stipulated that the state should work for the promotion
of the welfare of the people, including adequate means of livelihood for all.

Acquisition of property was placed in the Concurrent List in the Seventh
Schedule of the Constitution, i.e. it can be a subject matter for both state governments and the central government. In most instances the jurisdiction over
land acquisitions falls with the state government; however, the central government retains the option to take over responsibility for an acquisition of land.
The existing colonial legislation on land acquisition, the 1894 Land Acquisition Act, remained in force as the law that in practice regulated most land
transfers.

The first three five-year plans

The constitution of the Planning Commission in 1950 made it the central
coordinating organ for the proposed concentrated efforts by the Indian state to

forcefully promote economic development. The first five-year plan became the first effort to provide an overview of all the state's developmental activities in one volume (Planning Commission 1952). In reality, this was exactly what it was: An overview of those activities that had already been initiated by the states, by various ministries or by other administrative organs. The developmental activities that occupied a central position in the plan were precisely large irrigation and power projects. Some of them were so-called 'multi-purpose' projects because they catered to several objectives at the same time: Flood prevention, irrigation, power generation, possibly provision of drinking water and transportation. A key objective was to stimulate the production of food through the irrigation facilities provided by the large dam projects, two of which, the Damodar Valley Project and the Hirakud dam, will be dealt with later. The plan document focussed on the technical and economic aspects of the different projects (ibid.: 350). Only briefly was the problem of resettlement of those persons displaced by the projects mentioned. It was thus considered how it might be possible to put a tax on the increase in the commercial value of the land belonging to those peasants who would benefit from the irrigation projects in order to help finance the acquisition of new lands meant for resettling persons whose holdings would be submerged by reservoirs. This potential tax was called a 'betterment levy' (ibid.: 358–359). Of interest are also the considerations in the plan document on the advantages or disadvantages of minor or major dams and irrigation schemes, respectively (ibid.: 364). Nothing was mentioned, in this context, about the problems and disadvantages associated with the process of resettlement of people due to the large construction projects, however.

The second plan document represents the first serious attempt to prioritise and coordinate the Indian state's developmental efforts (and also to direct the efforts of the private sector) (Planning Commission 1956). The plan reiterated some of the concerns from the first plan. In the debate on minor vs. major projects, the plan settled for medium-sized projects (major ones having been initiated already) (ibid.: 170). It also mentioned some problems with implementing large projects (mostly technical ones, including substantial delays). It did touch upon 'social problems' when it stated that 'the preparation of a balanced scheme for a river basin is a complex engineering, economic and social problem' (ibid.: 179) and it repeated the possibility of using a 'betterment levy' to finance the resettling of displaced persons (ibid.: 183). Apart from these few scattered remarks, the plan showed little concern for the social costs of the large projects. On mining projects, nothing of the kind was mentioned, and on industrial projects social concerns showed only with regard to the goal of having a regional balance in the development of new industries (ibid.: 217) and the issue of land availability was indirectly addressed through a new scheme for 'industrial estates' that should be established to provide support for less land demanding village and small industries (ibid.: 237).

The formulation of the third plan provided an opportunity to reflect on the experiences from the two earlier plans. The plan included a chapter on 'public cooperation and participation', which mentioned that uneven distribution of the 'fruits of progress' would give rise to a sense of 'deep resentment and frustration' (ibid.: 292). More specifically, the plan document reflected on the problems involved in the implementation of minor irrigation projects (ibid.: 308ff.), but neither resettlements nor environmental damages were mentioned in this context. Technical, financial and administrative problems were mentioned, nothing else. On the larger irrigation and power schemes, the plan document noted the existence of various technical problems and financial problems, including the problems associated with recovery of 'betterment fees' (ibid.: 388), but there was no mentioning of the use of these fees to compensate or resettle those affected by the various schemes. Instead it focused on how to maximise local employment in the projects (ibid.: 393–394). The programme for establishing 'industrial estates' for small industries that was initiated during the second plan was regarded as being very successful – 60 were set up – and more estates were either under implementation (60) or proposed for the coming years (300) (ibid.: 449). Once again, nothing was mentioned about problems in acquiring land for the establishment of the estates. Similarly, in discussing the experiences from the setting up of large industrial projects in steel, fertiliser, heavy machinery etc. the plan document was mostly concerned with delays in implementation and with the escalating costs, none of which apparently were associated with the problems related to the displaced people or with environmental damages (ibid.: 452ff.). The one exception seems to be concern for the pollution of rivers by effluents from chemical industries (ibid.: 492). With respect to the establishment of new coal mines, it was briefly mentioned that 'legislation had to be passed to enable the public sector to acquire new areas' (ibid.: 511).

In sum, the planners involved in formulating India's three first and path-breaking economic plan documents seem to have had very little concern for the human and environmental costs involved in setting up large industrial, mining and infrastructural projects. The special concern for the welfare of Scheduled Tribes found in the Constitution of India, however, was being dealt with in a separate chapter of the third plan document, bearing the title 'Development of Backward Classes' and it is in that context that we find the only place where the downside of the grand development schemes was mentioned. The document here quoted from a report by The Scheduled Areas and Scheduled Tribes Commission (established in 1960):

> In Bihar, Madhya Pradesh and Orissa industrial and other development schemes have led to large-scale displacement of the tribal people. There is need, therefore, for strengthening and in some cases for reorganising the administrative set up for the scheduled areas.
>
> (Ibid.: 703–704)

What this would entail in practice is hard to guess. The plan document further mentioned that the number of families displaced ran into the thousands and that compensation needed to be sufficient to ensure effective rehabilitation. It was also recommended that future projects needed to take these concerns into account when determining the location of projects, and the report suggested that voluntary organisations might be helpful in arranging resettlement and rehabilitation (ibid.: 710). While not being very specific in how to deal with these problems associated with the rapid development efforts, the few formulations in the third plan document did demonstrate an awareness of the many potential problems. In the plan documents that followed even this limited awareness would be completely absent, however.[4]

The position of India's first prime minister, Jawarharlal Nehru, is of some interest here. Nehru was the head of the Planning Commission at the time, and he became famous for his 'temples of modern India' speech (in Hindi) at the inauguration of the large Bhakra Nangal dam in 1954:

> India has undertaken other big works which are not much smaller than this. Damodar Valley, Hirakud and the big projects of the South are going on apace. Plans are being made every day because we are anxious to build a new India as speedily as possible.... As I walked round the site I thought that these days the biggest temple and mosque and gurdwara is the place where man works for the good of mankind.... Where can be a greater and holier place than this, which we can regard as higher?... We have to press forward.
>
> (Nehru 1954)

Some years later, in 1958, Nehru apparently had developed a less enthusiastic standpoint with regard to large development projects. In a speech on 'Social Aspects of Small and Large Projects' he argued for the use of smaller projects that would not upset so many people that had to move out and seek rehabilitation (quoted in Guha 2005). Maybe this partial change of mind was what was reflected in the third plan document? In any case, it was not a change of mindset that would be visible in other policy documents from the period following his death in 1964.

The attitude of the Indian planners and the broader public can be illustrated by the fate of the large Damodar Valley Project and of the Hirakud dam.

Illustrative example 1: the Damodar Valley project

The largest early development project in India was undertaken in the area surrounding the Damodar River in the Eastern part of India. The ideas for establishing a large unified project with the purpose of flood control, irrigation, power production and possibly transportation facilitation had been circulated before Independence in 1947, but the ideas fitted well with the modernisation ambitions of the new independent government of India and the project was debated by the Constituent Assembly, where it found overwhelming support (Franda 1968: 71). Being situated in the border region between the states of Bihar and West Bengal made it a controversial affair to find an administrative and financial model for the project, especially when considering that most of the benefits of, for instance, flood control would go to West Bengal, while most of the disruptions caused by the construction of the dams would be located in Bihar (ibid.: 72–73). The central government would also take part in the financing of the projects, however. As it happened, most of the financing eventually came from the central government and it also assumed the actual control of the schemes. A separate Damodar Valley Corporation (DVC) was established as a formally autonomous entity uniting the two state governments with the central government in a unique combination.

It was officially estimated that about 75,000 people would be displaced by the initial dam projects. Nothing was indicated about people being indirectly affected by the projects (DVC 1956: 34). Later estimates give the figure of 93,874 displaced persons, and the associated industrial projects, like the Rourkela and Bokaro steel plants and the plants of the Heavy Engineering Corporation, have also displaced many families but on a smaller scale than the dams (Areeparampil 1996: 1527). The expansion of coal mining in the same area also resulted in a large displacement of local people, mostly indigenous people (Adivasis) (ibid.).

One contentious issue in the project was precisely the dispute over who should be responsible for the resettlement and rehabilitation of people displaced by the various dams and other constructions. Here the state of Bihar was put in charge of the rehabilitation process rather than the DVC itself (DVC 1956: 57–58). The rehabilitation of displaced people was clearly considered as a minor issue and it found no mention in the book by Marcus Franda (1968) despite his extensive field work in the region during 1962–1964. On the other hand, it is known that there had been some debate in the national parliament over how to treat people displaced by the Damodar Valley project, and officially the DVC was fully prepared to deal with the problem, cf. the following quotation from a contemporary DVC information booklet:

> The Corporation regarded itself not as a business concern but as a welfare organisation and arranged resettlement of the people in such a manner that the least possible hardship may be caused to them and that the people may be enabled to live under good conditions in well-planned villages. In fact, the hope was expressed that the displaced persons would 'exchange this hovel for a decent cottage, darkness for light and fanaticism for faith'. Unfortunately, this very commendable policy did not get the full co-operation of the local people. But the Corporation embarked on its programme of resettlement with a keen desire to improve the lot of the affected people. But instead of their co-operation or even understanding and sympathy, *there was distrust and cynicism, and propaganda by designing persons led astray the simple villagers* who were made to believe that the Corporation was not giving them a fair deal.
>
> (DVC 1956: 55, emphasis added)

The quotation shows that there were indeed protests from some of the affected local people and also that 'designing persons' had agitated for better compensation. The quotation also shows that the protests apparently had made only limited impression on the relevant officials.

In the official publicity magazine of the Planning Commission, *Yojana*, a gloating article written by the well-known author Khushwant Singh, described the new India that he saw emerging when he visited the large-scale projects in the Damodar Valley area:

> We went along the Grand Trunk Road through flat brown country. The only attractive feature was the Parasnath Mount which hovered 4,500 feet above the countryside. On its top were a series of Jain temples. Apparently thousands of pilgrims visit them every year. We did not. Our pilgrimage was to the 'new temples' of which Pandit Nehru has spoken.
>
> (Singh 1957)

No mention of any problem with land acquisition or with the displacement of local people! These problems seem not to have been visible to the enthusiastic visitor.[5]

Illustrative example 2: the Hirakud dam

A forerunner to the Damodar Valley project was the Hirakud dam in Orissa. The decision to construct the dam was taken in 1946, i.e. before Independence, but actual construction work only commenced in 1948 after a long period of widespread local protest (see Khagram 2004: 36–37; Nayak 2010). The protests were supported by local political leaders, but after a while the protests died out. Among the reasons for the failure of the protests to gather more widespread and long-lasting support were first of all police repression, with the arrests of many of the protesters. Second, and possibly even more important, was the withdrawal of support from political leaders higher up in the Congress Party hierarchy, including Mahatma Gandhi. Clearly, there was no interest from political parties to support a local agitation against an important development project. Later estimates would show that only 8–9 per cent of the approximately 100,000 people displaced by the project were eventually resettled (Nayak 2010: 72–73).

The two examples of large dam construction show that these projects were not established without local protests, occasionally even strong protest. The protests, however, did not lead to changes in the projects, let alone a halt in construction activities, and they also illustrate the apparent lack of concern by the involved authorities and of the leading national political party over the problems of resettlement, compensation and rehabilitation.

The industrial policy documents

If we move on to the more focused plans and policies for industrial develop-ment, we may start with a few documents that illustrate the general consensus on the nature and direction of the future economic development that had crys-tallised even before Independence (Roy 1965: ch. iii; Hanson 1966: ch. ii)

Three documents may illustrate this. The first is the so-called 'Bombay Plan' (Thakurdas et al. 1944–1945). The Bombay Plan was commissioned by a number of prominent Indian industrialists (it was also called the Tata-Birla plan), and it became famous for acknowledging the need for strong state inter-vention in the process of industrial development and for its recommendation of a focus on the development of basic industries, including electric power, mining and heavy machinery. At the opposite end of the political spectrum we find the 'Peoples Plan' authored by experts associated with the Indian labour movement (Banerjee et al. 1946). This plan put more emphasis on the development of agri-culture and the development of consumer goods, but it also recognised the need for developing basic industries – in particular during the first ten years – and for strong state intervention. Third, the (colonial) Government of India had in April 1945 issued a Statement of Industrial Policy (Government of India 1945). In it the government expressed the need for stronger control by the central gov-ernment – in contrast to the provincial governments – over industrial develop-ment, especially over the development of important (basic) industries like iron and steel, machinery, chemicals, coal and electric power. It also envisaged a system of industrial licensing to direct the activities of the private sector.

In sum, there is no indication in any of the documents produced before Inde-pendence of an awareness of the potential problems – of land availability or of environmental issues – associated with the large-scale projects that all relevant parties envisaged as being necessary for the future economic development of the country.

It is, given this background, less surprising that the policy statements issued by Independent India's new government shortly after coming to power in a similar manner seem to neglect these issues. Neither the Industrial Policy State-ment 1948, nor the more important and far-reaching Industrial Policy State-ment 1956 mention anything related to the acquisition of land, resettlement of people or environmental problems associated with rapid industrialisation (Gov-ernment of India 1948, 1956).[6]

Illustrative example 3: the large steel plants

Powered by electricity generated as part of the Damodar Valley project were the establishment of large industrial projects in the area. Important among these were the large steel mills – indeed whole 'steel towns' – that also benefitted from the availability of iron and coal in the region. There is little doubt that these projects displaced far fewer people than the large dams, but the available figures nevertheless point to significant numbers being displaced. One source estimates that the Bokaro steel plant alone displaced close to 13,000 families living in 46 villages in the chosen area (Areeparampil 1996: 1527). The Rourkela plant displaced more than 4,000 families (ibid.), most likely amounting to more than the 15,000 people living in 32 villages that another source mentions (Parry and Struempell 2008: 54). The same source mentions that the later establishment of the Bhilai steel plant affected a much larger number of villages (96) and a much larger number of people (ibid.: 55). In a dynamic perspective, the establishment of the steel plants and other industrial plants may have made an even greater impact on the local population than the figures indicate, as the establishment of the industries led to a rapid process of urbanisation that would involve additional seizure of agricultural land and a further displacement of local peasants from their land. On the other hand, industrial expansion also led to the creation of new jobs – in construction and elsewhere – and opportunities to earn a better income than before, although the opportunities did not always materialise due to the influx of better skilled workers from other regions of India (Strümpell 2014). As was the case with the constructions of large dams, there are examples of protest movements against the industrial projects. The eruption of protests and the severity of such protests seem to have been heavily influenced not only by the compensation packages offered by the authorities, but also by the ethnic composition of the people affected and by the local histories of conflicts and resistance against outsiders (Parry and Struempell 2008; Strümpell 2014). In many industrial projects, these factors were not present and there were few or no protests. As with the establishment of the Heavy Engineering Corporation plant in 1958 in Ranchi, where close to 13,000 people were displaced (Areeparampil 1996: 1527) the reaction was only passivity and resignation: 'They dispossessed the villagers, stomped all over their lands, and desecrated their ancestral faith. No one protested, no one resisted; they kept quiet because they did not know better' (Chandra 2013: 54).

In addition to the establishment of large industrial projects, the expansion of coal mining in roughly the same parts of Eastern India during the same period had also resulted in a large displacement of local people, mostly Adivasis, and although some were offered jobs in and around the mines, the new jobs benefitted only a minor part of the displaced persons (Areeparampil 1996: 1526).

This brief survey of some key documents on economic planning and on industrial policy, supplemented with scattered evidence on individual development projects confirm that although protests were happening in connection with many of the new development projects started in the early phase of India's modernisation process, the resistance against these early projects was 'sporadic, localised and disorganised', as summarised in a background report for the World Commission on Dams (Hemadri et al. 1999: xxvi). The different planning documents further show that there was at the time a very broad consensus on how economic development should be achieved: Emphasis should be on developing basic and heavy industries and the state should own or at the very least control all these industries, including the main infrastructural installations. In some sectors it may be necessary to admit foreign ownership, but the general rule would be state ownership in these industries. The acquisition of land to construct the industries would for this reason naturally be seen as serving an important public purpose, thus falling under the rules of public acquisition of land according to the law regulating this and to the rules given in the constitution. Acquiring land for private industrial projects – not so obviously a public purpose – might present a bigger problem. Foreign companies in particular might be expected to run into difficulties with acquiring land given the preference for nationally controlled development. Some foreign investment projects had during the 1950s apparently run into problems, but the central government at the time (in 1962) had responded quickly to the situation and had suggested an amendment to the land acquisition act to permit the take-over of land by the state government for purposes of 'economic development'. After some debates in parliament where agricultural interests voiced concern over the transformation of valuable agricultural land to industrial purposes, the government had to backtrack and settle with 'public purpose' as the motive for land acquisition, but it retained its right to ultimately decide the matter (Kust 1964: 76–78). This example shows a government willing to change laws in order to support industrial investors but also that protests from farming interests set political limits to how much support could be given.

As for the fate of those people who were evicted or otherwise affected negatively by the construction of the large projects, mostly the dams, Nehru's words to the displaced people from the Hirakud dam were probably quite representative of the mood among the political and bureaucratic elite at the time, not only in India but probably all over the world: 'If you are to suffer, you should suffer in the interest of the country' (cited in Khagram 2004: 37; and in Menon and Nigam 2007: 68).[7]

Political parties and political movements

Among organised political movements like political parties, trade unions, peasant organisations, etc. there seems to have been little concern voiced for the people being displaced by the early large modernisation projects. One might have expected left parties, especially the communist parties, to have been active in organising resistance, but if this happened at all, it seems to have been only sporadic and certainly not in a way that made it a concern for the parties at the national level. Most likely the left parties were both ideologically and in their political praxis in broad agreement with the industrialisation drive and they regarded the eventual social costs of the development projects as being both necessary and of a temporary nature. The industrial future would bring both employment and prosperity to those who would become the future working class. The influential Communist Party of India (CPI) seems at least in their programmatic statements to have been more concerned with fighting domestic landlords and monopoly capitalists plus foreign imperialism than with supporting poor Indians being uprooted by the advances of modern capitalism.[8]

The communist influenced peasant organisation, the All-India Kisan Sabha (AIKS), seems even to have had a quite different focus in its activities related to the impact of the large dam projects. As mentioned earlier, one suggestion to finance the costs involved in the resettlement of people being displaced by large dams would be to put an extra tax on those lands that would benefit from the new irrigation facilities – a betterment levy. The official history of the AIKS thus mentions twice how the peasant movement in the Punjab in the 1950s had agitated forcefully against the suggested betterment levy associated with the Bhakra Nangal project (Nehru's 'modern temple'). The organisation and the peasants they represented clearly regarded the 'betterment levy' as an unfair tax on the common peasant (Rasul 1974: 202, 230). Nothing was mentioned on the compensatory purpose of the levy and of the plight of the displaced peasants.

India's socialist parties, generally influenced by Gandhian ideas on decentralisation, might also have been expected to show concerns for people displaced by large projects. Indeed, in one instance the prominent socialist leader, Ram Manohar Lohia, led a struggle against the Rihand dam project in the early 1960s. Apparently he had little success with the struggle either at the local level or in attracting national attention to the problems (Hemadri et al. 1999: xxvi). In Rourkela, the Praja Socialist Party were for a time involved in organising the displaced people (Strümpell 2014), but otherwise the socialist parties – like the communist ones – do not seem to have shown a great interest in the issues (Hartmann 1982: ch. 5).

The evidence on the attitudes and activities of social and political movements related to the displacement problems associated with the large infrastructural or industrial projects are admittedly very scarce. The scarcity of evidence probably reflects a genuine lack of interest and lack of activities related to the issue among the relevant organisations. This once again confirms that in the early period with large-scale developments projects in India the consensus on the desirability and necessity of the projects was so widespread and overwhelming that the notion that another path to economic modernity and prosperity might be possible was unthinkable. A price had to be paid, someone had to pay it, but there was no other way forward. Myrdal's observation of the overwhelming dominance of the 'modernisation ideal' at the time seems indeed to be correct.

In addition to this, it is hard to neglect the fact that the people who were mostly affected by the many large projects have been among the most marginalised elements of the Indian society and this may indeed have played a major role in the widespread neglect of the problem of displacement. According to one estimate, around 40 per cent of those affected by the construction of large dams have been tribals (Adivasis) and around 20 per cent have been people from the lowest castes (Dalits) (Hemadri et al. 1999: xci). In the mental calculations of the possible social costs of modernity and progress by the political elites, these 'simple villagers' (to quote from the DVC pamphlet) would in those days hardly have been seen as sufficiently important to mention, and certainly not important enough to warrant any change in the projects.

Why do the dogs bark (more loudly) today? Some speculations

According to the evidence collected here, there seems to have been much less public protest against the acquisition of land for industrial, mining and infrastructural projects during the 1950s and early 1960s than has been evident in relation to development projects in recent years. Policymakers seem to have had very little concern for resettlement and rehabilitation issues in those days, and they were apparently not challenged by popular forces at the time. Today the situation has changed, and public protests have become the rule, not the exception, whenever new projects are being contemplated. The issues have reached the national political agenda and most policies and plans for new projects today will include considerations of the possible negative effects, be they in the form of displacement of people or damage to the natural environment.

Why is this so? The nature of development projects today is probably very similar to those of earlier times in the sense that they require access to large chunks of land and need to remove people from the land. This implies that it is probably not so much changes in the nature of the projects that has led to increasing protests but rather changes within the Indian society and possibly changes in India's relations with the outside world. Four main groups of possible causal factors will be suggested here as explanations for the rising protest wave, either individually or in various combinations.

- *Demography and the accumulation of development projects.* The population of India in the 1950s was around 400 million. With no increase in available land, the demographic pressure on land must have increased considerably in an India with 1.2 billion people, many of whom still reside in the countryside. As a result, the scarcity of land has increased and so have the conflicts over land use. Combined with the fact that the process of industrialisation, urbanisation and general modernisation has progressed much further – and the accumulated area used for past development projects has increased and that available for future development projects possibly decreased – it has become harder to, for instance, find vacant land to offer for development projects or for the resettlement of displaced families. Intensified land use has also made agricultural land more productive and more valuable. In combination, these accumulated processes have made the stakes involved in today's conflicts over land use much higher, thus leading to more intense conflicts. In addition, it may be of importance that many new projects related to the expansion of urban areas and the establishment of Special Economic Zones in semi-urban areas affect peasants that are relatively more resourceful, politically active and positioned higher in the social hierarchy than the people located in remote regions (often Adivasis). Apart from the geographical dimension of development projects this also links up with the increasing politicisation of civil society in India.[9]
- *Politics and the politicisation of civil society.* Several political changes may have led to a much more politicised situation today in contrast to earlier

times. The dominance of the Congress Party (and its associated 'developmentalist' ideology) in the 1950s and 1960s has been replaced by a political system with an increased number of eagerly contended political parties, nationally and regionally. This 'deepening of democracy' has also meant that new political parties directly organising the lower and more marginal elements of the Indian society, in particular the lower castes, have entered the local and national political scene, leading to intensified political competition. As a result, it is today much easier to politicise the concerns of these hitherto subordinate social groups. A major part of the people affected by large development projects have always been marginalised groups like Adivasis and Dalits, but these groups are today much better organised than they were previously. Many projects today probably also affect middle-caste peasant farmers that are politically much better organised than the socially more marginalised Adivasis and Dalits. The growth of NGOs engaged in social and environmental issues – nationally as well as internationally – have also contributed to enlarging the voice of those affected by large projects. Combined with the rise and globalisation of the new media (read: internet), this has worked to improve the organisation, enlarge the voice and increase the influence of the affected people.[10] In short, India has experienced what has been called 'a silent revolution' (Jaffrelot 2003) or 'a democratic upsurge' (Yadav 2000) and this has most likely made the development process in general more prone to social contestation. The contribution of international NGOs may have been considerable, particularly in the anti-dam protests, in terms of support with information, money and technical expertise and through their influence on the changing policies of international organisations like the World Bank, which is often involved in the financing of large projects, including dams.[11]

- *The privatisation of 'development'.* The early period of rapid industrialisation was largely undertaken by state-owned companies working for what was generally accepted as being 'public purposes'. Today, in the economically more liberalised India, many, if not most, new projects are happening in the private sector under the control of Indian or foreign companies. This could very well have led to considerably more public distrust as to who might be the ultimate beneficiaries of the various projects. There has always been a general mistrust in the general Indian public towards private enterprises and more so against foreign enterprises. It is thus much easier to mobilise public opinion and political parties – and not only the leftist parties – against profit-seeking Indian or foreign companies. This mistrust of private enterprises and in particular of foreign private enterprises is clearly visible in many contemporary agitations against new industrial projects. In addition to the increased prominence of private enterprises, one can speculate that the 'neoliberal' turn in India has changed the nature of the state – the public authorities – in such a manner that their chief purpose is no longer to ensure 'development' but to facilitate the expansion of private capital under the pretext that this would automatically lead to a faster and better 'development'. Indeed, some would argue that the promotion of a market-driven or private business led economic process of change is what today characterises the Indian state and the political regime and what today is defined as 'development' (Levien 2015; Chandra 2015).

- *The process of social learning.* A final explanation for the difference in popular reaction to large-scale industrial and infrastructural projects could finally be a very simple one, namely that people have learned from many years of experience with large projects. There is today a vastly greater reservoir of (mostly) negative popular experiences from the construction of large projects and from protesting against such projects. It is indeed also possible that both public authorities and private entrepreneurs have become better informed and have become much better at minimising whatever problems large development projects encounter. It is most likely, however, that the increase in competence in managing projects has been overtaken by a more rapid increase in peoples' knowledge of the many failures (and few successes) of large projects, especially when it comes to managing resettlement and rehabilitation. Participants in protests today often refer back to previous experiences and the fact that old conflicts over resettlement and rehabilitation (Damodar, Hirakud) have resurfaced and motivated people to seek compensation from the state for evictions taking place decades ago is testament to this.

Concluding remarks

This chapter has offered some scattered evidence on the very limited early popular protests against large development projects ('the dog that didn't bark') and on how the associated displacement problems have been perceived in earlier times among dominant social forces. In addition, it has offered some speculations on how today's very vocal reactions to large projects can be understood and explained. Changes in demography and land availability have over the years increased the stakes involved for the people affected by large projects and, in combination with the political changes and the mobilisation of civil society, this could explain why protests have become so widespread today.

The absence of many of the suggested causal factors can then explain why there was so little protest in the early phases of India's industrialisation experience. In more general terms, increased globalisation – more foreign investments and more attention to projects from international NGOs – has gone hand in hand with the consolidation and extension of democratic processes in India, including the growth of an active civil society. This combination has made economic development a politically highly contested process and even if one of the specific features of today's development – its 'neoliberal' or privatised character – is changed or moderated, protests and contestation will probably not go away. In that sense we are witnessing an irreversible process of social change.

Many activists involved in protest activities today, as well as many scholars studying these protests and studying the often repressive handling of protests by public authorities, often tend, almost by default, to see the early period in India's development in a more favourable light (Levien 2012, 2015; Chandra 2015). This chapter has demonstrated that in the early period, with a stronger influence by the state over development projects, the plight of the dispossessed people was for the most part completely ignored due to the overwhelming 'developmentalist' or 'modernist' consensus. The policies of the period may well have been beneficial for India's subsequent development, but the simultaneous neglect of the predicament of poor people deserves not to be forgotten.

Notes

1 The curious incident of the dog that didn't bark occurs in Arthur Conan Doyle's Sherlock Holmes story titled *Silver Blaze* from 1895.
2 For more numbers and a passionate indictment of the displacement process, see Sainath (1996: 71–77).
3 Some states have also passed similar laws.
4 I have briefly checked the fourth, fifth and sixth plan documents. Even the World Bank, who closely monitored the Indian planning efforts during the 1950s and 1960s, though occasionally highly critical towards many policies, apparently did not notice the large-scale evictions associated with the large projects. All the bank's reports from the period are now available on the World Bank website.
5 Interestingly, the problems of displacement caused by the Damodar Valley project are still alive. As late as in 2011, representatives of Adivasis displaced by the Damodar Valley project staged a demonstration at Jantar Mantar in New Delhi. See YouTube video online, available at: www.youtube.com/watch?v=NRD3ZXbF88U. One can also find beautiful videos on both the Hirakud dam and of the Damodar Valley project.
6 Only in 1980 would an Industrial Policy Statement mention ecological problems.
7 This attitude forms an intrinsic part of what Myrdal (1968) calls the modernisation imperative and McMichael (1996) simply calls 'the development project'.
8 The left faction of the party, later to be named the Communist Party of India (Marxist), in their separate programme adopted in1964 supported state planning and the emphasis on large-scale industrial projects without mentioning the associated social costs (Communist Party of India (Marxist) 1964).
9 For a discussion of the conflicts over SEZs, see Levien (2012) and Jenkins et al. (2014).
10 It is of course debatable to what extent NGOs and political parties represent the 'true interests' of the affected people. What seems certain is that the asymmetry in power between the affected people and the large corporate interests involved has decreased.
11 Khagram (2004) narrates in detail how the rise of international NGOs affected movements and debates in India.

References

Areeparampil, Mathew (1996). 'Displacement due to Mining in Jharkhand'. *Economic and Political Weekly* 31(24): 1524–1528.
Austin, Granville (1966). *The Indian Constitution. Cornerstone of a Nation.* New Delhi: Oxford University Press.
Austin, Granville (1999). *Working a Democratic Constitution. The Indian Experience.* New Delhi: Oxford University Press.

Banerjee, B.N., G.D. Parikh, and V.M. Tarkunda (1946). *Peoples Plan* (CD-ROM from the Institute for Studies in Industrial Development, New Delhi).

Bhagwati, Jagdish N. and Padma Desai (1970). *India. Planning for Industrialization*. New Delhi: Oxford University Press.

Chandra, Kanchan (2015). 'The New Indian State. The Relocation of Patronage in the Post-Liberalisation Economy'. *Economic and Political Weekly* 50(41): 46–58.

Chandra, Uday (2013). 'Beyond Subalternity: Land, Community, and the State in Contemporary Jharkhand'. *Contemporary South Asia* 21(1): 52–61.

Communist Party of India (Marxist) (1964). 'Programme'. Calcutta: Communist Party of India (Marxist).

Damodar Valley Corporation (DVC) (1956). *Eight Years of DVC*. Calcutta: DVC.

Fernandes, Walter (2007). 'Singur and the Displacement Scenario'. *Economic and Political Weekly* 42(3): 203–206.

Franda, Marcus F. (1968). *West Bengal and the Federalizing Process in India*. Princeton: Princeton University Press.

Government of India (1945). 'Statement of Industrial Policy, April 1945' (reprinted in Sharad S. Marathe, (1986). *Regulation and Development. India's Policy Experience of Controls over Industries*. New Delhi: Sage).

Government of India (1948). 'Industrial Policy Statement 1948' (reprinted in NABHI's New Industrial Policy and Procedure, New Delhi, 1992).

Government of India (1956). 'Industrial Policy Statement 1956' (reprinted in NABHI's New Industrial Policy and Procedure, New Delhi, 1992).

Government of India (1977). 'The Constitution of India'. New Delhi: Government of India.

Guha, Ramachandran (2005). 'Prime Ministers and Big Dams'. *Hindu*, 18 December.

Hanson, A.H. (1966). *The Process of Planning. A Study of India's Five-Year Plans 1950–1964*. London: Oxford University Press.

Hartmann, Horst (1982). *Political Parties in India*. Meerut: Meenakshi Prakashan.

Hemadri, Ravi, Harsh Mander, and Vijay Nagaraj (1999). 'Dams, Displacement, Policy and Law in India'. Contributing Paper to the World Commission on Dams. Cape Town: World Commission on Dams.

Jaffrelot, Christophe (2003). *India's Silent Revolution*. New Delhi: Permanent Black.

Jenkins, Rob, Loraine Kennedy, and Partha Mukhopadhyay (eds) (2014). *Power, Policy, and Protest: The Politics of India's Special Economic Zones*. New Delhi: Oxford University Press.

Khagram, Sanjeev (2004). *Dams and Development: Transnational Struggles for Water and Power*. Ithaca, NY: Cornell University Press.

Kust, Matthew J. (1964). *Foreign Enterprise in India*. Chapel Hill, NC: University of North Carolina Press.

Levien, Michael (2012). 'The Land Question: Special Economic Zones and the Political Economy of Dispossession in India'. *Journal of Peasant Studies* 39(3/4): 933–969.

Levien, Michael (2015). 'From Primitive Accumulation to Regimes of Dispossession: Six Theses on India's Land Question'. *Economic and Political Weekly* 50(22): 146–157.

McMichael, Philip (1996). *Development and Social Change*. Thousand Oaks, CA: Pine Forge Press.

Menon, Nivedita and Aditya Nigam (2007). *Power and Contestation: India since 1989*. London: Zed Books.

Myrdal, Gunnar (1968). *Asian Drama: An Inquiry into the Poverty of Nations*. New York: Pantheon Books.

Nayak, Arun Kumar (2010). 'Big Dams and Protests in India: A Study of Hirakud Dam'. *Economic and Political Weekly* 45(2): 69–73.

Nehru, Jawarharlal (1954). 'Temples of a New Age' (reprinted in Rakesh Batabyel (ed.) (1977). *The Penguin Book of Modern Indian Speeches*, New Delhi: Penguin, pp. 587–590).

Oskarsson, Patrik and Kenneth Bo Nielsen (2014). 'Development Deadlock: Aborted Industrialization and Blocked Land Restitution in West Bengal and Andhra Pradesh, India'. *Development Studies Research* 1(1): 267–278.

Parry, Jonathan and Christian Struempell (2008). 'On the Desecration of Nehru's "Temples": Bhilai and Rourkela Compared'. *Economic and Political Weekly* 43(19): 47–57.

Planning Commission (1952). 'First Five Year Plan'. New Delhi: Government of India (reprint).

Planning Commission (1956). 'Second Five Year Plan'. New Delhi: Government of India (reprint).

Planning Commission (1961). 'Third Five Year Plan'. New Delhi: Government of India.

Planning Commission (2002). 'Tenth Five Year Plan 2002–2007'. New Delhi: Government of India.

Rasul, M.A. (1974). *A History of the All India Kisan Sabha*. Calcutta: National Book Agency.

Roy, Ajit (1965). *Planning in India*. Calcutta: National Publishers.

Sainath, P. (1996). *Everybody Loves a Good Drought: Stories from India's Poorest Districts*. New Delhi: Penguin Books.

Sathe, Dhanmanjiri (2015). 'Land Acquisition Act and the Ordinance: Some Issues'. *Economic and Political Weekly* 50(26/27): 90–95.

Singh, Khushwant (1957). 'Damodar Diary'. *Yojana*, 22 September: 7–15.

Sinha, B.K. (1996). 'Draft National Policy for Rehabilitation. Objectives and Principles'. *Economic and Political Weekly* 31(24): 1453–1460.

Strümpell, Christian (2014). 'The Politics of Dispossession in an Odishan Steel Town'. *Contributions to Indian Sociology* 48(1): 45–72.

Thakurdas, Sir Purshotamdas, J.R.D. Tata, G.D. Birla, Sir Ardeshir Dalal, Sir Shri Ram, Kasturbhai Lalbhai, A.D. Shroff, and John Matthai (1944–1945). *A Memorandum Outlining a Plan of Economic Development for India*. Harmondsworth, England: Penguin Books.

Yadav, Yogendra (2000). 'Understanding the Second Democratic Upsurge: Trends of Bahujan Participation in Electoral Politics in the 1990s'. In: Francine R. Frankel, Zoya Hasan, Rajeev Bhargava, and Balveer Arora (eds). *Transforming India: Social and Political Dynamics of Democracy*, New Delhi: Oxford University Press, pp. 120–145.

3 From state-led development to embedded neoliberalism

India's industrial and social policies in comparative perspective

Stein Sundstøl Eriksen

In the literature, there are mixed opinions about the links between economic globalisation and social policies. On the one hand, it is argued that increased global economic integration compels states to promote their countries' economic competitiveness. In an increasingly liberalised world economy, this leads to a 'race to the bottom', in which states, in order to attract investment and prevent capital flight, must cut spending and reduce tax rates (Swank 2001; Brooks 2009). On the other hand, it is claimed that in the face of increased economic insecurity, citizens will demand more social protection by the state, as compensation for increased insecurity. According to this argument, increased economic liberalisation will be accompanied by expanded social policies, along the lines seen in Europe in the period of 'embedded liberalism', when welfare states were built. For India, similar arguments have been made by Partha Chatterjee, who argues that along with a (neoliberal) policy promoting the 'primitive accumulation of capital', the state has undertaken to 'reverse the effects of primitive accumulation' by funding programmes that provide alternative means of livelihood to those that have lost them (Chatterjee 2013: 214).

This chapter will assess the role of the state in industrial development and welfare provision in India. It will trace the evolution of state policies, focusing mainly on the period from the 1970s until today, to identify patterns of both continuity and change. It will focus on:

1   Economic policies, including the system of regulation, degree of state ownership and industrial policy (state ownership, licensing, trade policies, tax system);
2   Social protection (direct or conditional cash transfers, social assistance, pensions, unemployment benefits, public works, health and education).

Drawing upon the analyses of Chatterjee (2008), John Harriss (2011) and Atul Kohli (2012) among others, the chapter asks whether the Indian state is moving towards a liberal state form in which both the state's economic engagement and its emphasis on social policy are reduced, or, alternatively, whether we can observe what Polanyi calls a double movement, where market expansion is accompanied by an increasing emphasis on social policy.

My argument is that recent changes do not represent a move towards a pure neoliberal model, with minimal state regulation of the economy and very low levels of social protection. Nor do they, as argued by Chatterjee, point towards the emergence of a social-liberal state with broadly market-friendly economic policies combined with an expanding social safety net to compensate those who suffer from the effects of liberalisation. Instead, the kind of state that is emerging in India can be described, following Kurtz and Brooks (2008), as an embedded neoliberal state. Such a state would deregulate the domestic market (including the labour market), reduce trade barriers, privatise state owned enterprises and deregulate finance. At the same time, it can maintain other forms of state support to industry, such as export promotion, technology development and infrastructure. However, it would not pursue a redistribution or a substantive expansion of social safety nets. Hence, the limited degree of economic liberalisation is a result, not of a compulsion to provide social security – as argued by Harriss (2011: 138) – but of capital's interest in state support.

This chapter proceeds as follows: after placing the analysis in a theoretical context, I trace the evolution of policies over time and, on the basis of global data sets, place the Indian state in relation to other states in the global south. I then assess what kind of state the changes in policy during the last decades have led to. Finally, I discuss some possible explanations of the observed pattern, focusing especially on the impact of economic globalisation and the social basis of the state.

The state, globalisation, and liberalisation

In the debate about globalisation, a key issue is whether increased economic interdependence is leading to a convergence towards a liberal state form. Processes of economic globalisation have led to growing economic interdependence in at least three ways. First, international trade has increased significantly in scale, making each state more dependent on international markets. Second, both production and finance have become more globally integrated. Inputs for production at one location are provided through the import of parts, machinery, etc. from other locations, and investments are increasingly internationalised, in the sense that a growing share of total investments occurs in countries other than the investors' home countries. Finally, the liberalisation and expansion of finance has made capital more mobile than ever before, and states have become more dependent on international fluctuations.

It is frequently claimed that these changes have led to a convergence of policies in the direction of macroeconomic policies with a reduced economic role for the state (Grahl 2001; Ohmae 1995; Robinson 2004). To promote economic competitiveness, all states are compelled to deregulate their economies by (a) liberalising trade; (b) opening up markets for foreign investment; (c) privatising state-owned companies; (d) liberalising financial markets; (e) strengthening property rights; and (f) reducing levels of taxation. As a result, it is argued, there is a tendency towards convergence around a (neo)liberal model of economic policy. In addition to international market processes, convergence may also be a result of international political relations. Thus, states and organisations – the United States, IMF, the World Bank, WTO and EU – sanction countries deemed too 'interventionist', or with poor macro-economic balances (Gowan 1999; Wade 2003).

At the same time, there is a large literature that emphasises the continuing varieties of institutional configurations and policy regimes (varieties of capitalism, hereafter VoC) (Berger and Dore 1996; Hall and Soskice 2001; Kitschelt *et al.* 1999; Streeck and Yamamura 2001). These studies have challenged the idea that globalisation has resulted in convergence towards a single liberal capitalist model. Instead, they argue that because institutional structure varies between countries, the responses to the common pressures emanating from globalisation also vary. The mechanisms are often not linear, and the effects of a given regulatory or institutional change may differ. Thus, while international pressure clearly is important for explaining policy changes, there are also domestic sources of both continuity and change.

Both the globalisation literature and the VoC School have focused mainly on Western countries (Becker 2014; Peck and Theodore 2007; Streeck 2012). Expanding these frameworks to include developing countries could provide evidence of the diversity of contemporary capitalism or, alternatively, of the universality of trends towards convergence. Students of developmental states have argued that high-growth economies have emerged in countries where states have had the ability to play an active role, disciplining capital and labour, regulating markets and intervening to ensure that markets serve the overarching aim of promoting growth and industrialisation (Chibber 2003; Evans 1995; Hobson and Weiss 1995; Kohli 2005; Wade 1990).

Both economic and social policies are related to the drawing of the boundary between state and society (Bourdieu 1999; Giddens 1985; Weintraub 1997). Economic liberalisation entails restricting the scope of the state, limiting its direct economic engagement and separating it more clearly from the private sphere of the market. States moving in the direction towards a liberal model would therefore reduce their direct economic engagements (e.g. state-owned enterprises, production licences and subsidies) and expand the scope of market competition. Instead of such regulations and restrictions of competition, they would regulate the economy from 'the outside' through legislation and the enforcement of competition rules. This does not necessarily mean that the state becomes less important or less powerful. Rather, it represents a change in the *form* of regulation, from direct to indirect market regulation. The establishment or expansion of social policy represents a change in the opposite direction, expanding the scope of state responsibilities and thereby of state institutions.

All states with a market economy and a democratic political system are faced with two structurally defined demands. On the one hand, they must promote capital accumulation and economic growth. On the other hand, they must generate a minimum of legitimacy. First, since states mainly rely on the taxation of the private sector to fund their activities, accumulation in the market is the state's main material precondition. Consequently, the state's ability to regulate the market depends on its access, through taxation, to material resources generated in the market. States therefore have an interest in promoting economic development: The more capital accumulation in the private sector, the stronger the material basis of the state. Conversely, if the state intervenes in the market in ways that weaken growth and accumulation, it may undermine its own material basis.

At the same time, all democratic states rely on a minimum of legitimacy. Governments must win the support of citizens through elections, and to do this, they must convince voters that what they do serves the interests of voters. While they may not need the active support or positive endorsement of the majority, they at least need to limit active opposition and mobilisation of opposition groups. They must therefore always present their policies as promoting the common interests of citizens.

As states adopt more liberal economic policies, there is a risk that some sectors of society will be adversely affected. These sectors are likely to oppose the policies of liberalisation, and if they are large enough, the state will be forced to adjust its policies. This is the logic underlying Polanyi's idea of a 'double movement' (Polanyi 1957): The adverse consequences of economic liberalisation lead to protests and political pressure for reforms that compensate those who lose out. While economic liberalisation does not always lead to a legitimacy crisis and a 'double movement' (as Polanyi could be interpreted as claiming), it may have this effect. If people lose their livelihood (jobs or access to land), there is a risk of social instability. Expanding social protection – either from above as a pre-emptive strategy – or from below – as a result of popular mobilisation – can then be a way of maintaining social stability and preserving political legitimacy in the context of economic liberalisation.

The two demands (accumulation and legitimacy) may be in tension. Thus, policies that are effective in promoting growth may be unpopular, and popular policies may undermine accumulation. This raises the question of how states deal with the potential tension between the need for political legitimation (through the distribution of benefits/services to groups on whose support the government depends) and the promotion of accumulation and growth (through policies that promote growth)? Thus, there may be situations where the state is dominated by one social group (e.g. corporate capital) and economically dependent on the revenue raised by taxing it, while at the same time being dependent on the political support of groups who do not directly benefit from current policies. In such cases, the state is faced with a fundamental dilemma: The policies that are seen as necessary for promoting growth could be politically impossible to implement. In situations with increased political mobilisation, considerations related to the need to generate political support must to an increasing degree take the interests of newly mobilised groups into account.

However, in countries where a large proportion of economic activity takes place outside the formal sphere regulated by the state, the relationship between accumulation and legitimacy may be different. In such countries, state policies have less direct impact on citizens' living conditions. This, in turn, could imply that there is less pressure for improved social protection, and that, as a consequence, it is less likely that one will see a 'double movement'. At the same time, the state's interest in, and ability to, expand social protection is also likely to be limited, since, by definition, the regulation and governance of the informal sector is difficult.

In the following, I will analyse how the Indian state has dealt with this dilemma in the context of increased economic globalisation. Economic and social policies are particularly suited for such a focus. While economic policies are the main way that states seeks to promote accumulation, social policies are a key area for the generation of state legitimacy.

The evolution of economic and social policies in India

Industrial policy

In India, the state adopted a strategy of 'planned' economic development after Independence. The model was characterised by the state-led promotion of autonomous, self-reliant economic development, with limited integration into the global economy (Byres 1994; Chakravarty 1987; D'Costa 2005). The state took on the role of guiding and directing economic activity, occupying the 'commanding heights' of the economy. This strategy had broad political support, including the support of existing industry.

Industrialisation was seen as a key policy objective. Central elements of industrial policy, as expressed in the 1951 Industries Development and Regulation Act and the different five-year plans, were import substitution, the protection of infant industries, and state-led industrialisation with an emphasis on public sector enterprises. Policies also included restrictions on inflows of products, capital, and technology. The public sector was supposed to dominate key sectors. Major sectors like banking, insurance, mining, and oil were controlled by the state. Moreover, the state directed private investment in accordance with planned priorities. And although the private sector was allowed to dominate manufacturing, financing mainly came from public sector financial institutions (Mazumdar 2012). The state also came to be the principal medium for the inflow of external capital into India.

To promote industrial development, the government also set up special provisions for rural industry. More than 800 items were reserved for rural and small-scale producers, through a system of licensing, production controls, differential taxation, and direct subsidies, including handlooms, pottery, and match making (Mukherjee and Zhang 2007).

In the period after Independence, growth increased significantly. Moreover, the highest level of growth was recorded in the industrial sector, reflecting the priority given to this sector by the government. The sectoral growth patterns in the different sectors are presented in Table 3.1.

Table 3.1 Economic growth in India

	1931–1947	1952–1967	1968–1981	1982–1991	1992–2001
Agriculture	0.2	1.8	3.3	3.5	2.7
Industry	1.2	6.3	4.1	7.1	5.7
Services	1.7	4.8	4.3	6.8	7.6
GDP	0.8	3.4	3.8	5.6	5.6
Per capita GDP	−0.5	1.4	1.5	3.4	3.5

Source: Khan (2011).

From the mid-1960s, growth slowed down, especially in industry. In contrast to the developmental states of East Asia, the extent of industrialisation (as measured by the share of industry in GDP) has remained limited in India. Although industrial growth has picked up again since the 1980s, this is mainly a result of growth in the construction sector (Mazumdar 2010). In fact, for industry outside the construction sector, the proportion of GDP has declined slightly since the late 1980s. The fairly high overall growth rates since the mid-1980s have therefore been driven not by manufacturing growth, but by growth in services and construction. Table 3.2 below compares the sectoral distribution of GDP in India with China and other regions.

Hence, India did not experience the kind of broad industrialisation and overall economic transformation seen in countries like South Korea. One reason for this was that the Indian state failed to impose strict discipline on private capital (Chibber 2003). Big business firms, with the assistance of the discretionary decision makers in the state apparatus, routinely abused, manipulated, and circumvented the system of controls to their advantage. And although the public sector share of the economy increased over time, it constituted only about a quarter of national output by 1991 (Mazumdar 2012). Clientelism and corruption also became widespread, especially after circa 1970 (Kohli 2005; Virmani 2004).

From the late 1970s, and during the 1980s, attempts were made to reform this system. However, the attempts at liberalisation did not bring fundamental change. Some modest liberalisation was achieved domestically, including the de-licensing of some industries. But in terms of external liberalisation, business

Table 3.2 Structure of output (percentage share in GDP)

	Agriculture 1990	Agriculture 2009	Manufacturing 1990	Manufacturing 2009	Services 1990	Services 2009
LAC	9	6	23	17	55	63
SSA	18	13	17	13	48	57
China	27	20	33	34	31	43
India	31	8	17	15	41	55

Source: World Bank, world development indicators.

groups were sceptical of removing protectionist measures, and little was achieved.

After the period of modest reforms from the mid-1980s, India announced a new policy of liberalisation in 1991, which explicitly broke with the earlier strategy of state-led economic development. From this year, 84 per cent of manufacturing output was delicensed (Ghosh 2014: 199). The shift in policy was initially triggered by a foreign exchange crisis, but was supported by key business groups. As in the earlier strategy, there was consensus between the government and big business about the broad orientation of economic policy (Kohli 2012; Pedersen 2007).

Market forces and the private sector were now seen as the drivers of growth, and many parts of the regime of regulation and control were dismantled. However, the process of liberalisation has been cautious. Tariffs and capital controls have been reduced, but not abolished. Privatisation was undertaken, but only gradually, and often in the form of the partial privatisation of public enterprises. Hence, the public sector has remained significant, particularly in key sectors like banking, oil and mining.

The main reforms implemented in the 1990s were in the following areas (Kotwal et al. 2011):

1   *Restrictions on imports* (tariff and nontariff barriers). Before the reforms, India's import duties were among the highest in the world and rates above 200 per cent were common (Ahluwalia 1999). The level of protection was significantly reduced in the 1990s. Non-tariff barriers, mainly consisting of licensing, were also reduced, first for capital goods and later also for consumer goods.
2   *Restrictions on the foreign and domestic private sector.* Foreign investment had been either prohibited or restricted to a maximum of 40 per cent (unless special permission was granted). The threshold level was first raised, and subsequently removed, and the prohibition of FDI was removed in most of the sectors where it had existed. Restrictions on the domestic sector took the form of investment licensing and price controls. By the end of the 1990s, licenses were only required in a few sectors, such as alcohol, tobacco, and defence related industries. Price controls were abolished in several industries in the early 1990s, including iron and steel, coal, and phosphatic fertilisers.
3   *State control of banking and insurance.* Indira Gandhi had nationalised most of India's private banks. Through the 1990s, banking licenses were granted to allow the establishment of new private banks (national and foreign). However, most banks remain state owned.
4   *Public sector monopolies.* Until 1991, 18 industries, including iron and steel, heavy plant and machinery, telecommunications and telecom equipment, mineral oils, mining, air transport services, and electricity generation and distribution, were reserved for the public sector. With reforms, only atomic energy, defence aircrafts and warships, and railway transport remained reserved for public sector enterprises.

The support system for the small-scale industrial sector was also reformed. While the reservation of certain sectors of industry for this sector remained, there was a shift from non-tariff barriers to tariff rates, which gradually decreased. The result was that growth in small-scale units fell by more than half, from over 9 per cent in the period 1981–1986 to 4.3 per cent in 1996–2001. Hence, the reforms had a clear negative effect on the small-scale sector, especially rural manufacturing (Mukherjee and Zhang 2007).

Since the reforms started, the Indian economy has seen annual growth rates of 6–8 per cent for almost two decades. The higher growth rates have been attributed to the policy of liberalisation. Thus, proponents of liberalisation (such as Ahluwalia, Bhagwati and Srinavasan) claim that India's planning for industrial development was a failure, and that the recent growth is a result of liberalisation. However, a closer look at the figures show that growth accelerated in the 1980s, well before 1991 (Nayyar 2006; Balakrishnan 2010). While some studies attribute this to the reforms initiated in the 1980s, others have highlighted the impact of state intervention before the onset of liberalisation (Chaudhuri 2002; Khan 2011; Kohli 2005; Rodrik and Subrahmaniam 2004; Kochar *et al.* 2006), or that slow growth until the 1980s was the result, not of planning and state regulation, but of the choice of import substitution rather than export-oriented industrialisation (Chibber 2003).

Whether we see the 1980s or the 1990s as the turning point, this narrative shows that the economic policies of the Indian state have moved decisively in a liberal direction in recent decades. However, this does not in itself indicate the degree of liberalisation in absolute terms, or in relation to other countries. I will therefore first present some indicators of the degree of liberalisation in relation to an ideal-typical standard, and then a comparison with selected other countries.

To assess the degree of liberalisation, I use the OECDs Product Market Regulation Index (Wölfl *et al.* 2010). In this index, countries are given a score from 0 to 6, where 0 is fully liberalised and 6 is fully regulated. The index is composed of three main indicators: state control, barriers to entrepreneurship, and barriers to trade and investment. Each of the three main indicators and each of the sub-indicators are given equal weight. The main indicators are broken down in the following way:

> *State control* = scope of public enterprise, direct control over business enterprises, price control, and use of command and control regulation;
> *Barriers to entrepreneurship* = licencing and permit system, simplicity and transparency of rules and procedures, administrative burdens for start-ups, legal barriers to competition, and anti-trust exemptions;
> *Barriers to trade and investment* = tariffs, discriminatory procedures, other regulatory barriers.

Using this method, India's liberalisation score was 3.71 in 1998 and 2.85 in 2008. Hence, the direction of change is clear and the Indian economy has certainly liberalised. However, if we place India in a comparative perspective, a somewhat different picture emerges. Broken down to the sub-components, the extent of regulation is especially high in the area of state control.

To place India in a comparative context, the following table (Table 3.3) shows 2008 figures for product market regulation for India, OECD countries, Latin America, Eastern Europe, and the United States.

We see that on all three dimensions, the Indian economy is more regulated than economies in all other regions. However, the gap between India and other countries is especially large in the area of state control. Also, the difference between India and Latin America is smallest in the area of barriers to trade and foreign investment, indicating that, at least in relative terms, liberalisation has proceeded furthest in this area. Compared to other emerging economies, such as China, Indonesia, and South Africa, the picture is somewhat different. In comparison with these countries, the overall level of regulation in India is about the same as that in Indonesia and South Africa (Wölfl *et al.* 2010). The same applies to the three sub-indicators (state control, barriers to entrepreneurship, and barriers to trade and foreign investment). China, however, is more regulated, in particular in the area of state control.

The OECD data on product market regulation do not exist for earlier periods, but a similar index, the Fraser Institute's Economic Freedom of the World Index, has data for India for the period 1975–2008. In this index, countries are given scores from 1 to 10, with 10 as the maximum degree of economic freedom and 1 as the minimum. India's scores on this index are shown in Table 3.4.

As can be seen, India's score has increased on all sub-components, and its overall score has gone from 5.4 in 1970 to 6.5 in 2008.

Two conclusions may be drawn on the basis of these tables. First, it is clear that India's economic policies in general and industrial policy in particular have been significantly liberalised since the early 1990s. It has become more open to the world market. Tariffs have been reduced, and barriers to foreign investment have been removed. Internally, licensing has by and large been abolished, and tax concessions have been granted to businesses. Second, in a comparative perspective, India's liberalisation has been cautious, and the country still remains

Table 3.3 Product market regulation in India: an international comparison

	India	OECD average	Eastern Europe*	Latin America**	US
Overall indicator	2.85	1.49	1.82	2.08	1.03
State control	3.47	2.12	2.74	2.16	1.19
Barriers to entrepreneurship	2.57	1.46	1.44	1.94	1.20
Barriers to trade and foreign investment	2.56	0.97	1.35	2.31	0.73

Source: adapted from Conway and Herd (2009: 4).

Notes
* Bulgaria, Czech Republic, Hungary, Romania, Slovak Republic, Turkey.
** Brazil, Chile, Mexico.

Table 3.4 India's economic freedom, 1970–2008

	Size of government	Legal system, security of property rights	Access to sound money	Freedom to trade internationally	Regulation of labour and business	Summary rating
1970	5.9	4.4	6.7	–	5.2	5.4
1975	4.9	2.6	6.4	4.0	4.8	4.6
1980	5.0	6.3	6.3	4.3	5.2	5.4
1985	4.5	5.4	6.6	3.7	5.2	5.1
1990	4.9	4.8	6.6	4.0	5.3	5.1
1995	6.3	5.9	6.5	4.7	5.5	5.8
2000	6.8	6.0	6.9	5.5	6.1	6.3
2005	6.7	6.4	6.8	6.5	6.4	6.6
2008	6.8	5.9	6.7	6.8	6.2	6.5

Source: Economic Freedom of the World (2010) and Central Statistical Organisation.

among the least liberalised economies in the world. This especially applies to the area of state control. State ownership of firms is still prevalent in a variety of sectors, including banking, mining, utilities, and communications (Conway and Herd 2009: 11), and privatisation has been limited. Hence, while the direction of change has clearly been towards more liberalisation, in a comparative perspective, the scale of that change is still limited.

Social policies

In terms of social policy, the Indian state has, throughout the Independence period, defined the reduction of poverty as an overarching goal. Sen and Rajasekhar (2012) identify four phases in the evolution of social policies in India. During first phase, the 1950s and 1960s, social policies did not have a prominent place, and social protection was essentially limited to the organised workers in the formal sector of the economy, including the public sector. In this period, the promotion of growth was seen as the state's main priority, and rapid industrialisation and economic growth, it was argued, was the best way to fight poverty. Reduction of poverty and improved economic security for the poor was expected to follow from growth (Chibber 2012).

During the second phase, the 1970s and 1980s, specific programmes to combat poverty were set up, as part of Indira Gandhi's policy of *Garibi Hatao* (abolish poverty). The most important of these programmes were the Public Distribution System (PDS), which distributed subsidised food in special 'rations shops' (see below), and the Integrated Rural Development Programme (IRDP), which initially focused on credit provision to rural households, and later shifted towards an emphasis on employment generation and food-for-work.

A third phase was initiated from the late 1980s and early 1990s, with the onset of economic liberalisation. In this phase, the main emphasis was on cutting government expenditure, and on shifting responsibilities for service provision from the state to private actors. Also, the provision of government services became more target-oriented, reserving access to those citizens defined as being below the poverty line (BPL). Finally, Sen and Rajasekhar argue that we are now witnessing a fourth phase, where social security is redefined as based on rights (to food, work, and information), rather than as needs-based.

The most important of the long established programmes is the PDS, a system of food subsidies. Those holding a card documenting that they are poor are allowed to buy subsidised food and non-food items in special government shops. Commodities distributed include staple food grains, such as wheat, rice, and sugar, and kerosene. The PDS system originated during the Second World War, when so-called fair-price shops were set up to prevent speculative trading in a time of severe shortages (Sen and Rajasekhar 2012: 115). It was retained after the war to ensure food supply in areas with shortages, but was more or less neglected until it was revived as a result of drought and food shortages in the mid-1960s. During the first phase, distribution through the PDS was generally dependent on imports of food grain. In the 1970s, it was made a universal scheme, and from 1978 to 1991, it was greatly expanded, supported by domestic procurement and stocks. In this period, all households, rural and urban, with a registered residential address were entitled to subsidised rations. The fourth phase, from 1991 to the present, is one in which the policy of universal PDS has been replaced by a targeted policy, where only those defined as BPL are entitled to subsidised rations. The shift from universal access to targeting only those BPL households, which expresses the government's prioritisation of cutting expenditure and reducing the budget deficit, has led to great difficulties in identifying BPL households, and therefore to the exclusion of as many as 50 per cent of those who qualify (Harriss 2011: 133). Thus, the PDS has evolved from a rationing scheme in selected cities to a national universal programme of food distribution, and most recently, to a programme targeting only the poorest.

The Congress-led UPA government that came to power in 2004 established a set of 'flagship programmes' aimed at poverty reduction. The most important of these was the National Rural Employment Guarantee Act (NREGA), established in 2005. This programme is supposed to guarantee all rural dwellers employment for at least 100 days per year, with a minimum wage of US$2 per day. The programme is not yet fully implemented, and the degree of implementation varies between different states, but the average number of work-days provided under the programme is only 32 days (Jha 2013) and works and payments have often been delayed and the administration of the programme inefficient (Sen and Rajasekhar 2012).

Other programmes initiated by the UPA government include the Midday Meal Scheme, the National Rural Health Mission, the Integrated Child Development Scheme, and the Jawaharlal Nehru National Urban Renewal Mission. Common to all of them is that, in spite of high-profile rhetorical commitment, the allocation of funds has been inadequate. The result, as Harriss argues, is that 'most of them, in most states, actually reach very few of their intended beneficiaries' (2011: 135). At the moment, the government is also considering the introduction of a programme of cash transfers, which is seen as a major initiate in poverty alleviation. However, the form and extent of this programme is not yet decided.

Although these programmes do not reach all those who qualify for them, they could be seen as attempts to compensate those who have been excluded from the benefits of economic growth. They are also to a large extent a result of mobilisation and protest on behalf of the excluded. However, there are two reasons why they cannot be seen as true counter-movements in Polanyi's sense. First, they have not – at least not so far – led to substantive results in terms of expanded social protection. Second, they are the result, not of popular mobilisation from below, among those who are most in need of such protection, but of middle-class protest on their behalf. At best, therefore, they represent a nascent 'counter-movement from above' (Harriss 2011). Below, Table 3.5 gives an overview of the trends in social expenditure (as percentage of GDP) in India since the mid-1980s. The social sector is defined here as what comes under 'Social Services' and 'Rural Development' in the Indian budgets. Basically this means health, education, water and sanitation, housing, anti-poverty programmes, employment programmes, etc.

It is noteworthy that the long-term trend is moderately downward. It reached a peak at 7.7 per cent in 1987–1988, and by 2005–2006 it had gone down to

Table 3.5 Trends in social sector expenditure (SSE) of central and state governments combined, as share of GDP

Year	SSE as % of GDP
1980–1981	4.9
1985–1986	6.6
1987–1988	7.7
1988–1989	7.4
1989–1990	7.6
1990–1991	6.9
1991–1992	6.7
1992–1993	6.5
1993–1994	6.6
1994–1995	6.6
1995–1996	6.6
1996–1997	6.3
1997–1998	6.5
1998–1999	6.8
1999–2000	7.0
2000–2001	7.0
2001–2002	6.7
2002–2003	6.8
2003–2004	6.6
2004–2005	6.9
2005–2006	6.8

Source: Sen and Rajasekhar (2012) and Ramakumar (2008).

6.8 per cent (according to Sen and Rajasekhar, the increase in 1999–2000 and 2000–2001 was due to pay increases in the civil service).

To place these figures in perspective, it is instructive to compare India's spending on social protection with that of other Asian countries. Table 3.6, following, shows the proportion of central government spending allocated to social protection in selected countries in Asia.

Note that the figures are significantly lower than in Table 3.2. This is because this table only includes central government expenditures, and does not include government expenditure on health. However, as shown by Joshi (2006), the central government's relative share of social sector expenditure has increased in recent years.

What is clear from this table is that India, along with Bangladesh, spends significantly less on social protection than other Asian countries.

We may sum up the evolution of India's policy of social protection in the following points:

1   Overall, social protection has been a low priority for the Indian government. Total expenditure as a proportion of GDP has always been low, and has been slightly declining in recent years, despite the establishment of new 'flagship programmes'.
2   Since the 1990s, policies have shifted from state-based universal programmes to a more market-based system, combining privatisation and 'public–private partnerships' with targeting.
3   In comparison with other countries, India's expenditure on social protection is low.
4   Recently, the central government's share of social expenditure has increased, but at the same time, the states have reduced theirs.

To conclude this historical description: India's economic policy has evolved in a clear, albeit cautious, liberalising direction, especially in terms of external openness and integration into global markets. It is therefore clear that India is indeed moving towards a more liberal economic policy, and in this respect becoming more like most other developing countries. However, it nevertheless remains a relatively regulated economy, with a large public sector and significant

Table 3.6 Social protection expenditure for selected low and middle-income countries of the Asia Pacific for 2009 (as percentage of GDP)

	1990	1995	2000	2005	2007	2012
India	1.73	1.55	1.61	1.54	1.87	2.39
Bangladesh	0.71	1.10	1.12	1.17	2.04	2.59
China	5.20	3.19	4.70	2.76	5.01	6.83
Vietnam	2.50	4.99	4.06	4.21	6.04	6.28
Thailand	1.47	1.83	2.57	3.67	6.18	7.24

Source: ILO (2014).

market regulations. Hence, the Indian economy is considerably more regulated and 'statist' than the liberal model suggests. At the same time, social policy has remained a low priority, and expenditures have remained more or less constant in the period since the 1980s. The changes that have taken place are, first, that the central government spends more on such policies, while the states spend less; and second, that targeting has become more widespread. One cannot, from the pattern of government expenditure, see any trend of increased emphasis on social policies. The low and stable expenditure on social policies indicates that liberalisation has not been accompanied by a strong 'double movement'.

Globalisation, liberalisation, and social policies: understanding the evolution of the Indian state

Globalisation theory sees domestic policies (economic and social) as shaped (if not determined) by external pressure from the world market, which compels states to adopt ever-more liberal policies and cuts in government expenditure. Polanyian analyses on the other hand, focus on the relationship between ordinary citizens and the state, and especially on the need for the state to compensate for the increased risks and insecurity caused by increased marketisation.

The limited nature of India's liberalisation appears to go against the argument of globalisation theory, while the lack of increase in expenditure on social policies as liberalisation has proceeded indicates a lack of a Polanyian double movement. Hence, neither the globalisation thesis, which stipulates that all countries move towards a liberal, market based model, nor 'the 'Polanyi thesis', of economic liberalisation being accompanied by increased emphasis on social policies, appear to be vindicated by the Indian experience. While these perspectives cannot be completely dismissed, it seems clear that neither of them can fully account for the pattern of change seen in India in recent decades.

What kind of state is India evolving towards? Following Kurtz and Brooks' (2008) analysis of the evolution of the state in Latin America, we may classify the type of state that has emerged there as one of 'embedded neoliberalism'. An embedded neoliberal state, they argue, is one that promotes international integration through external liberalisation, while at the same time taking an active role domestically. In particular it retains significant state ownership, and supports domestic firms through what they term supply-side support, such as subsidies, technological development, and state support, to sectors such as energy, utilities, and other forms of infrastructure. It is characterised by close ties between the state and business, and state policies are used mainly to promote the interests of capital. At the same time, they argue that such a state provides little social protection, presumably because intensified global competition makes such policies difficult.[1]

In many ways, this model fits India. Economic policies have moved clearly in a liberal direction since the 1990s, with significant forms of deregulation and privatisation. At the same time, in a comparative perspective, regulation is relatively extensive. However, compared to the Latin American cases discussed by

Brooks and Kurtz, India is much less integrated into global markets, and has significantly more state control, in particular in the form of state ownership of enterprises. It is also less open in terms of trade and investment policies, though in these areas, the difference between India and Latin America is smaller. Hence, while India is less liberal than the Latin American countries analysed by Brooks and Kurtz in terms of economic policy, the changes of the last two decades have clearly been in a liberal direction.

According to Brooks and Kurtz, while embedded neoliberal states have significant state engagement and market regulation, they have low levels of social protection. India's expenditure on social protection is indeed low. However, in the case of India, this cannot be explained by pressure induced by globalisation to cut state expenditure (as Brooks and Kurtz imply), since India's level of globalisation is still quite low. This raises the following question: If neither the globalisation thesis nor the Polanyi thesis appears to be able to explain the evolution of India's economic and social policies, then how can it be explained?

In this section, I first discuss why the changes predicted by globalisation theory and Polanyian theory have not (or only to a limited extent) proved to be correct. This question can be split in two: First, why has India not liberalised more? Second, why has there been no increase in expenditure on social policies as liberalisation has progressed?

Why, then, has India not liberalised more, given the increasing global integration and hence increasing competitive pressure from global markets? To answer this question, it is useful to repeat why globalisation theory predicts a growing convergence towards economic liberalism. The main causal factor, which drives countries towards such a model according to the theory, is external pressure. Such pressure can take two forms, political or market compulsion. It is easy to demonstrate that neither of these types of pressure has been particularly strong in the Indian case. First, the Indian economy was in fact barely exposed to global competition when liberalisation was initiated. The size of its domestic economy, in combination with the inward orientation of its economic policies, meant that the country was fairly insulated from the world economy when it started liberalising in the 1990s. Thus, on the KOF index of economic globalisation, India's score in 1990 was only 19.5 on a scale from 1 to 100. The same pattern is seen if one breaks economic globalisation down into its two subcomponents, actual flows score (18.7) and restrictions on flows (20.5).[2] Thus, unlike what was the case in many other developing countries, liberalisation was not the result of external market pressure.

Moreover, unlike many other developing countries, the Indian state has not been dependent on foreign aid. Although it has received a substantial amount of aid, this has never been a major source of government revenue, and international aid agencies have never had significant influence on government policy.

Thus, almost 25 years after the onset of liberalisation, India remains among the world's least liberalised economies, as shown above. The country still has a high level of state ownership and extensive market regulation. Taken together, the nature and scope of India's external links probably means that the importance of such links for the evolution of the Indian state since Independence is likely to have been limited, at least in comparative terms.

Both the sources of liberalisation and its limited nature must therefore be sought internally, in the domestic political economy. During the first decades after Independence, the Indian state was dominated by the Congress Party. The ruling coalition in this period consisted of an alliance of industrialists, capitalist farmers, and civil servants (Bardhan 1984; Vanaik 1990). None of the three groups were able to fully dominate the others, and power had to be shared between them, in an uneasy balance where the relative strength of the different groups changed over time. Most notably the relative strength of capitalist farmers grew, while the bureaucracy's influence gradually weakened (Chibber 2003; Vanaik, 1990). The main form of political integration of the majority of the population during this period was patronage. Local elites acting as intermediaries were the main form of linkage between the political system and the majority of the voters.

However, by the late 1970s the dominance of the Congress Party had eroded. Since then, political fragmentation and multi-party coalitions made formal interventionist policies more difficult to formulate and enforce. At the same time, there has been a significant political mobilisation from below, among lower castes and classes who are increasingly breaking their dependence on the upper castes. With this mobilisation, local elites are no longer able to control their voting behaviour, and new parties, often caste-based, have emerged, which challenge the domination of the traditional elites (Jaffrelot 2001).

The fragmentation of the Congress Party marked a significant change, weakening the coherence of the ruling coalition. However, the fragmentation of the dominant party-system also made it more difficult for anti-business coalitions within the party to block big business interests. Paradoxically, this allowed pro-business policies to emerge explicitly and without significant opposition in the 1980s, long before liberalisation. The growing capitalist class had started to act as a pressure group for liberalisation in the 1980s (Khan 2011; Kohli 2012; McCartney 2009). This class had grown and developed under the protectionist regulation regime. Its power and influence had increased relative to landed elites and the bureaucracy, and it had emerged as the dominant class (Chatterjee 2008; Kohli 2012).

The growing political power of business in some sectors and regions, together with close ties between business groups and sections of the political and bureaucratic machinery, allowed them to demand greater freedom in resource allocation decisions and drove the opening up that happened in the 1980s. When the balance of payment crisis emerged in 1991, it became possible to embark on economic liberalisation. The crisis, together with the fall of the Soviet Union and the subsequent reorientation towards the United States, made it possible to push through this change in 1991, with the support of those sections of big business with an interest in liberalisation.

The dismantling of state regulation and increased openness to foreign capital associated with reforms have further increased the size and strength of the corporate capitalist class. And once these reforms had started, they resulted in a further growth in the size of corporate capital, whose influence on government policies therefore increased. Thus, the shift in domestic political economy was both the cause and the consequence of economic liberalisation, as reforms generated their own momentum, further strengthening the groups that benefitted from them (Mazumdar 2014).

However, it is quite clear that economic liberalisation is not popular among voters. This is clear from a number of surveys (Harriss 2011; Chandhoke 2005; Kohli 2012). This creates a dilemma for the ruling elite: How can sufficient support be garnered for a policy opposed by a majority of voters? Kohli identifies several ways in which the ruling elite has sought to create what he calls 'an illusion of inclusion'. In the electoral arena, the two dominant political parties (Congress and BJP), who are in basic agreement about economic policy and the need for continuing the policy of liberalisation, have tended to downplay liberalisation in connection with elections. Instead, election campaigns have focused on other issues, such as nationalism and identity-related issues such as caste and religion, in combination with populist rhetoric.

Also, liberalisation has been legitimised in practical, technical terms, thus depoliticising the reforms. Reforms have been sliced up and carefully phased, depoliticising them while politicising other issues, and care has been taken not to alienate too many groups at once. This is what Jenkins (1999) has referred to as 'reforms by stealth' (see also Kohli 2012). In line with this, responsibility for economic policy has been delegated to technical organs such as the Ministry of Finance. Moreover, the policy of decentralisation has meant that the central government has been able to shift the blame for government policies to the states, thus absolving itself from responsibility for its effects. Thus, a situation has emerged in which the state is dominated by corporate capital, and economically dependent on the revenue raised by taxing it, while at the same time being dependent on the political support of groups who do not directly benefit from current policies.

The answer to the question 'why has India not liberalised more?' is therefore twofold: First, capital has not pushed for radical liberalisation. At least some factions of capital are served well by a relatively regulated system, as long as the form of regulation is broadly consistent with their interests. And as shown by several authors (e.g. Kohli 2012: 58), there is agreement among India's business associations about moderate global opening, an opening that might maximise the interests of indigenous Indian capital. Second, while liberalisation is unpopular, the influence of the popular classes on policymaking is limited, and their views on economic issues have not been major issues in elections, which is the main channel through which they can influence the state. Still, awareness of its unpopularity may have contributed to the government's cautiousness, out of fear for electoral losses. Hence, the unpopularity of liberalisation also creates limits in terms of how far it can be pushed, without creating a political backlash. These limits are the effects of democracy: As long as the elite has to win support from the majority, it cannot go too far in a direction opposed by the majority of voters.

But why has liberalisation not been accompanied by more emphasis on social policies? After all, the last decades have seen a great increase in inequality. In a context of increased lower class- and caste-based political mobilisation, one could have expected that persistent widespread poverty and growing inequality would create more pressure towards redistribution and service provision for the poor majority – in other words that the need to secure legitimacy would compel the state to increase the emphasis on social policy. But, to use Polanyi's terms, there has been no strong double movement from below, to compensate the poor majority for increased inequality, poor social services and slow progress of poverty alleviation. Instead, issues of distribution and of social policies have been marginalised, and those who stand to benefit from better services and more progressive social policies have been too weak politically to push more forcefully for a stronger emphasis on such policies.

Three reasons can be pointed out for this weakness. First, while many groups have mobilised politically, they have done so in a fragmented manner, along caste lines and in regional movements. In a society where no less than 83.4 per cent of the workforce are estimated to be employed in the informal sector (OECD 2009), it is extremely difficult to mobilise for improved social protection. This has made it difficult to create a unified counterforce to the ruling coalition and the state–business alliance, who have little interest in prioritising social policies and whose main priority is to promote growth through a policy of continued liberalisation. Second, much of this mobilisation has focused on symbolic issues of recognition, such as the protection of minorities, reservations for lower castes in educational institutions and government employment rather than on economic policy and demands for redistribution (Jenkins 1999; Kohli 2012). Third, those political forces that have tried to mobilise opposition to the current economic policy, such as the left parties and the labour movement, have been weakened and fragmented.

This, then, has been the strategy used by the ruling elite: Promote accumulation through liberalisation and cooperation with capital, and avoid a legitimation crisis by proceeding cautiously with liberalisation while depoliticising economic policy and focusing political debates on other issues. In this way, the government has been able to continue the policy of liberalisation, even though the majority opposes it, while at the same time keeping social expenditure at a low level. In a socially fragmented country like India, this strategy has succeeded, at least in the sense of having prevented a serious legitimation crisis.

Concluding remarks

There are two main narratives about the state of the state in contemporary globalised capitalism. The first, neoliberal narrative claims that there is no alternative to neoliberalism. In this perspective, it is argued that because of intensified global competition, states are compelled to deregulate their economies and reduce the role of the state in terms of regulation and social protection in order to promote competitiveness. Hence, it is argued that states across the world are converging towards a neoliberal state form, with open trade, deregulated markets, and a minimal role for the state.

According to the other narrative, a pure neoliberalism will lead to social instability, and in order to prevent this, states must provide social security and insurance to compensate citizens for this insecurity. Hence, increased liberalisation will lead to pressure on the state to increase social spending. Economic liberalisation must therefore be accompanied by an expanded social safety net.

This chapter has analysed the evolution of the Indian state in the light of these debates. I have argued that neither the neoliberal nor the social-liberal model capture the character of the state in India. On the one hand, economic liberalisation, while significant, has not led to the creation of anything like a pure neoliberal state model. After 30 years of liberalisation, state ownership is still very important, both in industry and finance, and significant forms of non-liberal regulation persist. On the other hand, economic liberalisation has not been accompanied by an expansion of social safety nets. Rather, in spite of much political rhetoric about inclusive development and the launch of a few large-scale welfare programmes (NREGA, literacy campaigns), there has been a small reduction in the proportion of government expenditure allocated to social policies. And the mobilisation that has occurred has been a result of activism from middle class organisations acting on behalf of the poor rather than of mobilisation from below (Harriss 2011).

What is emerging in India, therefore, is a form of state–market relations which is quite neoliberal in terms of its lack of commitment to social protection, but less neoliberal in terms of economic policy.[3] Following Kurtz and Brooks (2008), we may call this model 'embedded neoliberalism'. This model conforms neither to the orthodox market model nor to the state-led developmentalist/dirigiste model. Nor does it look like the Western welfare state model. Like the pure liberal model, it is characterised by certain forms of domestic deregulation and increasing economic openness. However, like the dirigiste model, this is combined with active state intervention, state support to export, producer subsidies, provision of finance, and subsidised energy. Hence, it includes state responsibility for providing industry with the conditions for accumulation, not just through deregulation, but also through a public policy oriented toward technological development, subsidies, education, and provision of infrastructure. The policy, therefore, can be described as neoliberal in some ways and statist in others. However, it is statist mainly in ways that benefit the capitalist class. At the same time, social policies have been given quite low priority, and there has been no strong double movement, which could 'reverse the effects of primitive accumulation'. Hence, the scale of liberalisation has been relatively limited, while the effects of primitive accumulation associated with liberalisation (inequality, insecurity) are not being reversed.

One possible explanation for the lack of a double movement is that it is simply a result of insufficient liberalisation: If, or when, the economy is sufficiently liberalised, and labour is fully commodified and separated from the means of production, a 'double movement' will inevitably emerge. However, it is also possible that the form that liberalisation and the process of primitive accumulation has taken in India means that there are great obstacles to the emergence of a double movement. Perhaps the largest such obstacle is the fact that the surplus labour generated by the process of primitive accumulation is not being absorbed into the labour market. Industrial growth is limited, and the growth that has taken place has been far from labour-intensive enough to generate sufficient employment. Instead, those dispossessed from agriculture or old industries end up in the vast informal sector, as casual labourers, street vendors, and hawkers etc. – politically and economically fragmented in ways that make political mobilisation for better social protection extremely difficult.

The emergence of an embedded neoliberal state, I have argued, is a result of the ways in which the state has sought to combine the two imperatives of promoting accumulation and securing legitimacy. Accumulation has been promoted through gradual, but limited internal and external liberalisation, made possible by the close alliance between the state and business. In a context where this policy is unpopular, a crisis of legitimacy has been prevented (more or less) by a combination of limiting the extent of liberalisation, depoliticising economic policy, and displacing economic issues from the political arena by focusing on symbolic politics. And in a situation where the electorate is fragmented and so much economic activity and social life in general takes place in the informal sector, the pressure for more social protection has been fairly limited.

Notes

1 In this respect, their argument seems to contradict recent developments in Latin America, where moderate left governments in countries such as Brazil and Argentina have increased their expenditure on social policies. In this respect, it could perhaps be argued that their description of embedded neoliberalism fits India better than it fits Latin America.

2 In the index, Economic Globalisation is measured in the following way: (i) Actual Flows accounts for 50 per cent and is sub-divided into Trade (percent of GDP) (21 per cent); Foreign Direct Investment, stocks (percent of GDP) (27 per cent); Portfolio Investment (percent of GDP) (24 per cent); Income Payments to Foreign Nationals (percent of GDP) (27 per cent); ii) Restrictions accounts for 50 per cent and is sub-divided into Hidden Import Barriers (24 per cent); Mean Tariff Rate (28 per cent); Taxes on International Trade (percent of current revenue) (26 per cent); Capital Account Restrictions (22 per cent).

3 This goes against John Harriss' conclusion that the explanation for India's departure from the neoliberal model is its compulsion to provide social security (Harriss 2011: 138).

References

Balakrishnan, Pulapre (2010). *Economic Growth in India: History and Prospect*. New Delhi: Oxford University Press.

Bardhan, Pranab (1984). *The Political Economy of Development in India*. New Delhi: Oxford University Press.

Becker, Uwe (2014). 'Introduction'. In: Uwe Becker (ed.). *The BRICs and Emerging Economies in Comparative Perspective*, London: Routledge, pp. 1–26.

Berger, Suzanne and Ronald Dore (eds.) (1996). *National Diversity and Global Capitalism*. Ithaca, NY: Cornell University Press.

Bond, Patrick (2000). *Elite Transition: From Apartheid to Neo-liberalism in South Africa*. London: Pluto Press.

Bourdieu, Pierre (1999). 'Rethinking the State: The Structure and Genesis of the Bureaucratic Field'. In: George Steinmetz (ed.). *State/Culture: State Formation after the Cultural Turn*, Ithaca, NY: Cornell University Press, pp. 53–75.

Brooks, Sarah (2009). *Social Protection and the Market in Latin America* Cambridge: Cambridge University Press.

Byres, Terence J. (ed.) (1994). *The State and Development Planning in India*. Delhi: Oxford University Press.

Chakravarty, Sukhamoy (1987). *Development Planning: The Indian Experience*. Oxford: Clarendon Press.

Chandhoke, Neera (2005). '"Seeing" the State in India'. *Economic and Political Weekly* 60(11): 1033–1039.

Chatterjee, Partha (2008). 'Democracy and Economic Transformation in India'. *Economic and Political Weekly* 43(16): 53–62.

Chatterjee, Partha (2013). 'Subaltern Studies and Capital'. *Economic and Political Weekly* 43(16): 43–62.

Chaudhuri, Sudip (2002). 'Economic Reforms and Industrial Structure in India'. *Economic and Political Weekly* 37(2): 155–162.

Chibber, Vivek (2003). *Locked in Place: State Building and Late Industrialization in India*. New Delhi: Tulika Books.

Chibber, Vivek (2012). 'Organized Interest, Development Strategies and Social Policies'. In: R. Nagaraj (ed.) *Growth, Inequality and Social Development in India*. New York: Palgrave MacMillan, pp. 168–193.

Conway, Paul and Richard Herd (2009). 'How Competitive is Product Market Regulation in India? An International and Cross-state Comparison'. *OECD Journal: Economic Studies*. Online, available at: www.oecd-ilibrary.org/economics/how-competitive-is-product-market-regulation-in-india_eco_studies-v2009-art6-en.

Corbridge, Stuart and John Harriss (2000). *Reinventing India*. Cambridge: Polity Press.

Crouch, Colin (2005). *Capitalist Diversity and Change. Recombinant Governance and Institutional Entrepreneurs*. Oxford: Oxford University Press.

D'Costa, Anthony (2005). *The Long March to Capitalism*. New York: Palgrave MacMillan.

Evans, Peter (1995). *Embedded Autonomy*. Princeton: Princeton University Press.

Evans, Peter, Dietrich Rueschemeyer and Theda Skocpol (1985). *Bringing the State Back In*. Cambridge: Cambridge University Press.

Giddens, Anthony (1985). *The Nation-state and Violence*. Cambridge: Polity Press.

Gowan, Peter (1999). *The Global Gamble*. London: Verso.

Grahl, John (2001). 'Globalized Finance. The Challenge to the Euro'. *New Left Review* 8: 23–47.

Hall, Peter and David Soskice (eds) (2001). *Varieties of Capitalism: The Institutional Foundations of Comparative Advantage*. Oxford: Oxford University Press.

Harriss, John (2011). 'How Far Have India's Economic Reforms Been Guided by Compassion and Justice? Social Policy in the Neoliberal Era'. In: Sanjay Ruparelia, Sanjay Reddy, John Harriss, and Stuart Corbridge (eds). *Understanding India's New Political Economy*, London: Routledge, pp. 127–140.

Hobson, John and Linda Weiss (1995). *States and Economic Development: A Comparative Historical Analysis*. Cambridge: Polity Press.

Hollingsworth, J. Rogers and Robert Boyer (eds) (1997). *Contemporary Capitalism: The Embeddedness of Institutions*. Cambridge: Cambridge University Press.

ILO (2012). 'Statistical Update on Employment in the Informal Economy'. Online, available at: http://laborsta.ilo.org/applv8/data/informal_economy/2012-06-Statistical%20update%20-%20v2.pdf (accessed 20 February 2016).

Jaffrelot, Christophe (2002). *India's Silent Revolution*. New York: Columbia University Press.

Jenkins, Rob (1999). *Democratic Politics and Economic Reform in India*. Cambridge: Cambridge University Press.

Jessop, Bob (1990). *State Theory*. Philadelphia: University of Pennsylvania Press.

Jha, Raghbendra (2013). 'Welfare Schemes and Social Protection in India'. ASARC Working Paper 2013/10. Online, available at: http://dx.doi.org/10.2139/ssrn.2303988 (accessed 23 February 2016).

Joshi, Seema (2006). 'Impact of Economic Reforms on Social Sector Expenditures in India'. In: G.K. Karanth (ed.) *Dimensions of Social Development: Status, Challenges, Prospects*. Bangalore: Institute for Economic Change.

Khan, Mushtaq (2011). 'India's Evolving Political Settlement and the Challenges of Sustaining Development'. Online, available at: http://eprints.soas.ac.uk/12844/1/Khan%20India's%20Evolving%20Political%20Settlement.pdf (accessed 24 February 2016).

Kitschelt, Herbert, Peter Lange, Gary Marks and John D. Stephens (eds) (1999). *Continuity and Change in Contemporary Capitalism*. Cambridge: Cambridge University Press.

Kohli, Atul (2005). *State-Directed Development*. Cambridge: Cambridge University Press.

Kohli, Atul (2012). *Poverty amidst Plenty in the New India*. Cambridge: Cambridge University Press.

Kotwal, Ashok, Bharat Ramaswami, and Wilima Wadhwa (2011). 'Economic Liberalization and Indian Economic Growth: What's the Evidence?'. *Journal of Economic Literature* 49(4): 1152–1199.

Kurtz, Marcus and Sarah Brooks (2008). 'Embedding Neoliberal Reform in Latin America'. *World Politics* 60(2): 231–280.

McCartney, Matthew (2009). *India – The Political Economy of Growth, Stagnation and the State, 1951–2007*. London: Routledge.

Mann, Michael (1993). *The Sources of Social Power. Volume II: The Rise of Classes and Nation-states, 1760–1914*. Cambridge: Cambridge University Press.

Mazumdar, Surajit (2010). 'Indian Capitalism: A Case That Doesn't Fit?'. MPRA Paper 28162. Online, available at: https://core.ac.uk/download/files/432/12026881.pdf.

Mazumdar, Surajit (2012). 'Big Business and Economic Nationalism in India'. MPRA Paper 28160. Online, available at: https://mpra.ub.uni-muenchen.de/28160/1/MPRA_paper_28160.pdf.

Mazumdar, Surajit (2014). 'Continuity and Change in Indian Capitalism'. In: Uwe Becker (ed.). *The BRICS and Emerging Economies in Comparative Perspective*, London: Routledge, pp. 79–99.

Mjøset, Lars and Tommy H. Clausen (eds) (2007). 'Capitalisms Compared'. *Comparative Social Research* 24: 1–258.

Mooij, Jos and Mahendra Dev (2004). 'Social Sector Priorities: An Analysis of Budgets and Expenditures in India in the 1990s'. *Development Policy Review* 22(1) 97–120.

Mukherjee, Anit and Xiaobo Zhang (2007). 'Rural Industrialization in China and India: Role of Policies and Institutions'. *World Development* 35(10): 1621–1634.

Nayyar, Deepak (2001). 'Economic Development and Political Democracy: Interaction of Economics and Politics in Independent India'. In Niraja Gopal Jayal (ed), *Democracy in India*. New Delhi: Oxford University Press, pp. 362–396.

OECD (2009) 'Is Informal Normal? Towards More and Better Jobs in Developing Countries'. Online, available at: www.oecd.org/dev/povertyreductionandsocialdevelopment/42863997.pdf (accessed 24 February 2016).

Offe, Claus (1995). *Modernity and the State*. Cambridge: Polity Press.

Ohmae, Kenichi (1995). *The End of the Nation State: The Rise of Regional Economies*. New York: Harper Collins.

Peck, Jamie and Nick Theodore (2007). 'Variegated Capitalism'. *Progress in Human Geography* 31(6): 731–772.

Pedersen, Jørgen Dige (2007). 'The Transformation of Indian Business: From Passive Resisters to Active Promoters of Globalization'. Paper presented at the Sixth Pan-European Conference on International Relations at the University of Turin, Italy, 12–15 September.

Polanyi, Karl (1957). *The Great Transformation: The Political and Economic Origins of our Time*. Boston, MA: Beacon Press.

Ramakumar, R. (2008). 'Levels and Composition of Public Social and Economic Expenditures in India 1950–51 to 2005–06'. *Social Scientist* 36(9): 48–94.

Robinson, William (2004). *A Theory of Global Capitalism: Production, Class, and State in a Transnational World*. Baltimore, MD: John Hopkins University Press.

Rodrik, Dani and Arvind Subramanian (2004). 'From "Hindu Growth" to Productivity Surge: The Mystery of the Indian Growth Transition'. NBER Working Paper No. 10376.

Sanyal, Kalyan (2007). *Rethinking Capitalist Development*. New Delhi: Routledge.

Sen, Gita and D. Rajasekhar (2012). 'Social Protection Policies, Experiences and Challenges'. In: R. Nagaraj (ed.). *Growth, Inequality and Social Development in India*, Basingstoke: Palgrave MacMillan, pp. 91–134.

Streeck, Wolfgang (2012). 'E Pluribus Unum? Varieties and Commonalities of Capitalism'. MPIfG Discussion Paper 10/12. Cologne: MPIfG.

Streeck, Wolfgang and Kozo Yamamura (eds) (2001). *The Origins of Nonliberal Capitalism: Germany and Japan in Comparison*. Ithaca, NY: Cornell University Press.

Swank, Duane (2001). 'Political Institutions and Welfare State Restructuring: The Impact of Institutions on Social Policy Change in Developed Democracies. In: Paul Pierson (ed.) *The New Politics of the Welfare State*. Oxford: Oxford University Press.

Vanaik, Achin (1990). *The Painful Transition*. London: Verso.

Virmani, Arvind (2004). 'India's Economic Growth: From Socialist Rate of Growth to Bharatiya Rate of Growth'. Working Paper No. 122, Indian Council for Research on International Economic Relations (ICRIER). New Delhi: ICRIER.

Wade, Robert (1990). *Governing the Market: Economic Theory and the Role of Government in East Asian Industrialization*. Princeton, NJ: Princeton University Press.

Wade, Robert (2003). 'The Invisible Hand of the American Empire'. *Ethics and International Affairs* 17(2): 77–88.

Weintraub, Jeff (1997). 'The Theory and Politics of the Private/Public Distinction'. In: Jeff Weintraub and Krishan Kumar (eds). *Public and Private in Thought and Practice*, Chicago: University of Chicago Press, pp. 1–42.

Wölfl, Anita, Isabelle Wanner, Oliver Röhn, and Guiseppe Nocoletti (2010). 'Product Market Regulation: Extending the Analysis beyond OECD Countries'. OECD Economics Department Working Paper No. 799. Paris: OECD Publishing.

4 'Should the son of a farmer always remain a farmer?'

The ambivalence of industrialisation and resistance in West Bengal

Sarasij Majumder and Kenneth Bo Nielsen

When the Left Front (LF) government of West Bengal was re-elected for a record sixth consecutive time in 2006, the comfortable victory was widely interpreted as a popular endorsement of an electoral promise of rapid industrialisation in a state that had by then witnessed a prolonged industrial decline lasting for several decades. The LF's election manifesto's section on industrialisation had promised the electorate to set up industrial parks; to increase investments in industry; and to modernise and make competitive the traditional labour-intensive industries. The state would in addition establish a minimum of four Special Economic Zones (*People's Democracy* 2006), which would be earmarked as duty free enclaves operating under a relaxed and business friendly policy regime (see also Bedi, this volume). As the quote – from the then chief minister, Buddhadeb Bhattacharya of the Communist Party of India (Marxist) (CPI(M)) (cited in Da Costa 2010: 20) – in the title of this chapter indicates, the stated aim of this policy was to create meaningful employment opportunities for 'the sons of farmers' outside of an agricultural economy that was increasingly recognised as incapable of fulfilling the economic needs and aspirations of present and future generations. Yet, as is by now well known, the LF's policy of rapidly industrialising the state encountered resistance in several places, derailing the LF's plans and eventually contributing to its ouster from office in 2011.

In this chapter we are concerned with understanding the link between industrial policymaking and its manifestation and reception in specific localities in West Bengal. How has industrial policy evolved in the state over the past decades? How have the liberalisation-induced alterations of the federal terrain influenced the processes and forms of industrialisation in West Bengal? And how can we understand the deep sense of ambivalence and resistance with which specific industrial projects are often received in rural settings? To contextualise and engage with these questions the chapter proceeds through three main areas of discussion. We first review the governance record and key policies of the LF's years in office from 1977 up to 2006. This is a story of agrarian reform and democratic decentralisation coupled with industrial decline and a centralisation of power and social control in the hands of the CPI(M) that has been told often, and we therefore only reproduce this story in condensed form here.

To understand how the LF's more recent industrial policies were received in particular settings, we use the case of the attempted – but eventually stalled – setting up of a Tata Motors car factory in Singur in the state's Hooghly district. The case of the Tata Motors factory in Singur made headlines not simply because of the visible resistance it encountered, but also because it – in social activist circles – was portrayed as paradigmatic of the state-led dispossession associated with industrialisation in contemporary India (e.g. Bidwai 2007). Yet in fact, the Tata project was met with a variety of responses, ranging from fierce protests against it by some of the dispossessed, to groups of ordinary villagers marching in its favour. Frequently, individual villagers would even express both points of view simultaneously, strongly endorsing the idea of generating more off-farm employment, while in the next breath decrying the setting up of the Tata factory in the vicinity. While recent anthropological research in particular has shown how a multiplicity of often contradictory aspirations, dreams, and anxieties converge with particular intensity upon large-scale industrial projects (e.g. Cross 2014), such ambivalence within communities and individuals as they encounter industrialisation is still often glossed over in popular representations (Majumder 2010; Nielsen 2014), but to us, it is of crucial importance for understanding how industrial policies are received and understood locally. More specifically, we argue that deeply ambivalent, localised perceptions of the relative merits of rapid industrialisation need, in the context of West Bengal, to be analysed in the light of the long-term formation of specific, and often contradictory, land-based identities and subjectivities, the origin of which precede LF rule, even if the LF's governance practices gave them a more concrete form. Land-based identities in contemporary West Bengal, we argue, embody contradictory aspirations insofar as they simultaneously produce a desire for land *and* for respectable off-farm employment. These contradictory aspirations, in turn, make a policy of rapid industrial rejuvenation an exceedingly difficult and delicate balancing act. As an epilogue, we examine how the incumbent Mamata Banerjee-led Trinamul Congress (TMC) government that replaced the LF in 2011 has, in rhetoric and policy, sought to engage with the vexed question of industrialisation.

Before we proceed, however, we would like to clarify how we believe our emphasis on historically produced land-based subjectivities as crucial for understanding how industrialisation evolves in practice, relates to other approaches to this question. While we certainly agree that the ideological dominance of business on industrial policymaking in India has been growing – evidenced in the current virtual consensus among all major political parties about the priorities of rapid economic growth led by private investments (Chatterjee 2008: 57) – actual processes of industrial development or urbanisation are surely shaped by a more complex and contingent set of factors. Most obviously, as Chandra (2015) has recently noted, this ideological dominance has not yet been successfully wedded to a matching political dominance, thus producing very different outcomes in different contexts (Nielsen and Oskarsson 2016). What we need to ask, then, is why and how industrialisation, land conversion, and urbanisation may, in one location, proceed with little or no resistance, and elsewhere encounter a lot of resistance. For that reason, we are concerned here with the relative pace and frictions – their presence, absence, and expressions – implicated in processes of industrialisation, and with how these interact with governing practices and complex local social hierarchies. In grappling with these issues, we take inspiration from an emerging scholarship (Corbridge 2011; Jenkins *et al.* 2014; Sud 2014; Bedi and Tillin 2015) that sees state-specific political, economic, and social environments as key factors that help explain the considerable variation, across India's federal geography, with industrialisation-induced land acquisitions and resistance in the context of economic liberalisation. As Bedi and Tillin (2015) argue, state governments legislate not just to attract capital, but also to appease key constituents and manage political consequences at the state level. And yet, an optic that emphasises the role of the state, its policies, and state elites, tends to obscure the perspectives of people in concrete sites of industrial development, people who are already engaged in diversifying livelihoods and seeking social and spatial mobility (Nielsen 2015). Studying what may be called the 'social life' of industrial policies – their emergence, implementation, and reception – brings us into contact with important, locally embedded popular sentiments about industrial development, sentiments that are as much about emotions, affect, ambiguity, aspirations, feelings, and anticipation as they are about rational cost–benefit calculations. As indicated, we later invoke the idea of land-based identities and subjectivities to unpack these sentiments and their role in shaping local responses to industrialisation in West Bengal. Our analysis will thus seek to bring out the importance of subjectivities, desires, and feelings implied in processes of industrialisation, over structures and institutions. We begin, however, at the policy level.

LF policy: foregrounding agriculture

The late 1960s and early 1970s, which witnessed the rise of the left parties in West Bengal, has aptly been described as 'a decade of chaos' (Kohli 1997: 342).[1] It was a period marred by several spells of emergency rule, urban terrorism, a Maoist-inspired rural insurgency and the often violent land grab movements encouraged by the left parties, particularly the CPI(M) (Ruud 2003). By 1977 the CPI(M) had penetrated rural Bengal by spearheading many of the land occupation movements. Thus, when the LF government came to power the same year, the CPI(M) had already built up a massive rural support base, which it has generally taken care to nurture and maintain since. Most significantly it has done so through a number of rural reform programmes that have centred on pro-poor agricultural development through the redistribution of ceiling surplus agricultural land, that is, land held in excess of the legal ceiling. In addition the rural reforms have included the revamping of the *panchayat* (village council) system of decentralised governance, as well as numerous other measures, including (following Webster 1992): (1) Operation *Barga*: Recording the names of *bargadar* (sharecropper) and securing them the legal rights to fixed and heritable tenure and a fixed share of the harvest; (2) efforts to detect, vest and distribute ceiling surplus land; (3) giving institutional credit to the recipients of vested land to break ties of debt and bondage; (4) assigning permanent title to homestead plots in order to prevent the eviction of landless agricultural workers and sharecroppers residing on the landowners' plots as permissive occupiers; (5) restoration of land alienated due to distress sale; and (6) providing irrigation, subsidies, exemption from revenues, and designing food-for-work programmes.

Most observers regard the LF government's rural reforms as having been relatively more successful than in many other states in India, where land reforms have often been carried out in a very limited form. During the 1980s, rural poverty in West Bengal declined significantly, the conditions of the rural poor gradually improved, and the agrarian impasse that had characterised West Bengal ever since Independence (Bhattacharyya and Bhattacharyya 2007) gave way to a decade of sustained and high agricultural growth from the mid-1980s.[2] These redistributive rural reforms have been instrumental in reinforcing the widespread rural support for the LF government, which remained intact until recently. Thus, when the LF took stock of its first 25 years in office in 2002, it highlighted land reforms and fighting vested rural interests as among its most important achievements (LF 2002). Both politically and symbolically the LF government has thus, throughout its years in office, been closely associated with the agrarian sector and the peasantry, and especially improved land access for the rural poor.

In contrast, the LF's stock-taking exercise from 2002 did not include a discussion on industrialisation. This is perhaps not surprising given how, as we elaborate on below, the LF government has generally presided over a gradual industrial decline. This decline assumed increasing significance when it became evident by the mid-1990s that the impressive rates of agricultural growth had relapsed into relative stagnation. The increasing population density in rural areas coupled with the accelerating fragmentation of land holdings[3] made intensive and mechanised forms of cultivation difficult, and in many places the potential inherent in high yield variety (HYV) seeds and the like had already been exhausted. With regards to rural employment, the most recent Human Development Report for West Bengal (WBHDR) concluded that these (and other) difficulties in agriculture had led to a situation where non-agricultural activities had become 'preferable' for many smallholder rural households – and not least for many a farmer's son – but that there 'quite simply was not enough jobs' (WBHDR 2004: 42, 89). Given these mounting problems in the agrarian economy, the industrial sector has increasingly been promoted as the sector most likely to provide solutions to the challenges of mounting under- or unemployment. The LF government's stand on industrialisation around the time of the 2006 elections had thus been designed and promoted to give a boost to industrial production, but the zeal with which this policy would later be pursued in rural areas such as Singur and Nandigram, and the pride of place it occupied in the LF's election manifesto, needs to be understood in light of the longer history of West Bengal's industrial decline.

Whereas West Bengal was once India's industrial powerhouse, it has witnessed a significant relative decline in industrial production since Independence, resulting from increased competition from other states, especially in Western and Southern India (Pedersen 2001: 649); and from the configuration of centre–state fiscal relations in the era of Nehruvian development thinking, underpinned by policies such as the Industrial Development and Regulation Act and the policy of freight equalisation. The latter made steel and coal available at common all-India prices everywhere, thereby 'in one stroke [removing] whatever locational advantage this state had due to proximity of coal, steel, etc.' (Roy 1996: 1095). Industrial decline gathered speed during the mid-1960s when West Bengal was hit hard by reductions in central government investments intended to hold back drought induced inflation; and the labour militancy that characterised the decade of chaos from 1967 onwards led to industrial closure and a further flight of capital (Kohli 1997: 352–353). By the early 1970s the industrial output of the state which made up 23 per cent of the all-India output in 1964 had dropped to around 10 per cent (Ram 1986: 17).

By the time India embarked on its path of economic liberalisation around 1991, West Bengal's problem of 'limited industrial dynamism' (Kohli 1997: 361) persisted. Thus, while Manuel Castells (2003: 267) has rightly remarked that India's economic liberalisation would soon induce an economic boom around areas such as Ahmedabad, Mumbai, Bangalore, and New Delhi, economic 'quasi-stagnation' would continue around other major metropolitan centres, and perhaps Kolkata especially, in spite of the LF government's pro-active response to the opening of the Indian economy. In West Bengal, the rising importance assigned to private industrialists was visible in the concerted efforts, from the 1990s, by the state government to involve the private sector in its economy by running advertising campaigns, organising investment-promotion road shows, and offering incentives to attract investors (Sinha 2005). The LF government introduced a new incentive scheme for investments in 1993, followed by a new industrial policy in 1994 (Pedersen 2001: 657–658) which in tone and tenor marked a clear departure from its earlier standpoint. When the LF came to power in 1977 it had spoken of 'lessening the stranglehold of the monopoly houses and of the multinationals', and of increasing the control of the workers over the industrial sector (Government of West Bengal 1978). Now, it spelt out its commitment to take the fullest advantage of the withdrawal of the freight equalisation policy and industrial delicensing; welcomed foreign technology and investment 'as may be appropriate'; recognised the importance of the private sector in providing accelerated growth; and stressed the need for 'harmonious industrial relations' (Government of West Bengal 1994: 6–8, 15). Later, in 2000, this was supplemented by the West Bengal Incentives Scheme for Industrial Projects (Government of West Bengal 2000), which was, in turn, superseded by a new incentives scheme in 2004 (Government of West Bengal 2004). Both schemes included an extensive list of incentives 'applicable to all large/small sale projects' (Government of West Bengal 2004: 6). These included capital investment and interest subsidies; refunds on stamp duty and registration fees; waiver of electricity duty; employment generation subsidies; and remission of various duties and fees. Yet this wooing of Indian and foreign investments did not produce the desired results, and by the late 1990s, West Bengal's share of the all-India industrial output had dropped to 5 per cent.

The reasons why West Bengal has found it so difficult to revive its industrial economy are complex. While they include the state's anti-investor image under LF rule (Guruswamy *et al.* 2005: 2154), an important additional explanation is that in today's competitive environment, many Indian states have entered the competition to attract industrial investment. Following economic liberalisation in 1991, the Indian states have acquired a much freer hand in attracting private investments directly, and the competition to do so is often fierce. To Jenkins (1998), this has produced a highly competitive race to the bottom – a kind of 'provincial Darwinism' – where the Indian states outbid each other through subsidies, cheap loans, tax waivers, land and the like to attract investments to their state. While Eastern India is often seen as somewhat of an exception to this pattern insofar as states such as Bihar, Jharkhand, and perhaps also Uttar Pradesh, for a long time more or less completely managed to ignore the 'compulsions' of economic liberalisation (Corbridge 2011), Jenkins's argument is compelling in the context of West Bengal, where ambitions and hopes of reviving the state's glorious industrial past persist among policymakers and a larger public, even as these ambitions are often frustrated.

When West Bengal headed for elections in 2006, the share of manufacturing in the state domestic product compared unfavourably with all major Indian states apart from Bihar and Kerala (Cortuk and Singh 2015: 93) who are hardly industrial powerhouses. Compared to its earlier policies, the LF government's recipe for industrial revival *anno* 2006 similarly relied on lucrative incentives, but the efforts to improve the image of the state as a favourable investment destination for industrialists were made in a more vigorous manner, and the endorsement of capitalism made more unambiguously than before. Under Chief Minister Bhattacharya's stewardship, private industrial investments – including foreign ones – were more aggressively courted, and investors reassured with promises of improvements, industrial peace, and administrative revamping (Basu 2007: 289). The LF's main campaign slogan was 'agriculture is our base, industry our future', and when the chief minister spoke at the LF's victory rally in Kolkata in late May 2006, he reiterated his government's commitment to industrialising Bengal: 'New employment opportunities have to be created for the people below the poverty line and hungry masses in the unlit villages whose misery we are aware of.... More capital to set up industries has to be generated' (cited in *The Statesman* 29 May 2006).

One of the earliest high-profile industrial projects to come out of this policy was the Tata Motors small car factory in Singur block, located some 40 km north of Kolkata. The Tata Motors project entailed the acquisition of 997 acres of fertile farmland from several thousand land owners. A majority of them consented to the acquisition in exchange for cash compensation, but a significant minority mobilised to resist the land acquisition from going ahead. While the land was acquired in December 2006 and construction work commenced in January the following year, the protests continued and finally, in October 2008, Tata Motors had had enough and decided to abandon their factory in Singur for greener Gujarati pastures. By then, another local group had organised to 'save the Nano', marching in rallies and putting up posters to encourage Tata Motors to stay in Singur. To explore why an industrial policy would meet with such diametrically opposite responses, and with many villagers often supporting both positions at the same time, we next turn to the analysis of the land-based subjectivities and identities we touched upon in the introduction. Here, we draw on Gidwani's (2008) notion of 'politics of work' and Majumder's (2012) idea of a 'politics of land', and use local practices of work and leisure geared towards subtle rural class politics and distinctions as our analytical starting point.

Contradictory aspirations: industrialisation, land-based identities, and the politics of land and work

Work has rich symbolic connotations.[4] It is aimed at furnishing material needs but simultaneously enables the creation and re-creation of one's identity and self-understanding in particular contexts. Rural households distinguish themselves by their ability to withdraw family labour, either partially or completely, from a commoditised labour circuit. This process, which Gidwani calls devalourisation, renders certain kinds of work less important or acceptable (2008: 142). Villagers' symbolic priorities, and not simple rational calculations, underlie this historical process of devalourisation of certain kinds of work that forms the bedrock of social distinctions that are both costly and risky to maintain in a village setting. They therefore require a certain political and economic wherewithal, such as land ownership. In addition to this 'politics of work' perspective, an idea of the 'politics of land' is thus necessary for understanding rural subjectivities and class relations in a context in which a major segment of the rural population is drifting away from agriculture toward a disorganised non-farm sector (Gupta 2015). Importantly, this drift does not transform rural villagers into proletarianised wage labourers – the antithesis of corporate capital – nor do they remain pristine peasants outside the formal ambit of capitalism; they rather become pluri-active (Lindberg 2012), straddling multiple economic and political worlds. In this context, the politics of land and work intertwine and manifest themselves in localised, complex, ambivalent responses to industry-induced land acquisitions, as we show later.

In contemporary West Bengal, the politics of land and work combine to simultaneously stabilise and destabilise the status of small landholders in the symbolic playing field of rural life. Land ownership continues to offer important social and economic leverage that enables one to have socially valued leisure time, to educate a male child for a non-farming career, to negotiate a dowry on the marriage market, to give orders to landless labourers, to drive hard negotiations with the land broker, and also to realise the speculative value of land if need be. Because it is a symbolic and material marker of distinction, ownership of land can work to sublimate unfulfilled hopes and desires, while at the same time representing possibilities for a better future because it can be leveraged to obtain the resources necessary to enter sought-after non-farm vocations. Herein lies the capacity for engendering desires and aspirations for a non-agricultural middle-class life sustained by employment in a government, white-collar, or factory setting that offers a regular salary and retirement benefits. Small land-holding villagers see, and measure, progress, development, and industry in the light of these aspirations, through which they position themselves in new rela-tionships with each other, and to the class of landless villagers and migrants, and their own small plots of land. As land holdings fragment and plot sizes dwindle, regulating the commodification of land increasingly depends on the availability of socially appropriate non-farm work – or other appropriate avenues of earning cash – that can be used to buy land rather than being pressured to sell it. The paucity of appropriate non-farm work thus tends to decommodify both land and work. This closely intertwined nature of the politics of land and work makes it immensely difficult to ascertain clear, unambiguous intentions and aspirations behind local responses to industrial projects.

The politics of land and work in Singur

We will now turn to the case of Singur and use the historical emergence of land as a symbolic good, and of salient land-based identities, to analyse the ambiva-lence and contradictions that characterised the Singur villagers' view of the industrial project that was slated to come up in their back yard.

Historian Sugata Bose (1994: 284) writes that the social structure of southern West Bengal in the 1920s contained three categories of people: The landlords of the Brahman or Kayastha[5] castes; the *chasis*, or small landholding farmers of agricultural castes, such as Mahishyas, Sadgopes (Goala), and Aguris; and labourers drawn from the Bagdi or Bauri lower castes and from indigenous San-thals. In districts like Hooghly, where Singur is located, Bose writes that in the 1920s, small landholding farmers of the Mahishya and Sadgope castes would lease land from the landlords and exploit the labour of Bagdi, Bauri, and Santhal sharecroppers to sustain agricultural production. Bose's account reveals an important internal hierarchy of supervisory smallholders and subordinate agri-cultural labourers among the so-called peasants of Hooghly. This situation is particularly instructive for the intertwining of the politics of land and the pol-itics of work insofar as it dissociates small-scale landownership from actual self-cultivation: In pre-Independence rural Bengal, caste hierarchies and social distinctions arose and were maintained along a division of labour between supervisory work versus heavily physical agricultural work.

The traditional supervisory status of small landholders acquired new political meaning under the Marxist regime, which used the land redistributions we dis-cussed earlier as a tool to win over this group, culturally and politically. In the context of the abolition of the *zamindari* system and the decline of *zamindari* influence, these targeted reforms ensured that the smallholders who gained ownership of, or legal sharecropping access to, the landlords' land remained loyal supporters of the LF. Smallholders' land was, in contrast, only rarely targeted for redistribution among agricultural labourers from lower castes (see Bardhan and Mookherjee 2010; Bhattacharya 1999). The Mahisya and Goala smallholders would eventually reap dividends of the productivity-enhancing improvements in agriculture that we also touched upon above: the installation of deep tube wells, the use of HYV seeds, etc. At the same time, as Bandyopahay explains, the leftist parties did not have enough suitable active members to field candidates for the full 65,000 seats in the 1977 *panchayat* (local government) elections (*Ekak Matra* 2008). The landless members of the CPI(M) did not have sufficient political capital and networks to contest elections so, subsequently, small landholders took the opportunity to join the rank and file of the CPI(M). As a result, small landholding households benefited from both the land redistribution policy *and* from political decentralisation, at the expense of the completely landless groups. The Marxist strategy of rural class consolidation transformed the self-understanding and identity of small landholders, such that they perceived themselves as more civilised than the agricultural labourers from lower castes or tribal groups. This heightened importance of older hierarchies articulated through a farmer, or *chasi*, identity provided the cultural basis of Marxist rule (see also Ruud 2003). And, because these intermediate *chasi* castes were numerous and influential in the Singur area, including both within and beyond the resistance movement, we focus particularly on them here.[6]

Haranath Kolay,[7] a resident of Gopalnagar village in Singur,[8] is an exemplary case to demonstrate the effects of political and policy shifts in rural Bengal, and their effects on people's aspirational subjectivity and engagement with the state and protest politics. As a schoolteacher, Haranath was respected in the village but also envied for his permanent government job, which came with retirement benefits and enough disposable income to speculate in land. Haranath never wasted time in *adda* (social gossip) at the village level, and instead devoted a major section of his morning time to supervising the labourers he hired to work his land, before he left to teach at school.

During co-author Majumder's fieldwork, Haranath expressed a deep desire that his two sons would leave their jewellery work in Gujarat and Maharashtra and return to Gopalnagar to perhaps set up small businesses near the new highway. While such small businesses were likely to thrive with the arrival of the Tata factory, Haranath lamented the land acquisition for the new Tata factory:

> This Marxist government gave us land; why are they taking that away? The plot that we got during the land redistribution went a long way to bring up my brothers and my children. How can I let it go? Additional income from the land will help us to send our grandchildren to schools and colleges. These days they charge a lot of money in the private engineering colleges. Won't they go to schools and colleges? Farming is no longer a respectable person's occupation.

By 'farming' Haranath meant supervising Muslim or low-caste, landless agricultural labourers. He recounted that his father had owned a small patch of land but would also informally lease land from the Kayastha *zamindar*[9] in Gopalnagar, land that he would plough with the help of other agricultural labourers: 'In those days land was not as productive as you see it now; it would only give one season of rice. Now it gives us two seasons of rice, potatoes, jute, and vegetables', he explained. His father apparently valued the leased plot he cultivated because it was his household's mainstay. Still, his family always lived under the threat of the *zamindar*, who could take the leased land away, thus reducing their income and status.[10]

Haranath's father had been a loyal subject who rarely disobeyed the *zamindar*, but other small landholders and sharecroppers had gradually started defying feudal power under the backing of Marxist politicians in the village. After the left parties first came to power in 1967, Haranath and his friends and brothers started directly defying the *zamindar* by occupying his land and identifying ceiling surplus land that each *zamindar* held with the active help of the police. As a result of this policy-driven activism, Haranath's father received ownership of the plots he was cultivating (with the help of hired labour) as well as legal access to the rest of the plots (i.e. a formal lease that protected him from eviction).

At the time Haranath also began actively shaping the village public sphere by performing in locally staged plays. He initiated a group called Samajsevak Sangha (Social Welfare Society). The Sangha organised cultural programmes celebrating Tagore, Nazrul, and Subhash Bose's birthdays. As key members of Samajsevak Sangha, Haranath and his friends would also organise camps to educate people about Indian history and leftism, teach them literacy, and inculcate values consistent with good moral character so that people would not drink, would respect women, and would wear slippers on social occasions instead of going barefoot.

These concerted efforts to wean society away from a hegemonic feudal culture also gave rise to new gendered moral codes and class distinctions in village public life. The camps challenged 'age-old' caste prejudices and feudal tendencies that shaped village habitus, and cultivated pride in a *chasi* identity. Haranath claimed that villagers were very lazy and superstitious, believing that supernatural forces affected their lives, which the Sangha also tried to address. Yet while Haranath was thus combatting sloth, superstition and debauchery, he detested the fact that women of Mahishya families worked with their husbands, just like many lower-caste families whose women worked and drank alongside their men. He claimed:

> We stopped that among the Mahishya. Women should not soil their hands. We also worked among the lower castes but they remained the same, some of them took us seriously but most of them remain lazy drunkards. They still remain underdeveloped.

Haranath proudly claimed that 'villages are the backbone of the nation', but that villagers and farmers like him are neglected in India. He acknowledged that local small landowners acquired some voice after the LF came to power and institutionalised the local *panchayats*; but he also lamented the increasing politicisation of community and household affairs that had accompanied the penetration of the left parties – and especially the CPI(M) – as people would now even marry along political lines. Local village CPI(M) leaders would also exercise socio-political control by targeting the disloyal small landholding households by not giving them welfare benefits, or by selectively formalising the access of the landless labourers to their land so that the small landholders would not be able to evict them from the fields. This was possible because the LF had never fully implemented the formal right of access to the land tilled by mostly Bagdi and Bauri landless labourers, retaining this policy as a means to penalise those smallholders who were disloyal, or were suspected of voting against the left parties. Yet Haranath added that many of the more powerful small landholding households in fact counteracted the LF's strategy by having family members in every political party, so that they could influence decisions concerning land regardless of which party won the local elections. Such strategising was important insofar as land, he emphasised, was his family's single most important asset: 'It is like gold; its price increases even if weeds grow on it. You sell gold only if you are distressed, so everybody waits for the right time. Why would we sell now?'

He pointed out that without their land the smallholders would become like the landless villagers: They would have to go to work every day and would lose the leisure time (and status) that supervision afforded them. Haranath lamented that whereas in his generation the children of *chasi* households would start going to the fields very early, 'these days, my sons and grandsons do not want to go to the fields. Since the time we taught them to wear shoes, they would not go to the fields, not even to supervise work'. But although interest in farming was thus declining within the family, Haranath claimed that formal rights to land had simultaneously increased rivalries among siblings. Brothers continued subdividing the plots held by their fathers or grandfathers and would build dikes to separate their portions of the field. Houses were also divided, he said, the kitchen and hearth sometimes being separated. He regretted the way that legal entitlement to individual plots had divided families and often led brothers to fight over miniscule patches of land.

Haranath's younger brother, Komol, gained some interest in farming after he lost his job in a factory near Kolkata that was shut down when the workers' union demanded a wage hike. Komol was not an enthusiastic farmer but had started accompanying Haranath to the field. He did not want to give up his land for the car factory, even if he was fairly compensated, because he earned some cash by selling whatever the labourers he employed grew on the land. He said that when he worked in the factory, he had to go to work every day; now he could relax some days and do odd jobs on other days. Yet he was at the same time unhappy about the closure of the factory he used to work in, which he attributed to the 'unnecessary trade unionism of the Marxist party'. 'I am sure'

Komol said, 'they [the Marxists] will encourage trade unionism here [at the Tata factory] and this will be closed'. He also expected that had he been able to continue working in the factory for just a few more years, he would have saved enough money to buy a few more plots by the highway and start a business: 'There is nothing like being your own boss and supervising others' Komol affirmed.

Haranath's account of the changes in village social and political life in the post-land reform years demonstrates how land emerged as an important marker of moral and social status in the villages. As a status marker, ownership or access to a plot of land structured the life history and socio-political practices, or *work*, of the individuals from small landholding households. Ownership of *land* gave one a sense of belonging to the village community and a higher status than agricultural workers. Small landholders' position of privilege also structured their sense of belonging to the nation, and with that came a responsibility to morally reform those social practices in the village that they viewed as backward. Thus, an intertwined politics of land and work served as the foundation for small landholders to internalise certain aspects of the development or improvement discourse promulgated by national and local politicians, Marxist or otherwise. But the problem of dwindling plot sizes and lack of non-farm employment close to the villages kept haunting them. Subdivision of plots affected the politics of land and work by making it increasingly difficult for small landholders to straddle the multiple worlds of politics and the economy, and maintain their status vis-à-vis agricultural workers.

In response to the crisis in land productivity caused by the dwindling size of holdings, the LF had earlier implemented two major coping strategies. First, new government primary and secondary schools became a viable employment option for many educated smallholders to find a new economic foothold without migrating out of the village. The second major option was petty trade of diverse kinds. On the one hand, male villagers of Haranath's generation, who had attended college, successfully found jobs in the many new local schools. But, on the other hand, the schools also created a new generation of male youths who went on to get college degrees, only to find themselves in a situation of industrial decline and diminishing employment prospects, as we described above. Their aspiration to make it in life via off-farm employment thus faced a gloomy future to the extent that even committed teachers like Haranath discouraged young boys from completing high school. In this situation, the default option was to engage in the many newly established jewellery workshops looking for apprentices; or to migrate to other cities in India. Thus, dwindling plot sizes and the absence of alternative employment options hindered the decommodification of labour on which the politics of work is based. At the same time, however, with people leaving the villages to work elsewhere, migrant remittances enhanced possibilities of speculating in land and recouping rural high status. The migrating male relatives could also return to their native villages to enjoy this enhanced status, a therapeutic experience in the context of their often isolated and difficult lives as wage-labourers in big cities. This life situation explains why giving up land for industrialisation would jeopardise the politics of land and work, which remained central to the constitution of the small land-holders' self-understanding and identity. Tellingly, returning migrant villagers from small landholding households, who had worked as jewellers in Mumbai and Ahmedabad, would deplore Kolkata as a 'second-class city' that could neither generate steady orders for the jewellery they made, nor evolve into an industrial hub like Mumbai.

The bustling bazar of Singur block near the villages was indicative of the second major non-farm livelihood choice – petty trade – undertaken by rural men who chose not to migrate. Entrepreneurial ventures in the bazaar included shops for anything from televisions and electronics to agricultural machinery, jewellery, fertilisers, books, and machine parts. Two short, ethnographic vignettes will demonstrate the subjectivities of these 'farmer-traders'.

Sapan Sahana was a well-to-do businessman whose father was a small land-holder. A jeweller, he had left Gopalnagar to work in a jewellery factory in Mumbai years ago. He later returned to the village to start a jewellery factory there that employed local young men. On the side, however, Sapan was a land broker and contractor who supplied materials for paving roads and building houses. He also belonged to a group of 300 local entrepreneurs who supplied labour and materials for building the Tata factory.

While the protests against the Nano factory dominated national media, there was an inordinate amount of excitement for the upcoming plant in the market area, where local entrepreneurs like Sapan anticipated increases in local busi-nesses in the form of shops, restaurants and a subsequent increase in land prices. The dream of having a non-farm income option in the vicinity of their native lands was exciting. The idea was that with the sprouting of diverse ventures one may find new livelihoods without having to butter up to party honchos or gov-ernment bureaucrats.

Sapan and other entrepreneurs like him were thus providing the non-farm employment that small landholders coveted. His various businesses therefore provided alternative avenues of employment to government jobs, which required the right party connections. Entrepreneurs such as Sapan also lent money to villagers seeking to start their own small business ventures. However, Sapan and other entrepreneurs like him were supporters of the opposition party, the TMC. While these entrepreneurs clearly did not have the capacity to provide jobs for *all* the small landholding villagers looking for non-farm employ-ment, their growing influence with the local youth nonetheless constituted a major threat to the LF, which had realised that land redistribution alone was not enough to forever retain the political loyalty of small landholders in the light of their rising demand for non-farm employment. The jobs that entrepren-eurs like Sapan generated enabled them to influence the village youth to support the TMC – which spearheaded the resistance to the Tata factory – and to oppose the ruling Marxists in local and provincial elections. Hemanta, a devout TMC supporter, was one such youth who also participated in, and sometimes led, demonstrations against the Tata factory.

Even though Hemanta's family owned substantial amounts of farmland, he genuinely deplored village life. He never wore a *lungi* or t-shirt in public, as middle-aged men did, nor did he favour the casual shorts and t-shirts that most men of his generation wore. He always dressed neatly in trousers, with his shirt tucked into the waistband and was never seen hanging out with other village youths; but, he was prominently present when the anti-factory protests dominated village life, only to disappear from the scene again when they eventually subsided: He wanted to get ahead in life and would not waste time talking to 'lazy villagers'. Towards this end, he worked as an agent for numerous private insurance companies, and Majumder regularly accompanied him when he sold insurance products to clients.

Hemanta thought that his reputation as an insurance agent would suffer if he worked as a farmer. He feared his clients would not trust him and would show little respect for his recommendations. For that reason, he had not been to his farm in four years. He said:

> These days you need not go to the field to supervise the labourers. We lease our land out and the plot goes to the highest bidder, that is, whoever will give us the most cash after growing and selling crops in our field. If the lessee fails to keep his promise, we look for a better one.

In most cases the lessee would be a landless agricultural worker of a lower caste.

Hemanta felt that selling insurance gave him independence and freed him from having to engage with agricultural workers every day: 'It is hassle-free', he claimed. Still, he was trying to invest some of the money he earned as an insurance agent in land in order to profit during the years ahead. He expected that if the factory was forced to leave its erstwhile site it would move to some other location roughly 15 km north of Gopalnagar, a move that would help him realise his dreams of profiting from land speculation. To him, the rationale was clear:

> How can one oppose the factory? We need factories, but we do not want them on our land. We are all developed and civilized people; there are backward areas 15 kilometers to the north. The government should set up the factory there.

He himself, of course, would not want to work in a factory since this entailed keeping regular work hours. He preferred to set up a shop and sell insurance, which gave him the personal freedom he valued.

The above ethnography brings out the complicated, often ambivalent, relationship between landowners and their land. Possession of land is fundamental to the stabilisation of their identity and self-understanding; yet these are *also* stabilised through a straddling of the divides between the urban and the rural, and between farm and non-farm spheres, in which industrialisation and off-farm work become crucial. To the extent that off-farm work is unavailable, or industrialisation absent, local identities and self-understandings are threatened and potentially destabilised. This produces an ambivalent and seemingly paradoxical public sentiment that is, in the context of land acquisitions, both for and against industrialisation. It is also a sentiment that political parties and ruling regimes seek to utilise and manage through promises, rhetoric, and – sometimes – policy. In the next section, we briefly examine how the current TMC-led state government has sought to manage these sentiments after coming to power in the state in 2011. We do so by examining the TMC's view on industrialisation in light of the arguments we have made so far.

Industrial policy under TMC rule

As a starting point it is important to note that even at the height of the popular resistance against the factory in Singur, the TMC's stand on industrialisation was conspicuously ambivalent. For example, speaking in Singur in August 2008, Mamata Banerjee had addressed Ratan Tata thus:

> Mr Tata, are you listening to me? Land [in Singur] has been acquired. Please accept the advice of the people of the area and return the 400 acres to the farmers.[11] We are pleading for both industry and agriculture so that people in industry and agriculture can smile.... There is still a solution.... We have a one-point programme: Let there be agriculture as well as industry.
> (Cited in Dam 2008)

This one-point programme would often, during and after the controversy in Singur, be reflected in populist slogans such as 'industry with cheers and not tears', or 'let both agriculture and industry smile' (Majumdar 2008), as well as in the TMC's promise to deliver a government that would uphold and defend the interests of *ma, mati, manush* – mother, earth, and humanity. But while the emphasis on *mati* – indexing land not just in an economic sense, but as something people are wedded to, around which their lives revolve (Gupta 2012: 95) – echoes land-based sentiments expressed in the conflict over the land acquisition in Singur, the TMC was not inclined to take a clear stand against industrialisation and urbanisation. Rather, in the development plan it submitted to the central government soon after winning the elections, it pledged to turn Kolkata into London. And, as we elaborate below, it advocated a policy of industrial rejuvenation surprisingly similar to that of its predecessor (albeit with some notable exceptions), with chief minister Mamata Banerjee proclaiming – at the 2016 Bengal Global Business Summit – that her government would 'not harass any industry. If problems crop up, we can always negotiate and sort it out amicably. Our aim is to make Bengal the no. 1 industrial destination' (cited in Mazumdar *et al.* 2016). Such contradictions in large part reflect the popular sentiments and ambivalences that we outlined above.

The TMC government's position on industrial development was most clearly articulated in its 2013 'Investment and Industrial Policy of West Bengal' (Government of West Bengal 2013). The policy stressed the urgency of providing stimulus measures for industries in the state. To this end, it intended to rapidly build and improve infrastructure – via public–private partnerships – to enable industrial growth at a rate of 20 per cent year on year. This, it claimed, would double the share of manufacturing of the state GDP in only five years. Other strategies to achieve this included the creation of a business friendly environment and a tax friendly regime; a disciplined work atmosphere; welcoming FDI; establishing a single-window system for industrial start-ups; promoting industrial corridors; creating land banks; undertaking strategic disinvestment in PSUs; and reducing red tape. Particular industrial sectors were also identified as especially important, including textiles, food processing, aquaculture, leather, gems, jewellery, IT, jute, tea, and chemical and petrochemical industries.

When set against the LF's 1994 policy the continuities are more striking than the differences, although the tone and tenor of the two policies differ somewhat. In 1994 FDI was welcomed where appropriate; 'harmonious industrial relations' were emphasised; improvement and upgradation of industrial infrastructure highlighted as indispensable; and IT, petrochemical, textiles, leather, food processing, aquaculture, chemicals, gems and jewellery identified as key sectors. The policy had an incentives scheme to assist in establishing new units or expanding existing ones, a scheme that contained many tax concessions; it even had a single-window set-up for clearances, the *silpabandhu*; and it promised 'quick decisions' in all fields of decision-making. At the policy level, the TMC's industrial policy *anno* 2013 was, in other words, not fundamentally different from that of the LF 20 years earlier. Yet where they differed crucially was in the field of providing land for industrialisation, a topic that was barely mentioned in 1994, but which in 2013 had its own subsection, underpinned by a separate land allotment policy, passed in 2012. Here, it was stated that 'the state government is against any kind of forcible acquisition of land' (Government of West Bengal 2013: 29). Instead, industrialists would have to purchase whatever land they needed directly from the land owners; or as a minimum, they would need their consent to have the government step in and acquire the land for them. But industrialists would not be left to fend entirely for themselves: The government claims to have worked to free up land for industries by other means, for instance by setting up a land bank which is claimed to have around 100,000 acres at its disposal (Wadke 2015). In spite of what may thus appear to be a somewhat stilted land scenario, the state has not been given the cold shoulder by investors. Rather, because of the many hurdles – administrative, political, and otherwise – associated with freeing up land for industries or real estate, land has (as in many other states)– become *the* booming sector in West Bengal, each hurdle and delay adding to its speculative value (Sud 2014).

Conclusion

In this chapter we have adopted a bottom-up view of the question of industrial policymaking and its ambivalent manifestations, focussing on how industrialisation is received and understood in a particular site proposed for industrialisation.

Using the case of the now aborted Tata Motors car factory in Singur in West Bengal as our empirical reference point, we have argued for an approach that takes as its point of departure an analysis of the long-term formation of specific, and often contradictory, land-based identities and subjectivities. These land-based identities in contemporary West Bengal, we have shown, embody contradictory and very ambivalent aspirations insofar as they simultaneously produce a desire for land *and* for respectable off-farm employment. Importantly, these sentiments are as much about emotions, affect, ambiguity, aspirations, feelings, and anticipation as they are about rational cost–benefit calculations of material benefits. This is not to suggest that landowners in rural West Bengal are not acutely aware of the fluctuations of land prices, or of the economic risks involved in relinquishing a regenerative resource (land) for a perishable one (jobs prone to downsizing; cash). Indeed, such concerns figure in the ongoing stabilisation and destabilisation of identities that we described in the ethnographic section. But, popular perceptions and receptions of practices of rapid industrial development are not reducible to such abstract, cost–benefit calculations.

While the Singur case is not paradigmatic, the argument that we have made with reference to this particular case has two implications that may find resonance in other, comparable contexts. First, our claim about the inherent ambivalence implied in processes of industrialisation, land-use, and resistance makes it exceedingly difficult to structure accounts of popular movements opposing land acquisitions for industrialisation in clear-cut, unambiguous terms. And second, it goes some way towards explaining why populist political rhetoric and discourse on rapid industrialisation is often so contradictory and contextual. As West Bengal heads for elections in the spring of 2016, we are likely to see such fluid rhetoric and policy statements flourish once again.

Notes

1 This section draws on Nielsen (2010).
2 This was also propelled by intensive cultivation, higher wages, improved seeds, small-scale irrigation, and deregulation of the local market (Bhattacharyya 2009: 59).
3 An average land holding in West Bengal is around 0.8 acres. More than 95 per cent of the state's farmers are classified as marginal (80+ per cent) or small (app. 15 per cent).
4 This section draws on Majumder (2012).
5 The Kayastha caste-group appears in Bengal and Orissa and occupies the lowest position in the hierarchy of the three upper castes in West Bengal, after the Brahman and Baidyas.
6 For an analysis of how e.g. landless, Dalit agricultural labourers perceived their own role in local social life and the economy, and in the movement against the Tata factory, see Nielsen (2016).
7 All names are pseudonyms.
8 This section is based on Majumder's fieldwork in the villages of Singur block between 2006 and 2010. Nielsen carried out fieldwork in the same area between 2007 and 2009.
9 Feudal lord.
10 They also had to give a significant portion of their harvest to the *zamindar*.
11 In the TMC's estimate, the so-called unwilling farmers owned around 400 acres of the land acquired for the Tata factory.

References

Bardhan, Pranab and Dilip Mukherjee (2010). 'Determinants of Redestributive Politics: An Empirical Analysis of Land Reforms in West Bengal, India'. *American Economic Review* 100(4): 1572–1600.

Basu, Partha Pratim (2007). 'Brand Buddha in India's West Bengal: The Left Reinvents Itself'. *Asian Survey* 47(2): 288–306.

Bedi, Heather, and Louise Tillin (2015). 'Inter-state Competition, Land Conflicts and Resistance in India'. *Oxford Development Studies* 43(2): 194–211.

Bhattacharya, Dwaipayan (1999). 'Politics of Middleness: The Changing Character of the Communist Party of India (Marxist) in Rural West Bengal (1977–90)'. In: Ben Rogaly, Barbara Harriss-White, and Sugato Bose (eds). *Sonar Bangla? Agricultural Growth and Agrarian Change in West Bengal and Bangladesh*, New Delhi: Sage, pp. 279–302.

Bhattacharyya, Dwaipayan (2009). 'Of Control and Factions: The Changing "Party-Society" in Rural West Bengal'. *Economic and Political Weekly* 44(9): 59–69.

Bhattacharyya, Maumiti and Sudipta Bhattacharyya (2007). 'Agrarian Impasse in West Bengal in the Liberalisation Era'. *Economic and Political Weekly* 42(52): 65–71.

Bidwai, Praful (2007). 'West Bengal on the Wrong Track? The Singur Syndrome'. In: Dola Sen and Debashis Bhattacharya (eds). *Singur and Nandigram and . . . – The Untold Story of Capitalised Marxism*, Kolkata: Kanoria Jute and Industries Limited' Sangrami Shramik Union, pp. 36–37.

Bose, Sugata (1994). 'A Typology of Agrarian Social Structure in Early Twentieth-Century Bengal'. In: David Ludden (ed.). *Agricultural Production and South Asian History*, New Delhi: Oxford University Press, pp. 267–301.

Business Standard (2012). 'Bengal Government Identifies Nine Lakh Acres for Land Bank'. 6 March. Online, available at: www.business-standard.com/article/economy-policy/bengal-govt-identifies-nine-lakh-acres-for-land-bank-112030600072_1.html (accessed 24 June 2015).

Castells, Manuel (2003). 'Rise of the Fourth World'. In: David Held and Anthony McGrew (eds). *Global Transformations Reader: An Introduction to the Globalization Debate*, New York: Blackwell, pp. 430–439.

Chandra, Kanchan (2015). 'The New Indian State: The Relocation of Patronage in the Post-Liberalisation Economy'. *Economic and Political Weekly* 50(41): 46–58.

Chatterjee, Partha (2008). 'Democracy and Economic Transformation in India'. *Economic and Political Weekly* 42(16): 53–62.

Corbridge, Stuart (2011). 'The Contested Geographies of Federalism in Post-reform India'. In: Sanjay Ruparelia, Sanjay Reddy, John Harriss, and Stuart Corbridge (eds). *Understanding India's New Political Economy: A Great Transformation?* London: Routledge, 66–80.

Cortuk, Orcan and Nirvikar Singh (2015). 'Analysing the Structural Change and Growth Relationship in India: State-level Evidence'. *Economic and Political Weekly* 50(24): 91–98.

Cross, Jamie (2014). *Dream Zones: Anticipating Capitalism and Development in India*. London: Pluto Press.

Da Costa, Dia (2010). *Development Dramas: Reimagining Rural Political Action in Eastern India*. Delhi: Routledge.

Dam, Marcus (2008). 'Let Agriculture and Industry Co-Exist'. *Hindu*, 23 August. Online, available at: www.hindu.com/2008/08/23/stories/2008082360821200.htm (accessed 17 April 2013).

Ekak Matra (2008). 'Interview with Debabrata Bandyopadhyay', November 2006.

Gidwani, Vinay (2008). *Capital, Interrupted: Agrarian Development and the Politics of Work in India.* Minneapolis, MN: University of Minnesota Press.

Government of West Bengal (1978). 'Industrial Policy for West Bengal'. *Social Scientist* 6(66/67): 103–108.

Government of West Bengal (1994). 'Policy Statement on Industrial Development'. Calcutta: Government of West Bengal.

Government of West Bengal (2000). 'West Bengal Incentives Scheme for Industrial Projects'. Online, available at: http://dcmsme.gov.in/policies/state/westbengal/ipwb.htm (accessed 11 March 2016).

Government of West Bengal (2004). 'West Bengal Incentive Scheme'. *Kolkata Gazette,* 31 March. Online, available at: www.google.no/url?sa=t&rct=j&q=&esrc=s&source=web&cd=1&cad=rja&uact=8&ved=0ahukewiwkpxny7jlahxchjokhrycbqiqfggbmaa&url=http%3a%2f%2fwww.wbidc.com%2fimages%2fpdf%2fwest_bengal_incentive_scheme_2004.pdf&usg=afqjcnea52b_irb34fiaiq4sswzdn4mcsw&bvm=bv.116573086,d.bgs (accessed 11 March 2016).

Government of West Bengal (2013). 'Investment and Industrial Policy of West Bengal'. Kolkata: Government of West Bengal.

Gupta, Dipankar (2015). 'The Importance of Being "Rurban": Tracking Changes in a Traditional Setting'. *Economic and Political Weekly* 50(24): 37–43.

Gupta, Monobina (2012). *Didi: A Political Biography.* Noida, India: Harper Collins.

Guruswamy, Mohan, Kamal Sharma, and Prakash Jeevan Mohanty (2005). 'Economic Growth and Development in West Bengal: Reality versus Perception'. *Economic and Political Weekly* 40(21): 2151–2157.

Jenkins, Rob (1998). 'The Development Implications of Federal Political Institutions in India'. In: Mark Robinson and Gordon White (eds). *The Democratic Developmental State,* Oxford: Oxford University Press, pp. 187–214.

Jenkins, Rob, Loraine Kennedy and Partha Mukhopadhyay (eds) (2014). *Power, Policy and Protest: The Politics of India's Special Economic Zones.* New Delhi: Oxford University Press.

Kolhi, Atul (1997 [1990]). 'From Breakdown to Order: West Bengal'. In: Partha Chatterjee (ed.). *State and Politics in India,* New Delhi: Oxford University Press, pp. 336–366.

LF (2002). '25 Years of Left Front Rule in West Bengal'. Online, available at: www.cpimwb.org.in/upload_all_docs/pdf/lf_govt/25_Years_of_Left_Front_in_West_Bengal_Booklet.pdf (accessed 10 March 2016).

Lindberg, Staffan (2012). 'Rural India 1970–2005: An Arduous Transition to What?' *Indian Journal of Labour Economics* 55(1): 61–75.

Majumdar, Diptosh (2008). 'UPA, CPM Government Betrayed Me: Mamata Banerjee'. *IBN Live,* 3 September. Online, available at: http://ibnlive.in.com/news/upa-cpm-govt-betrayed-me-mamata-banerjee/72752-37-single.html (accessed 17 April 2013).

Majumder, Sarasij (2010). 'The Nano Controversy: Peasant Identities, the Land Question and Neoliberal Industrialization in Marxist West Bengal, India'. *Journal of Emerging Knowledge on Emerging Markets* 2: 41–66.

Majumder, Sarasij (2012). '"Who Wants to Marry a Farmer?" Neoliberal Industrialization and the Politics of Land and Work in Rural West Bengal'. *Focaal: Journal of Global and Historical Anthropology* 64: 84–98.

Mazumdar, Rakhi, Madhuparna Das and Tasmayee Laha Roy (2016). 'Bengal Global Business Summit: Mamata Banerjee Hardsells State as the Place for Ease of Doing Business'. 11 January. Online, available at: http://articles.economictimes.indiatimes.

com/2016-01-11/news/69678998_1_bengal-global-business-summit-state-youth-mamata-banerjee (accessed 24 February 2016).

Nielsen, Kenneth Bo (2010). 'Contesting India's Development? Industrialisation, Land Acquisition and Protest in West Bengal'. *Forum for Development Studies* 37(2): 145–170.

Nielsen, Kenneth Bo (2014). 'Saving the Farmland: The Making of Popular Anti-Land Acquisition Politics in Singur, West Bengal'. Unpublished PhD dissertation: Department of Social Anthropology, University of Oslo.

Nielsen, Kenneth Bo (2015). 'Between Peasant Utopia and Neoliberal Dreams: Industrialisation and its Discontents in Emerging India'. In: Arve Hansen and Ulrikke Wethal (eds). *Emerging Economies and Challenges to Sustainability: Theories, Strategies, Local Realities*, London: Routledge, pp. 79–91.

Nielsen, Kenneth Bo (2016). 'The Politics of Caste and Class in Singur's Anti-Land Acquisition Struggle'. In: Uday Chandra, Geir Heierstad and Kenneth Bo Nielsen (eds). *The Politics of Caste in West Bengal*, New Delhi: Routledge, pp. 125–146.

Nielsen, Kenneth Bo and Patrik Oskarsson (2016). 'Development Deadlocks of the New Indian State'. *Economic and Political Weekly* 51(4): 67–69.

Pedersen, Jørgen Dige (2001). 'India's Industrial Dilemma in West Bengal'. *Asian Survey* 41(4): 646–668.

People's Democracy (2006). 'LF Election Manifesto Reiterates Pro-People, Pro-Poor Agenda'. *People's Democracy* 30(9).

Ram, Mohan (1986). 'Västbengalens Marxister Friar till Kapitalisterne' [West Bengal's Marxists Court the Capitalists]. *Sydasien* 10(1): 16–17.

Roy, S.N. (1996). 'West Bengal's Industrial Development Policy'. *Economic and Political Weekly* 31(18): 1094–1096.

Ruud, Arild Engelsen (2003). *Poetry of Village Politics: The Making of West Bengal's Rural Communism*. New Delhi: Oxford University Press.

Sinha, Aseema (2005). *The Regional Roots of Development Politics in India: The Divided Leviathan*. Bloomington, IN: Indiana University Press.

Sud, Nikita (2014). 'Governing India's Land'. *World Development* 60: 43–56.

Wadke, Rahul (2015). '"We Have a Land Bank of 1 Lakh Acres for Industrial Use": Amit Mitra'. *Hindu Business Line*, 15 September. Online, available at: www.thehindu businessline.com/economy/we-have-a-land-bank-of-1-lakh-acres-for-industrial-use-amit-mitra/article7656005.ece (accessed 23 February 2016).

WBHDR (2004). 'West Bengal Human Development Report'. Kolkata: Development and Planning Department, Government of West Bengal.

Webster, Neil (1992). *Panchayati Raj and the Decentralisation of Development Planning in West Bengal*. Calcutta: K.P. Bagchi.

Part III

Governing nature and society

5 Coal for national development in India

Transforming landscapes and social relations in the quest for energy security

Kuntala Lahiri-Dutt

In India, coal is much more than just a fossil fuel, a mere commodity in the nation's power supply.[1] I have previously argued that coal is seen as key to the country's sovereignty as a nation-state; is equivalent to modernity; and is crucial for an energy secure future for India (Lahiri-Dutt 2014a). At the same time, mining was arguably the earliest (and possibly the key) agent of transformation of landscapes and social relations in the coal-bearing regions of the country. As it charts new pathways into lands that have so far been claimed by indigenous communities (Adivasis, the original inhabitants, or known officially as the Scheduled Tribes), coal continues to redefine lands and social relations, making new territories and new worlds. This raises the question: Is the meaning of coal the same for the nation and the people? And what shapes these meanings? If the meanings of coal are not the same, then would it be possible to imagine more than one economy of coal in India? In this chapter I argue that there are multiple coal economies, which are intricately interlinked with local and national politics of resources and identities, each drawing upon different notions of mining, morality, and the material values of coal, in turn defining these meanings and values through a logic that is unique to each of them. The different coal economies transform the landscapes and social relations of the coal-producing regions in dramatic ways in the quest for national energy security.

I argue that the state-owned enterprise, Coal India Limited (CIL), represents the 'national coal' economy; the private entrepreneur-owned collieries producing coal that is captive to power plants represent the 'neoliberal coal' economy; the non-legal small-scale mines in India's northeast produce 'statecraft coal'; and last, but not the least, the innumerable poor, spread throughout India's coal-bearing tracts, illegally produce 'subsistence coal'. Each of these economies has different labour and resource regimes, and varying degrees of formal recognition that give rise to confusion over whether they are really four or five economies (or possibly even more 'sub-economies' hidden within the four identified so far). The production of four different coals from these diverse collieries, and the various actors, their interests and (sometimes conflicting) norms and values, make up the diverse worlds of coal in India. This chapter highlights the complex links between these economies, and the people who build them through their work. By doing so, it brings to light the intricate and dynamic relationships between people and coal, and situates the various ways in which this form of resource extraction transforms landscapes and social relations within the context of India's history and current economic growth trajectory.

To help understand these multiple economies of coal in India, I argue that coal as a mineral resource is not only a material *thing* but is co-produced by its utilitarian values of meeting the perceived needs of Indian society at given points in time. A part of this utilitarian value is embodied in the regulatory framework around coal; the plethora of laws around coal protects the legal eminence of the material resource. For example, the Mines and Minerals (Development and Regulation) Act 1957 (MMDR) classifies coal and lignite as 'major minerals' listed in Schedule A, which is reserved exclusively for the public sector. Through the legislation, the material commodity assumes wider social, cultural, and political meanings to associate itself with economic development, nationalism and nation-building, allowing the extraction of it by the state to represent a moral endeavour. The attachment of the resource to nation-building drives the state to attribute an iconic status to coal in India. Legal provisions such as the Coal Bearing Areas (Acquisition and Development) Act 1957 (CBAA) gives coal mining priority over all other uses of land as it takes precedence over other legislative measures. The CBAA was passed to: 'Establish greater public control over the coal mining industry and its development, [and] provide for the acquisition by the state of unworked land containing coal deposits or of rights in or over such land'.[2] By invoking CBAA, the state can overrule tribal or indigenous communities' ownership of land, even though this ownership is supposed to be non-transferable or inalienable. In coal mining, the CBAA and the (now repealed) Land Acquisition Act 1894 (LAA) together give the state the ultimate power of usurping any property belonging to any citizen for the extraction of coal. This legislation remains in place in spite of liberalisation. In fact, these laws can nowadays be utilised for the acquisition of land in favour of private entrepreneurs to expand coal mining for thermal power production.

The other law specific to coal is the Coal Mines (Nationalisation) Act 1973. Again, this 1973 Act reinforces the spirit of the MMDR because, by nationalising the mines, it has firmly consigned coal to the purview of the public sector. The Act categorically states that: 'No person, other than the central government or a government company or a corporation owned, managed or controlled by the central government shall carry on coal mining operation in India, in any form'.[3] Through these laws, coal and the nation become intimately associated, and assume the same meaning, allowing the state to adopt the high moral position. At the same time the legislation meant to protect the interests of poor indigenous communities and the environment assume a less important position to resource nationalism, implying that the need for coal for nation-building is superior to the need for the citizenry to claim rights over the land. Interestingly, the high moral position of the state on coal has developed significant fissures that allow other actors to adopt similar positions about their rights to extract coal according to their own moral logic, creating serious confusion over who (or what action) is right and what is wrong, in turn diffusing the ways in which coal extraction actually operates.

The chapter starts with a discussion on the material and symbolic values of coal. This theoretical discussion is followed by a look at the history of coal extraction in India, leading to a section that details the different worlds of coal and their respective forms of governance. The next two sections discuss, in turn, how coal transforms social relations and landscapes before connecting these transformations with the national quest for coal.

The material and aspirational qualities of coal

The need to expand India's domestic coal production by restructuring the coal mining industry has followed a rising sense of national crisis in the availability of energy. This availability is usually framed as part of military and strategic needs to maintain sovereign political power by the rapidly growing Indian economy. The sense of crisis is most acutely felt (and conveyed) in thinking about (the finiteness of) coal in terms of the (growing) population of India. The compelling reasons for increasing coal production lie in ensuring energy security, as the Planning Commission (2006: xxiv) elaborates. Given that coal accounts for around 55 per cent of India's current commercial energy consumption, and that about 75 per cent of total coal consumed in the country is used for power generation, coal is clearly and inextricably linked to the goal of ensuring India's energy security. Not only are resources constructed in these policy discourses by their utilitarian value in meeting human needs, they also assume wider cultural meanings associated with economic development, nationalism and the building of a modern nation. The procurement of certain physical quantities of material is framed as a problem – essentially one of there being less supply than is required. In documents such as the Planning Commission report (2006), the availability of electricity is equated with development. A picture of insecurity and a bleak future is drawn to convey the sense of urgency in dealing with the problem, often complemented by per capita comparisons of energy use between India and countries with a higher living standard, typically in the West but increasingly with China (Malik 2002; Garg and Shukla 2009).

In presenting coal as a 'more than material commodity', my argument draws upon ongoing debates in human geography, enlivened in particular by Ingold (2007), Castree (1995), and Richardson and Weszkalnys (2014), and their views of resources as co-constituted by nature and humans. Like other material things, coal traverses complex social and political spaces in its journey from being a material thing to being a resource, and then turns into a commodity; one can say that the material is created and re-created by those who use it in different ways. In the process, coal acquires meaning and assumes utility through its interactions with human society. To explain these diverse worlds of coal, I use here the framework proposed by Gibson-Graham (2006: 71), who argues that an economy can be seen as being organised by transactions, labour, and enterprise, each of which has alternative components to those generally subject to mainstream analyses that focus purely on formal market transactions, paid labour (waged and salaried), and capitalist enterprise. In particular, I explore what she describes as 'novel economic "positivities"' in articulating the politics of energy scarcity and crisis, where she observes (2006: xxxiv):

> Any contemporary economic politics confronts an existing object: An economy produced, through particular modes of representation and calculation, as a bounded sphere whose internal mechanisms and exchanges separate it from other social processes. This economy is not simply an ideological concept susceptible to intellectual debunking, but a materialization that participates in organizing the practices and processes that surround it, while at the same time being formatted and maintained by them.

Unless we fracture and dislocate India's coal economy, it remains impossible to recognise the diverse worlds that remain hidden within it, and how these in turn rework social and environmental relations. In this chapter, I will not only reveal four different coal production regimes and their sizes, but also touch upon the different 'rules' – the organising practices and processes – of these economies. The use of the analytical framework is justified by coal's deep and extensive influence in India, and by the extent and nature of these economies. The influence is clear from the fact that India is host to a separate Ministry for Coal, probably the only one in the contemporary era, and unparalleled in human history except in industrial revolution Britain. With a dedicated Ministry of Coal, coal obviously occupies pride of place in contemporary India, shaping the nation's energy future and influencing its economic and political milieu. The material acquires meaning and assumes utility through its interactions with Indian society, and the haze of coal smoke writes the capital–labour and capital–nature relations as they unfold in India. Within this context, it is possible to consider coal as something produced as much by humans as by nature.

Early geographical work on resources by Zimmerman (1951) suggested that 'resources are not, they become' (1951: 14). A similar vein of thought can be detected in the works of the Chicago-school of geographers who studied why human communities live in areas prone to natural hazards (for example White 1945). A social constructivism is clear in this line of thinking; it turns resources into a dynamic category – rather than resources 'being', they 'become'. That is, what counts as resource depends on the interaction between biophysical heterogeneity, technology and social institutions. However, geographical literatures in recent years have critiqued this weak form of social constructivism; Bakker and Bridge (2006: 18) critique the previous claims about resources as 'cultural appraisals of nature' for their rigidity in positioning resources within the pure realm of nature. In other words, they claim that Zimmerman's conceptualisation of resources is based on the idea of natural realism that treats resources unproblematically as a given category that is external to society. They suggest that the actual practices of resource acquisition demonstrate that this resolutely physical understanding of materiality is something of a fiction.

Disciplinary debates have centred on whether or not resources are 'out there' as part of nature and separate from humans, their perceptions and needs. Ingold (2007) put forth a critique of Gosden's (1999: 152) broad division of the material world into two components, landscape and artefacts – thereby placing the human mind as the 'other' of landscapes and artefacts. Ingold argues that greater attention to the materiality of objects makes it quite impossible to follow the multiple trails of transformations that 'converge' on a material. He proposes that a shift of focus should occur from the materiality of objects and measurable properties of materials to the subjective qualities of materials that are 'in here' (as against 'out there'). In other words, the qualities are perceived in our mind, as the ideas that each individual has about material things (such as coal). At the same time, Ingold criticises the establishment of a dichotomy between material properties and qualities because 'it takes us straight back to the polarisation of mind and matter from which our enquiry began' (Ingold 2007: 9), and concludes that there is a distinction between the 'material world' and the 'world of materials'. He explains that:

> The properties of materials, regarded as constituents of an environment, cannot be identified as fixed, essential attributes of things, but are rather processual and relational. They are neither objectively determined nor subjectively imagined but practically experienced. In that sense, every property is a condensed story.
>
> (Ibid.: 16)

One can, therefore, say that coal bears different meanings and presents different values to different people, depending on how they experience the material, and their usage. Such a subjective conceptualisation of materiality reduces the ambivalences that exist within research on the social construction of nature, and allows us to consider the taken-for-granted beliefs about the essential nature of resources by showing how particular concepts and categorisations of the material world have been produced and sustained over time (Demeritt 2002: 769). Materiality, in this formulation, occupies an inconsistent position that changes with the actors, the norms and values that guide their actions, and their politics. Such fluidity imbues the material fact of coal within the reality of the social lives of coal in India to create what Gibson-Graham (2006: 618) described as 'diverse' economies.

A symbol of colonialism becomes a symbol of national wealth

Coal mining was one of the pivotal 'modern' industries associated with India's colonial trajectory, but the industry assumed a new role as a national symbol after the Independence of the country. The mining of coal created a unique working class of rural and tribal migrants in the early colonial collieries. After

Independence, it was the collieries where the birth of the trade union movement was initiated to protest the ruthless exploitation of workers. Since the
nationalisation of coal mining in India beginning in 1971, the state-owned CIL
has been the equivalent of India's coal mining industry. India's resource nationalism is embodied in CIL, and one can say that the coal produced by it is
'national coal'.

Whereas old coal mining areas present widespread urban tracts with a bleak
outlook and decaying agriculture, in recent years the supremacy given to coal
mining has led to its expansion into forest-covered frontier areas that were
traditionally used by Adivasis and rural communities. Large, open-cut coal
mining operations have dispossessed and pauperised many such communities,
depriving them of their rights to retain the ownership of their lands (Sharan
2009). This strong version of resource nationalism on coal has been synonymous
with state capitalism in India. Often, the compelling need for coal is presented
as the need to produce electricity; a need that has prevented the Indian state
from engaging with the impending realities of a climate-changed future.

Modern, industrial coal mining is closely linked to the consolidation of colonial rule in India; 'discovered' in 1774 by two Englishmen, John Sumner and
Suetonius Grant Heatly (Ghosh 1977: 34), real growth began in the third
quarter of the nineteenth century after the construction of the railways. Simeon
(1996: 85) identified three main groups of actors that controlled the economic
regime of the colonial coal mines, operating in informal modes of regulation
that developed out of a pre-industrial social context supported by legal structures that, through inertia and laxity, accommodated the system. These were
the landlords who were rentiers and mine-owners, the managing agency houses,
and the Railway Board – the latter two firmly in British hands. While the first
group, the *zamindar* mine-owners, were arguably replicating the production relations known to them from agrarian feudal structures in order to ensure a steady
supply of labour, the managing agency houses and the Railway Board were effi-
ciently generating surplus by controlling trade and the market. The British managing agency system was created to serve the urban-industrial enclaves, and it
led to demand-centred organisation of the mining industry. In this organisation,
the managing agency houses, located usually in Calcutta, had evolved out of the
earlier commercial concerns that had traded in agricultural commodities and
functioned as 'primordial banks' (Tripathi 1979; Singh 1966).

Colonial collieries were the largest employers of mineworkers including
Adivasi men and women, and lower caste rural peasants from surrounding districts. India's indigenous communities and oppressed castes began their transformation into a proletarian working class in the highly exploitative and risky jobs
in collieries. Nonetheless, the trade being controlled by the British, colliery tracts
remained a resource periphery; the industry was a secondary enclave meant to
serve the primary industrial enclave of the metropolis. By the First World War,
the Indian coal industry fully displayed characteristics that one can still detect:
semi-feudal production relations and rural roots of labour, displacement of agriculture, environmental degradation in surrounding areas, and urbanisation.

Soon after India's Independence, coal's symbolism began to shift from colonialism to nationalism, primarily led by trade union movements. Trade unions became stronger in the collieries, some of which were owned by local landlords and were characterised by feudal labour and production relations (Kumar 1996). Union leaders united the workers to demand better and regular wages, increased safety, and more secure jobs. The new India aimed to become a socialist power that developed its own iron and steel plants, and the coal mines played a key role in fleshing out this dream of self-sufficiency. Under the five-year plans, state policies favouring industrial development further enhanced the demand for coal. Coal as a raw material was rapidly becoming the driver of the Indian industrial sector, and by mid-1960 had become a significant factor in achieving an industrially strong India (Kumarmangalam 1973). Around this time, electricity began to reach urban homes, and many urban households made the transition from biomass fuels to coal-fired cooking ovens. Coal became a source of comfort as well as the material with which to build a nation. These developments subtly shifted coal's symbolism from its past association with colonialism and its description as 'death pits' by socialist leaders (Dange 1945) to a contemporary nationalist project. The ideological wave was such that bringing all the collieries under state control by creating a major state enterprise appeared to be the most logical option for the Indian State.

Coal mining was brought under public ownership in several phases between 1971 and 1973, followed by the Coal Mines (Nationalisation) Act, passed by the Indian Parliament in 1973. In September 1975, the nationalised coal industry was restructured with the establishment of CIL, a holding company with its headquarters at Calcutta. CIL currently controls eight subsidiary companies, seven of which are coal-producing entities directly engaged in the extraction and distribution of coal. The eighth, Central Mine Planning and Design Institute Limited (CMPDIL), is solely engaged in mine planning and design. CIL has not, throughout its lifetime, met the expectations of a socially and environmentally responsible corporation – including the need for due diligence in land acquisition, resettlement of displaced people, rehabilitation of the environment, and financial viability. Yet, it has been remarkably resilient in surviving the new economic environment ushered in by the liberalisation of the Indian economy in 1991 when important responsibilities such as health and education were devolved to the private sector. Despite an absence of widespread support, CIL has continued to remain the largest player, limiting the extent of coal mining liberalisation to primarily the partial deregulation of coal pricing, and grants of mining leases to privately-owned companies to mine coal for thermal power production, the latter referred to as captive mining.

The multiple worlds of coal in India

Since the nationalisation of the coal industry, CIL has been the primary actor. This giant company[4] is labelled as a '*Maharatna*' (literally, the top gem), and is one of the 'nine gems' (*Navratna*) amongst the many public sector units (PSUs) that came into existence as a result of the 'commanding heights' policy adopted by the pro-USSR India, and continues to occupy a near-monopolistic position in official policy. CIL is the largest coal-producing company in the world, contributing about 81 per cent of total coal production in India. In 2012, CIL operated 471 mines spread across eight states. Of these, 273 are underground, 163 are open cut, and 35 use mixed mining methods, producing 450 million tonnes of coking and non-coking coal. In this chapter, the coal produced collectively by CIL and other smaller public entities is referred to as 'national coal'.[5]

However, the national coal is not entirely produced by employees hired by the CIL. Like the rest of India's formal sector economy, there is a large 'shadow' economy following CIL. As noted earlier, CIL's production relies both on in-house employees and on outside 'contractors' The contractors are privately-owned 'job-companies', which take the responsibility – against a contract, hence the name – to remove the overburden, mine coal, transport it to depots, load it in trucks, and fill up the voids created in the process. It is now more common for CIL to hire contractors to perform significant amounts of production-related tasks. The substantial numbers of labourers used by these contractors are not a part of the formal employment by CIL, they are purely informal-sector workers without a written job offer working at extremely low wages, often earned on a weekly or daily basis. They are often recruited from amongst the local displaced communities, and are in addition to the CIL work-force. There is no official record of employment of these numbers. An interview with one of the very senior managers of CIL held that the proportion of contractors' labourers adds another 50 per cent to the numbers hired officially by CIL. One might designate the contractors' labourers as the informal shadow of formal employment within the CIL. I assume that the other government-producers also employ a similar proportion of informal labourers. These low-wage temporary labourers are not included in calculating productivity, but their contributions are included in CIL's production figures. Gibson-Graham would describe this as a classical example of a 'hidden economy' (2006: 137).

The economic liberalisation of the Indian economy has led to divestment and privatisation of several important industries, but the Coal Mines (Nationalisation) Amendment Bill, proposed in 2000 to fully liberalise the coal industry, is still waiting consideration by the Indian Parliament. The 1973 Act was amended in 1993 to grant mining leases to privately-owned companies, primarily to produce coal meant only for designated power plants. In other words, these collieries are 'captive' to the thermal power plants they supply coal to (Lahiri-Dutt et al. 2014a). The captive private producers are mines owned by Indian entre-preneurs in search of capital gains from the ongoing and rising demands domesti-cally for energy, but operating in incongruous circumstances in which coal is accorded iconic and special status as a key agent of nation-building and national prosperity. The captive private producers collectively produce 6.5 per cent of the coal the Indian Government records as the official total production of coal within the country (Economic Times 2015). Captive coal mines are a result of the Indian state's attempts to deregulate the coal mining sector post-1991 in response to the growing energy demands in India. This is why I describe this coal economy as 'neoliberal coal'. The deregulation is nowhere near complete, as evident from the hegemony of CIL in coal production, but these mines have been in the news for a number of reasons in recent years: Their larger ecological footprint than the old CIL mines; the corruption involved in selected privately-owned companies' acquisition of mining leases in certain coal-blocks; and the underhand and undemocratic methods applied by some of these colliery owners in getting access to the coal-bearing lands. These collieries are generally open-cut with large ecological footprints, and their production feeds into power stations located nearby. Locally, these companies employ contractual labour and show only very limited employment figures on their websites. In the absence of officially available recorded data, I assume that the proportion of formal–informal employment in captive collieries will be similar to that of CIL.

The third coal economy comprises 'statecraft coal'. The government coal production figures show that five million tonnes of coal are produced annually in the northeastern state of Meghalaya. This coal economy exists far away from public vision, concealed inside the forested hill tracts of remote northeastern India, primarily in the state of Meghalaya (see Karlsson, this volume). This state enjoys the special status as a Sixth Schedule state in the Indian Constitution. Under this schedule, the land-owners in Meghalaya – generally local 'scheduled tribe' or indigenous communities – reserve the right to enjoy the natural resources of the land, including the mineral resources below the surface. Generally, the Indian Constitution attributes to state governments the ownership of minerals lying at a depth greater than six inches under the surface. However, the special status of Meghalaya has created a grey area of non-legality that denies a straightforward distinction between legal and illegal. Whilst coal as a major mineral cannot be mined by individual entrepreneurs (as per MMDR), the land-owners in Meghalaya, by virtue of the special status awarded are owners of the coal. The special status was attributed to Meghalaya to bring the territory within the territories of the Indian state. This non-legal coal mining economy is located within the political expediency of territory-building by the state, a practicality that provided sovereign rights over resources to the local people unlike anywhere else in India. The coal produced in Meghalaya, therefore, is best described as 'statecraft coal'.

In tracing the history of the cultural politics of coal in Meghalaya, where ethnic identity is used as a cultural tool to justify coal mining by indigenous mine owners, and the contradictory legal rules around land and mining, Das (2014: 79) argued that governance of such non-state spaces is problematic. I describe the coal mines of Meghalaya as 'non-legal' to underline the problematic nature of resource governance frameworks, and to imply the placement of such mining in an unclear position versus coal legislation. Consequently, the mining of statecraft coal presents a phenomenon that is not even qualified for or phrased in the manner in which law has presented or practised the governance of resources. The statecraft coal economy is firmly a part of the informal sector.

Since these collieries are small in size, no official record of their employment exists. One can say that these collieries themselves are a part of India's informal economy by virtue of poor regulation, the nature of production and labour regime. However, because of their location in a state that enjoys a special status, the coal that is produced cannot be designated either as illegal or legal. To put it simply, the law itself has created a crack, through the space of which a non-legal zone has come into existence. One can say that the statecraft coal economy of northeastern India is informal (non-legal). Meghalaya's statecraft coal production data were sourced from government reports and the informal non-legal labour regime existing there was supplemented by field surveys.

The fourth coal economy comprises 'subsistence coal' produced from innumerable small-scale collieries run by the local political and social leaders on village common land and privately-owned land, usually bordering formal mines. The production and trade of this coal, usually in small-scale, artisanal forms of mining, is important for the livelihood of these villagers. In previous works, I have shown that such mining is closely linked to the displacement of the peasantry, due to either the expansion of open-cut collieries with poor environmental practices (Lahiri-Dutt 2014b) or the occupational shifts and increasing urbanisation of coal tracts (Lahiri-Dutt 2001). Such mining takes place well outside the legal domains, but the illegal coal economy comprises a small part of the informal sector that makes up 83 per cent of Indian economy (Harriss-White 2002). One can say that the coal produced by innumerable, dispersed producers – often displaced from their own land and disenfranchised from rights over their resources – is 'subsistence coal' as it provides the livelihoods for the rural poor. Technically, such coal mining is illegal because the regulatory framework in India allows no individual entrepreneur to mine for coal at small-scale. Official production figures definitely do not include the sizeable amount of coal produced throughout the coal-bearing tracts of eastern and central India. I have classified this as informal (illegal) coal production.

Subsistence coal production by informal illegal labour was estimated through an initial field survey and extrapolated to the coal-bearing areas in eastern India as a function of local urban demand. The survey indicated a figure of 2.5 million tonnes in the early 2000s (Lahiri-Dutt and Williams 2005). To estimate its growth, a more recent survey was conducted in 2012; the latter survey gave an estimate of 3.7 million tonnes (Lahiri-Dutt et al. 2014b). The estimates of subsistence coal, albeit calculated conservatively in both these surveys, were for the eastern states of Jharkhand and West Bengal, covering the major parts of Eastern Coalfields Limited (ECL), Bharat Coking Coal Limited (BCCL), and Central Coalfields Limited (CCL). The amount produced by the subsistence coal economy does not include other routes for informal coal delivery other than by cycle, thereby again presenting a rather limited estimate. These two states account for 25 per cent of the total coal production of India (as per Provisional Coal Statistics 2013–2014, Government of India, Ministry of Coal, and the Coal Controller's Organisation, Kolkata). To account for these other sources, the 2012 estimates have been increased approximately four times, assuming that similar levels of activity in informal mining occur around the coalfields elsewhere in the country. The extrapolated figure captures the total illegal coal production from the other coal-bearing tracts of India, putting the total amount at 15 million tonnes. Table 5.1 gives an overview of the volume of these four different coal economies.

A point that is relevant for this chapter is the continuation of semi-feudal production systems at the operational level. Even when collieries were brought under state ownership, CIL did not substantively change many of the old relations of production but created an additional, formal, centralised edifice of management. Consequently, some of the entrenched pre-modern labour relations can still be found on mine sites. For example, the system of labour replacement or *badli* – in which a relative or a village friend might undertake the tasks of a salaried worker against a mutually agreed amount, with the company choosing not to deal with the informal replacement arrangement – continues even today. Moreover, the formal sector enterprise hires 'contractors', often locally through individual mining area offices, to give out most of the production-related tasks. A significant portion of mining, including overburden removal, land rehabilitation and even actual coal production, is carried out by these contractors. The contractors hire casual labour at extremely low wages that are paid on a daily or weekly basis. Thus, within CIL's official 'total production' figures, there is an invisible segment of coal that is produced by a non-formal and casual workforce. One can say that this is the fifth coal economy that is not easily detected, and even the production figures of coal hide this fifth economy.

Market, labour and enterprise, and transactional differences are the key aspects of the diverse economies framework presented by Gibson-Graham. The differences in these coal economies are illustrated in these aspects. Whereas there were four coal economies when only coal production was dealt with, one can detect the existence of five (or even six) 'worlds of coal' in thinking about the different production and labour regimes therein. I can only describe the different labour regimes in the five interlinked economies based on my empirical data. The first aspect, 'market' is artificially protected, monopolised, state-regulated, and generally fixed for national and neoliberal coal produced by CIL and the captive collieries in the formal sector. The contractors' labourers produce coal for CIL, and although they work through informal arrangements,

Table 5.1 Production of coal in four economies, 2014 (million tonnes)

Economy	Production
National coal	520
Neoliberal coal	34
Subsistence coal (illegal)	15
Statecraft coal (non-legal)	5

Sources: Data taken from Provisional Coal Statistics (2013–2014), Government of India, Ministry of Coal, Coal Controller's Organisation, Kolkata (2014). Rounded production values for 2012–2013: total national 520 Mt; captive/private 34 Mt.

no alternative market exists for the 'hidden national' coal produced by them. However, statecraft coal is produced informally but within a non-legal space and its market is naturally protected through the constitutional provisions, and usually a 'niche' in Bangladesh due to the remote location of Meghalaya state in the northeast. The alternative to this market is also local, informally controlled trading. The last, subsistence coal produced informally and illegally, again has a niche market within the coal-tracts: In local small factories and workshops, in brick kilns and small businesses and domestic consumers. The alternative to market exchange of this coal is informal barter, underground and shady dealings, local trading systems and credits that are beyond the purview of formal financial systems. A similar pattern presents itself in considering labour regimes: Whereas the salary scales of employees are determined by the state in consultation with unions for CIL and captive collieries, wage rates are determined locally by village leaders and contractors' ground staff. Usually, payments for labour are made in cash for CIL employees, but some parts of the wage can be paid in-kind to the informal labourers working for the contractors.

With regard to the laws and rules that apply to each world of coal, as well as the main 'actors' therein, the importance of formalised laws decreases from the national coal produced by CIL to the neoliberal coal produced by the captive collieries, to the statecraft coal produced informally but non-legally, to subsistence coal produced by innumerable poor. For example, the national coal world is ruled by laws such as CBAA and LAA to acquire land; Indian Mines Act for labour safety; and MMDR that gives mineral classification and determines who will be involved in its production. The two main actors here are the employees in MoC and CIL. One could say that for the informal labourers hired by contractors for producing coal on behalf of CIL, the Factory Labour Act should be implemented, but in reality there is poor implementation of the rules of this Act. There are many more actors within the informal part of the national coal economy; contractors, when hiring labour negotiate through layers of local social and political rules, and must involve local leaders. Therefore, besides CIL Area Office employees, actors also include local administrators and political leaders (such as *gram panchayat pradhaans* or elected village councillors) and regional political figures, and displaced local or migrant communities who provide the wage labour.

Captive collieries producing neoliberal coal are also ruled by laws such as those around CIL (CBAA and LAA, Indian Mines Act and MMDR) but have a wider range of actors like the informal part of the national coal economy, including the MoC; CIL officials; local administrators, political leaders, and regional political figures, and local/migrant communities. Statecraft coal, produced in Meghalaya within the informal, non-legal, domain, is ruled by the Indian Constitution (sixth schedule) that gives the state the special status, and MMDR for mineral classification and production rule, but not CBAA or the Indian Mines Act, or even the Factory Labour Act. The actors in this coal economy include the Mining Department officials at the state level; the leaders of indigenous groups and tribes, the *gram panchayat pradhaans* and state political figures. Indigenous landowners generally own the deep shaft collieries, but the labourers are generally migrant communities that come from Nepal and Bangladesh, who are willing to take enormous risks for earning cash incomes unavailable in their source areas.

The subsistence coal economy, operated at the ground level by the rural poor, generally locals and in most cases displaced either from their land or from their traditional occupations and within the informal illegal domain, is guided by completely different logic and rules. Here, customary norms and values that are shared by communities rule people's actions, and the key actors, besides the *gram panchayat pradhaans* and local political figures, are these local/migrant communities that labour in the unsafe, risky, insecure, and poorly paid jobs. Clearly, the latter worlds of coal are ruled by alternative and/or less visible norms that are different from the nation-building agenda of industrialising India. Labour becomes less secure, wages are lower, and jobs less safe. Pre-modern forms of production – such as family labour units – become visible.

In sum, each of these worlds of coal is governed by different sets of norms and values, and different actors operate within them. An analysis of the diverse rules that govern the economies show that formal laws put in place by the Government of India and the Ministry of Coal assume less significance, and localised forms of authority – such as the *gram panchayats* (village councils) – assume power.

Thinking through the different rules and actors allows us to reinterpret what constitutes India's diverse worlds of coal. They also reinterpret informality in India, a sector designated as 'unorganised'. Often, studies of the informal economy present a dichotomy between the formal and the informal, designating the co-existence of the two as 'dual economies'. These diverse coal worlds clearly highlight the importance of looking beyond official data to explore rules and norms that dictate labour conditions. The analysis here shows that instead of a clear-cut formal–informal division, the worlds of coal are multiple, overlapping and indeed varied. For example, CIL and the contractors who undertake various mining-related works for CIL, together present not a duality but more a likeness to Russian dolls, whereby the informal contracting economy hides its informal labour arrangements *within* the formal CIL economy. The coal produced by both serve the same market, yet in employment terms the contractors' labourers remain informal. To what extent such an economy shadows the privately-owned captive collieries needs to be investigated further. The diverse worlds also show that legal and illegal coal economies do not inhabit mutually isolated spaces, and leave much grey space in between them. I argue that the findings presented here not only have far-reaching implications for our understanding of the materiality of coal as a resource, its multiple values and its governance, but also for what meanings coal holds for millions of people involved in insecure jobs in mining, or facing dramatic changes to their physical environments as a consequence of these coal economies. Consequently, coal as a fossil fuel, a resource seen by geologists, policymakers, and even environmentalists, as an inert substance, needs to be understood as an active agent in nation-building as well as shaping lives and landscapes.

Social relations of production in different coal economies

Social relations in the coal economies comprise of those working in some capacity related to coal and those who have lost jobs and ways of living as a consequence of expanding coal. Coal labour and the coal displaced are often seen as in opposition to one another. By discussing the four coal worlds we might, however, begin to see that these categories are much more fluid. We find multiple, contradictory trends that include increased mechanisation coupled with a growing informalisation of labour via outsourcing; and displacement, which forces people into scavenging coal for a living.

If one looks at employment instead of production volumes, then using a combination of data for labour and employment sourced from surveys and interviews, the sizes of the coal economies need to be rearranged. Table 5.2 presents the numbers of people involved (or employed) in producing these different amounts of coal in the different 'economies'. Through the lens of labour one can see that the national coal economy can actually be split into two – the formal employees recorded by CIL, and the informal labourers hired by its contractors. The presence of this large informal labour contributing to the production of national coal is neither acknowledged, nor recorded. The least number of employees are in the neoliberal coal economy. The estimate for employment in the other government colliery organisations is based on the assumption and field-knowledge that their employment patterns are similar to that in CIL. It is likely that the captive mines also use contractors to produce part of the coal by hiring cheap daily or weekly wage labourers locally, but we have insufficient information on this aspect. If this is the case, then using the same estimate,[6] employment in captive mines should be 90,000 rather than 60,000, with another line added indexing 'Captive coal (informal)': 30,000. The CIL employees and the contractors' labourers together comprise the second largest number of people mining coal.

It might be noted that these figures do not present the numbers of people within the miners' families who are dependent on coal for their livelihoods. If this is taken into account then subsistence (illegal) coal mining supports the largest number of people. The statecraft (informal, non-legal) coal production

Table 5.2 Labour in diverse coal worlds in India (2014)

Economy	Employment
National coal (formal)	450,000
Subsistence coal (illegal)	400,000
National coal (informal)	200,000
Statecraft coal (non-legal)	100,000
Neoliberal coal	60,000

Note
No informal labour identified in captive production, but other public miners (e.g. Singareni) assumed to have similar proportion of contractors as per CIL.

employs the next significant numbers. With regard to per-employee output (that is, productivity), the output from CIL and captive collieries together is about 1,200 tonnes per year. Coal mined informally (and illegally) is transported by cycles that deliver 250 kg coal on average every other day, and hence the productivity from this sector can be estimated as 36 tonnes per year per worker.

The question of rights and access to the land and its natural resources is at the centre of such debates over unauthorised coal mining (Fernandes 1998). The protection of common pool resources to help poor communities survive in colliery tracts is crucially important, as is the need to find ways to vest the power to co-manage mineral extraction with the local communities. Much of the land that is being acquired for large-scale coal mining is inalienable (or 'non-transferable') tribal land. Some of these lands have been used by these communities for generations, but without ever having been being recorded in revenue records. These are *gair majurwa* (or land without official records or deeds), that is, commons. These lands had played important roles for local communities and in absence of such forest or farm lands, the local poor communities are forced to change their livelihoods. As increased coal extraction changes the material and environmental basis of livelihoods, the lives of these communities become fundamentally altered.

A significant number of workers are still able to provide for their families in a reliable manner by holding on to unionised jobs in national coal. It becomes clear from the numbers in Table 5.2, however, that a majority of people who work with coal are informally employed, whether in the formal or in the non-legal and illegal sectors. Uncertain and temporary jobs here become the norm, largely outside of legislation on working conditions. With particularly hazardous working conditions in the non-legal and illegal sectors we are able to see that work in coal is not very different from other forms of labour in poverty-affected coal regions.

If the coal resources of India are truly vested in the national interest, then the state should ensure that opportunities benefit the nation equitably. In mining coal, the Indian state presents a sense of urgency that accompanies the framing of an energy crisis. This sense of urgency has encouraged and allowed both private and public companies to invest in coal extraction. Some of the coal-bearing tracts are owned (or used generationally) by indigenous communities who have also moved into coal mining. Often, they would describe their new livelihood as 'coal collection', as though the collection of coal has replaced the collection of fruits and game that they were used to in their hunting-gathering ways of life in the past. It is also important that a wide debate occurs among social scientists, planners, international agencies, and members of civil society on the issue of justice in coal mining areas. It is understandable that the public sector would resist any attempts to implement regulatory and technological changes that reduce its monopoly power. The resistance is unlikely to be explicit, but most likely will be mounted through administrative delays and bureaucratic bottlenecks, long identified as the primary restrictions to the efficiency and expansion of coal mining in India.

Transforming landscapes

At the heart of large-scale landscape transformations in coal extraction lies the technological choice of using underground or open cut extraction methods. Open cut mines are where the coal is accessed from the surface level via a large, open cut into the ground often measuring several kilometres in circumference and at times as much as several hundred metres deep, thus representing a serious change in land use. This change is additionally largely irreversible, even with the best post-mining reclamation approaches, given the large and very expensive amounts of material, usually many million tonnes of soil and rocks, which need to be shifted to even attempt to level the land. A focus on productivity in coal production means that no new underground mines are to be opened by CIL. India's planned expansion in coal is not only dangerous for its carbon release but also for its vast landscape alterations, as close to a doubling of output is expected by the Ministry of Coal (2015), to reach one billion tonnes extracted annually by 2020.

The devastating impact of coal mining on the local environments of coal-bearing tracts have been manifold: Forest clearance and degradation, other changes in the land-use and complete alteration of the flora and animal species, decay of local agricultural economies, and urbanisation. Specific to older coal mining areas are coal fires that have desiccated forests, destroyed villages, and literally undermined human security (Saxena 2002). Some of these underground coal fires have been burning for decades, rendering the ground unstable over large areas and even more prone to subsidence (Lahiri-Dutt and Gangopadhyaya 2007). In addition, there are subsidences due to underground voids, and pollution of rivers by coal washeries.

Mining projects extract mineral resources accumulated under the land and use up some of the natural capital critical in sustaining the well-being of the local communities who live in areas immediately surrounding the mining operation. In other words, large mining projects located in resource-rich areas create wealth or extract value from environmental resources for a wider market, from the ecosystem comprising the subsistence base for long-established communities. These communities include marginal ethnic groups who bear the costs associated with environmental degradation. Inequities are ingrained in the very nature of the industry: Highly capitalised, large scale mining is connected to national and global economies, but at the same time causes environmental (such as deforestation, water and air pollution) and social impacts (such as social, cultural and occupational displacement) in the coal regions, where local communities live and interact with environmental resources (Lahiri-Dutt 2015).

It is well known that mineral resource extraction tends to 'reproduce' rather than 'reduce' inequalities in wealth and livelihood opportunities (Bridge 2004), and if women and men have unequal access to, and control over, resources, then mining enhances these inequities. In their eagerness to extract minerals, mining corporations tend to focus on individual and isolated parts of the environment while neglecting others. Indigenous communities consider the environment holistically, presenting a persistent pre-modern worldview that refuses to reduce the environment into its various parts. Land (and its resources such as forests above and minerals below the surface) and water are intimately enmeshed in this life-world.

Open cut mining is closely associated with the present expansion of formal mining in national and neoliberal coal. This is where large land concessions are granted and where companies have the funds and machinery required to manage the excavation not only of the coal body but also of the overburden, which, like the coal, measures in the millions of tonnes per year for a large mine. The storage of overburden waste requires additional space measuring hundreds of hectares per mine, thus creating additional land use pressures and waste compared to underground operations. The land use of non-legal and illegal coal is in comparison significantly reduced, with most of this mining carried out either in smaller, underground 'rathole' mines with only minor land use above ground, or simply scavenged from formal mining sites, including the coal transport infrastructure. The dangers to labourers in non-legal and illegal coal are thus not matched by similar dangers to landscapes.

The North and South Karanpura fields in Jharkhand can serve as an example of an area that comprises frontier territory where Adivasi communities have been displaced to make way for open cut collieries. Scholars have demonstrated that the local poor, particularly the indigenous community, receive the least benefits from mining developments, and are among the most affected (Dias 2005). For many such displaced local community members, 'coal collection' has now replaced hunting-gathering from the now vanished forests. The very coal that has led to their displacement from traditional lands is now providing a very basic subsistence, albeit at a great cost. Their day-to-day survival depends on coal, the very commodity that has undermined their livelihoods and that has turned them into illegal citizens.

Conclusion: coal as national development

Mine planning has for quite some time been unable to meet the demand for coal, and has faced growing protests against land acquisition for mining, the displacement of villagers, and general unrest in the mining tracts that extend from Jharkhand through Odisha to Chhattisgarh and Andhra Pradesh (Bhushan and Hazra 2008). A shift of attention from the material properties of resources such as coal to their qualities and meanings can here enliven the many subjective and hidden worlds where humans are enmeshed with things in their everyday lives. As shown in this chapter, those involved in the diverse worlds of coal hold different values and believe in different qualities of coal. Those who dictate the policies and establish the laws see coal differently from those whose lives are intricately linked to legal, illegal and non-legal economies of coal. This is why in describing the multiple worlds of coal, I have chosen not to concentrate on the 'matters of coal' as they are usually discussed in resources and energy policy debates, but have tried instead to illuminate how different actors create and recreate these worlds.

Yet, the regulatory edifice is not irrelevant in framing these different worlds; as I have shown, the nature of legality and the extent of formality (and hence acceptability of these worlds to those who make development policies) vary. These laws, by attributing notions of legitimacy to some worlds, hide other worlds from public attention. Even when they do make an appearance in public discourses, those that are defined by illegality are usually portrayed as causing harm and contrary to nation-building purposes rather than noting the livelihoods they support. Innumerable lives are involved in India's diverse coal worlds. A majority are among the poorest, made poorer by the large-scale, nation-building project of coal mining. For the poor, the mining of coal is not related to the nationalist project or the growing alarm over energy security, but is simply a matter of daily survival and subsistence. Therefore, the manner in which India's coal economy is debated in public discourse needs to be rephrased to accommodate the livelihoods of the poor who, displaced from their traditional lands and livelihoods, are exerting the small amount of autonomy they might have been left with. Unfortunately, India's resource nationalism over coal is such that interpretations of this autonomy and resistance assume an illegal perspective. Thinking through the diverse worlds, one can see that the governability or manageability of India's coal offers a deeper problematic than earlier envisaged.

Clearly, a simple and hegemonic move – a governance plan – for India's coal is impossible as there are economies that, according to Gibson-Graham (2006: 58) 'have slipped from their locations in discourse and landed "on the ground", in the "real" [world]', not just separate from but outside of the governance frameworks that have conventionally imagined coal mining. The other social spheres that comprise the diverse worlds remain elusive in the conventional framing of resource governance problematic. The informal illegal and non-legal economies remain beyond the periphery of policies and laws. The laws formulated for the formal domain have far-reaching effects, yet their expressions do not always belong only to this domain. More interestingly, instead of a binary relationship between formal and informal economies, we see that they overlap and interact with each other, and a significant amount of informality is hidden within what is generally seen as the formal sector. Each of these coal economies operates with its own distinct forms of landscape transformations and employment relations, and consequently dramatic variations in coal extraction and livelihood outcomes.

These diverse worlds of coal have important policy implications. Freese (2003: 1) suggests that the values a society puts on coal are sourced through the perceived needs of a particular time and place, and the multiple worlds of coal in India show us that coal's impact is far from over (ibid.: 2). The need for coal, more of it, is closely associated with the post-liberalisation need for faster economic growth, but is often couched in the language of nation-building. This addiction to coal drains local livelihoods and degrades the environment but, at the same time, creates coal-dependent livelihoods in the same areas. It also entrenches the related beliefs that there is nothing untoward with the way we consume and use resources; that nothing is wrong with its ownership, allocation or distribution, and that no alternatives exist to large-scale coal extraction. The concept of energy security is conceived on simplistic assumptions such as direct linkages between population-growth leading to environmental degradation; scarcity leading to decreased economic activity and migration; and the weakening of states resulting in conflicts and violence. This conceptual position has equated energy security with strategic and military security; on the one hand, resources have become the environmental trigger of conflicts and crises; and on the other, the sense of urgency has helped the Indian state to shed ethical values and its responsibility to its poorest citizens.

In India's coal-bearing tracts, the sense of urgency that accompanies the framing of crisis has allowed private companies to invest in resource extraction in peripheral areas. But the land and mineral ownership laws have remained of colonial vintage. The growing resentment and resistance to land acquisition for mining-industrial–urban requirements is rooted in the reality that the local poor receive the fewest benefits from such developments. At its best, they are hired either as wage labourers by the contractors or are pushed into informal coal mining that is presented as an illegal activity in lack of other more appealing alternatives among the dispossessed and those living in degraded environments. The acquisition of non-transferable tribal land for coal mining and related projects by privately-owned companies, and the state's complicity in facilitating the various formal and informal strategies adopted by the companies to gain access to land, have encouraged the dispossessed local rural communities to take a share of the coal for themselves. The cases of illegal and non-legal coal economies graphically illustrate how outdated the mineral governance framework is, and how purely cosmetic changes of laws fail to adequately protect the interests of the weak and the poor.

Notes

1 This article draws on Lahiri-Dutt (forthcoming) in its analysis of the four coal economies of India. I thank the Australian Research Council (grant ID: DP130104396, Beyond the Resource Curse) for funding part of this study. My gratitude is to Dr David Williams for assisting me with the assessment of the different coal economies in terms of production and employment. I also thank Ms Anindita Kumar for her assistance with reviewing some literature on the materiality of resources.

2 The full text of CBAA is online, available at: www.coal.nic.in/cba-act.pdf (accessed 17 March 2013).

3 See the full Act online, available at: www.indiankanoon.org/doc/72652/ (accessed 17 January 2013).

4 CIL has assets of INR79,807 *crore* (as at 2013–2014) and a profit after tax of INR23,000 *crore* in the same financial year. Source: Annual Report, CIL, 2013–2014. Online, available at: www.coalindia.in (accessed on 17 March 2016).

5 Included here are the other government collieries of which SCCL (Singareni Collieries Company Limited) is the largest producer. SCCL is jointly owned by the

Government of Telangana and Government of India, and produced about 50 million tonnes of coal in 2012. CIL produces around 450 million tonnes; the remainder comes from various other public entities.

6 As noted earlier, 50 per cent of formal employment as recorded in the company's human resources data.

References

Bakker, K. and Gavin Bridge (2006). 'Material Worlds? Resource Geographies and the "Matter of Nature"'. *Progress in Human Geography* 30(5): 18–48.

Bhushan, Chandra and Monali Zeya Hazra (2008). *Rich Lands, Poor People: Is 'Sustainable' Mining Possible?* New Delhi: Centre for Science and Environment.

Bridge, Gavin (2004). 'Contested Terrain: Mining and the Environment'. *Annual Review of Environmental Resources* 29: 205–259.

Castree, Noel (1995). 'The Nature of Produced Nature: Materiality and Knowledge Construction in Marxism'. *Antipode* 27: 13–48.

Dange, S.A. (1945). *Death Pits in Our Land: How 200,000 Indian Miners Live and Work.* Bombay: New Age Printing Press.

Das, Debojyoti (2014). 'Border Mining, State Politics, Migrant Labour and the Land Relations along the India–Bangladesh Border'. In: Kuntala Lahiri-Dutt (ed.). *The Coal Nation: Histories, Politics and Ecologies of Coal in India*, Aldershot: Ashgate, pp. 39–62 and 79–104.

Demeritt, David (2002). 'What is the "Social Construction of Nature"? A Typology and Sympathetic Critique'. *Progress in Human Geography* 26: 767–790.

Dias, Xavier (2005). 'World Bank in Jharkhand: Accountability Mechanisms and Indigenous Peoples'. *Law, Environment and Development Journal* 1: 73–79.

DRET (Department of Resource, Environment and Tourism) (2008). 'Water Management: Leading Practice Sustainable Development Program for the Mining Industry'. Canberra: Commonwealth of Australia.

Economic Times (2015). 'Captive Coal Mine Output Adds up to 53 MT for FY15'. 17 April. Online, available at: http://articles.economictimes.indiatimes.com/2015-04-17/news/61253458_1_coal-blocks-coal-production-coal-imports (accessed 16 March 2016).

Fernandes, Walter (1998). 'Development Induced Displacement in Eastern India'. In: S.C. Dubey (ed.). *Antiquity to Modernity in Tribal India, Vol. 1*, Delhi: Inter-India Publications, pp. 217–301.

Freese, Barbara (2003). *Coal: A Human History*. London: William Henemann.

Garg, Amit and P.R. Shukla (2009). 'Coal and Energy Security for India: Role of Carbon Dioxide (CO2) Capture and Storage (CCS)'. *Energy* 34(8): 1032–1041.

Ghosh, Amiya Bhushan (1977). *Coal Industry in India: An Historical and Analytical Account, Part 1*. New Delhi: S. Chand.

Gibson-Graham, J.K. (2006). *A Postcapitalist Politics*. Minneapolis, MN: University of Minnesota Press.

Gosden, C. (1999). *Anthropology and Archaeology. A Changing Relationship*. London: Routledge.

Harriss-White, Barbara (2002). *India Working: Essays on Society and Economy*. Cambridge: Cambridge University Press.

Ingold, Tim (2007). 'Materials against Materiality'. *Archaeological Dialogues* 14: 1–16.

Kumar, Shobha (1996). *Mining and the Raj: A Study of the Coal Industry of Bihar, 1900–1947*. Patna: Janaki Prakashan.

Kumarmangalam, Surendra Mohan (1973). *Coal Industry in India: Tasks Ahead*. Calcutta: Oxford India Book House Publishing Co.

Lahiri-Dutt, Kuntala (2001). *Mining and Urbanization in the Raniganj Coalbelt*. Calcutta: World Press.

Lahiri-Dutt, Kuntala (2014a). 'Introducing Coal in India: Energising the Nation'. In: Kuntala Lahiri-Dutt (ed.). *The Coal Nation: Histories, Politics and Ecologies of Coal in India*, Aldershot: Ashgate, pp. 1–37.

Lahiri-Dutt, Kuntala (2014b). 'Stranded Between the State and the Market: "Uneconomic" Mine Closure in the Raniganj Coal Belt'. In: Kuntala Lahiri-Dutt (ed.). *The Coal Nation: Histories, Politics and Ecologies of Coal in India*, Aldershot: Ashgate, pp. 129–143.

Lahiri-Dutt, Kuntala (2015). 'The Silent (and Gendered) Violence: Understanding Water Access in Mining Areas through the Rights Lens'. In: Stephanie Boechler and Anne-Marie Hansom (eds). *A Political Ecology of Women, Water and Global Environmental Change*, London: Routledge, 38–57.

Lahiri-Dutt, Kuntala (Forthcoming). 'The Diverse Worlds of Coal in India: Energising the Nation, Energising Livelihoods'. *Energy Policy*.

Lahiri-Dutt, Kuntala and David Williams (2005). 'The Coal Cycle: A Small Part of the Illegal Coal Mining in Eastern India'. *Resources, Environment and Development* 2(2): 93–105.

Lahiri-Dutt, Kuntala and Prasun K. Gangopadhyaya (2007). 'Subsurface Coalfires in the Raniganj Coalbelt: Investigating their Causes and Assessing Human Impacts'. *Resources, Energy and Development* 4(1): 71–87.

Lahiri-Dutt, Kuntala, David Williams and Justin Imam (2014a). 'Revisiting coal cycles in Eastern India: Report of 2012 survey'. Online, available at: http://asmasiapacific.org/wp-content/uploads/2015/01/Coal-Cycles-Report-2014.pdf (accessed 29 June 2016).

Lahiri-Dutt, Kuntala, Radhika Krishnan, and Nesar Ahmad (2014b). '"Captive" Coal Mining in Jharkhand: Taking Land from Indigenous Communities'. In: Kuntala Lahiri-Dutt (ed.). *The Coal Nation: Histories, Politics and Ecologies of Coal in India*, Aldershot: Ashgate, pp. 165–182.

Malik, R.P.S. (2002). 'Water-Energy Nexus in Resource-poor Economies: The Indian Experience'. *International Journal of Water Resources Development* 18(1): 47–58.

Ministry of Coal (2005). 'The Expert Committee on Road Map for Coal Sector Reforms'. New Delhi: Government of India.

Ministry of Coal (2006). 'Annual Report 2005–06'. New Delhi: Government of India.

Ministry of Coal (2015). 'Annual Report 2014–15'. New Delhi: Government of India.

Planning Commission of India (2006). 'National Mineral Policy: Report of the High Level Committee'. Online, available at: mines.nic.in/File_link_view.aspx%3Fltp%3D1%26lid%3D116 (accessed 11 January 2013).

Richardson, T. and G. Weszkalnys (2014). 'Introduction: Resource Materialities'. *Anthropological Quarterly* 87(1): 5–30.

Saxena, N.C. (2002). 'Jharia Coalfield Today, Tomorrow and Thereafter'. Dhanbad: Centre for Mining Environment, Indian School of Mines.

Simeon, Dilip (1996). 'Coal and Colonialism: Production Relations in an Indian Colliery, c.1895–1947'. *International Review of Social History* 41: 83–108.

Sharan, R. (2009). 'Alienation and Restoration of Tribal Land in Jharkhand'. In: Nandini Sundar (ed.). *Legal Grounds: Natural Resources, Identity, and the Law in Jharkhand*, New Delhi: Oxford University Press, pp. 105–125.

Singh, S.B. (1966). *European Agency Houses in Bengal, 1783–1833*. Calcutta: Saraswati Press.

Tripathi, A. (1979). *Trade and Finance in the Bengal Presidency, 1789–1833*. Calcutta: Saraswati Press.

White, G.F. (1945). 'Human Adjustment to Floods: A Geographical Approach to the Flood Problem in the United States'. PhD dissertation, University of Chicago.

Zimmerman, E. (1951 [1933]).*World Resources and Industries: A Functional Appraisal of the Availability of Agricultural and Industrial Resources*. New York: Harper and Brothers.

6 A different story of coal

The power of power in Northeast India

Bengt G. Karlsson

While entering the town of Margherita in upper Assam you are greeted by a huge mural with the text 'Northeastern Coalfields – Excavating Happiness from the Depth of Darkness'. Underneath you see workers, machines, factories, and powerlines, as well as people enjoying music, theatre, and sports. The mural is reminiscent of the communist aesthetic you would find in the former states of the Soviet Union, celebrating heavy industry, human labour, and ingenuity in taming nature. The message conveyed is that coal, and the extraction of coal, is the very foundation of industrial society in the service of humans.

Margherita came into being around the rich coal deposit in this part of the Himalayan foothills. The extraction has being going on for more than a century,

Figure 6.1 Mural in the town of Margherita in upper Assam (source: author).

initially as an underground mine as a private colonial undertaking, and later as an open-pit mine under the public sector venture known as the North Eastern Coalfields Ltd., part of the larger Coal India Ltd. To get to the coal seam the company has to dig deep and remove enormous quantities of overburden. The senior manager of the Tirap Colliery, a vast open-pit mine outside Margherita, told us this during a guided, private tour of the mine. As we approached the bottom of the pit, we could see the layer of coal 3–4 m wide that yellow Volvo excavators were busy extracting. The manager picked up a piece of coal and gave it to me. It was surprisingly light and dry and flaky in its texture. The coal glimmered beautifully in different shades of black and blue. It made me think how it is that something so delicate has come to unleash such massive forces of change, not least the 'industrial revolution', which for better or worse has permanently altered the conditions of life for people on earth.

Even if access to coal and energy more generally is a prerequisite for industrial development, places where you find coal are not necessary the most industrialised ones. In fact, the reverse is often the case. As Kuntala Lahiri-Dutt put it in a new book on coal in India: 'Today India's coal-bearing tracts are cursed by this natural endowment, the extraction of which is leading to inequities, the decay of agriculture, and the displacement of the indigenous and poor classes' (Lahiri-Dutt 2014: xxi).[1] Regions holding coal rarely reap the benefits, like access to electricity and subsequent modern amenities, but are left with the costs of a polluted environment and loss of land. As much as 90 per cent of the coal deposits are within indigenous or tribal areas, and these are the communities with the highest levels of poverty and, in other ways, are the most marginalised people in the country (Bhushan and Hazra 2008: 9). The same will be true for other minerals like iron ore or bauxite; 'the land is rich but the people remain poor' (for bauxite, see Padel and Das 2010).[2]

In this chapter I will pursue an analysis of what I call the 'power of power', by which I refer to the critical role energy plays in modern, industrial societies. The ways in which different sources of energy are extracted, produced, refined, transported, and consumed enable or produce certain social arrangements and eventually condition the very structure of society. Power, in other words, is loaded with power. I will draw on the recent work by historian Timothy Mitchell. In his book *Carbon Democracy: Political Power in the Age of Oil* (2011), Mitchell relates the usage of fossil fuels to the emergence and constraints of democracy or democratic politics.[3] As he shows in the case of coal in late nineteenth- and early twentieth-century Western Europe and North America, the material properties of coal, and how it was appropriated and used, allowed for labour protests and eventually democratic political demands. Coal empowered steam engines and other machines that enabled large-scale manufacturing and the modern city to develop, i.e. it was now possible to concentrate people into larger cities without direct access to agricultural land for energy production. But the modern city was highly vulnerable due to the dependence on constant access to coal. The mining and transport of coal, with loading and unloading at several junctions of the transport chain, offered critical sites where the labourers could 'slow, disrupt or cut off its supply' (Mitchell 2011: 19). This became most effective when mineworkers collaborated with workers in the railways, docks and shipping, possibly calling a general strike. Workers hence could use their power over the supply of energy to make political claims for higher salaries, regulated working hours, pensions and other benefits, which, Mitchell argues, 'radically reduced the precariousness of life in industrial societies' (2011: 27). Things were rather different with oil, which eventually came to take over the fossil fuel regime in Europe and North America after the Second World War. Mitchell writes:

> Governing the global supply of oil, like most things that we call 'global', rested on the control of a comparatively small number of sites – a few dozen major oilfields, pipelines, and terminals, and the handful of bulk tanker fleets that journeyed between them.
>
> (Mitchell 2011: 67)

This system is more difficult to interrupt for labourers in a particular place or country. Strikes, for example, became less effective. Oil – its material properties and the way oil is produced, transported and consumed – seems to lend itself to or enable more authoritarian or anti-democratic social arrangements, according to Mitchell. The separation between the sites of production and consumption of the energy is especially critical. Coal mining areas were usually located in the same country, directly linked to or adjacent to large centres of industrial production (ibid.: 21). Oil was different. Not only in terms of the geographical distance between source and users, but also in terms of the enclave nature of oil production, where oil companies in a most thorough way seek to keep the surrounding society out, often with the use of a well-developed security apparatus (see Appel 2012; Watts 2005). This is particularly the case with off-shore oil production (Ferguson 2006).

What is being suggested is the need to look into the intimate interrelation of energy, infrastructure, and societal forms. Also taking cue from Mitchell's work on carbon fuels, the anthropologists Dominic Boyer calls for a new 'anthropology of energy' that is attentive to the ways in which control over energy are interrelated with emergent forms of governance. Boyer refers to this as 'energo-politics' (2011: 5). Along such lines, I will address the present conjuncture of coal, politics, and development in the state of Meghalaya in Northeast India. Not only is coal extraction an important industry in its own right in Meghalaya, but as more than half of all the energy consumed in India comes from coal, the extraction, circulation, and consumption of coal is critical to the country's industrialisation. Following Mitchell, this chapter therefore analyses the social arrangements that underpin and are shaped by India's most important source of energy.

The material properties of specific 'natural resources' obviously require different types of extractive infrastructures, which again lend themselves to or allow for, different levels of political autonomy, democracy, and economic development. For example, the large hydro-projects presently underway in Northeast India are technically rather complex and require large infrastructure investments, expertise, and capital brought from outside, which ultimately bring people of this frontier region more directly into the power grid of the nation-state. Coal mining carried out in the northeastern hill areas, on the other hand, is largely a low-tech affair that requires minimal investments and skills that can be arranged locally. Climate change concerns have rendered hydro-power the new green source of energy and it is believed to be, more than anything else, the future of Northeast India.[4] Coal, as we will see, seems to harness more unruly qualities in this part of the world.

Coal

Let us re-state some of the basics. Coal consists of organic matter – plants, or remains of plants – that for hundreds of millions of years has been compressed and stored under high temperatures. The type of coal you get depends on the type of vegetation that existed before in that particular place. It is the solar energy that these plants once absorbed that now is being appropriated. A central feature of coal, its material properties, is its bulkiness. Transport has therefore always been a critical aspect in the extraction of coal. When the coal-fields in Assam were opened in the late nineteenth century, the solution was to build a railway to transport the coal to the markets outside. To honour the Italian chief engineer in charge of the construction of the railway, the new town was named Margherita after the Italian queen.[5]

Coal holds a particular place in the Indian national imaginary. It speaks of freedom and development; 'excavating happiness'! Coal is, as mentioned, the most important source of energy in the country and new coal mines are approved and new coal-fuelled power-plants are being built all over India. This despite global pressures on India, being one of the world's major emitters of carbon dioxide, to turn away from a carbon-based energy system to one that is more environmentally sustainable. Climate change, one would think, renders coal something of the past. But, obviously, it is a past that is still lingering on.[6]

Instead of the large-scale mechanised coal mining that is being carried out by Coal India in places like Margherita, my concern here is with the less discussed coal mining that is going on in the hill areas of Northeast India. Even if there are contractors and traders and other interests from the plains involved (Kikon 2014), coal mining is to large extent in the hands of the indigenous or tribal communities themselves. I will mainly discuss coal mining in the hill state of Meghalaya, but also make a few remarks regarding coal in Northeast India more generally. There is a longer history of colonial incorporation of these frontier areas as an extractive zone – providing elephants, limestone, tea, oil, coal, and timber – which structure present-day resource extraction. Yet, as I will argue, there is a particularly critical internal power dynamic that I would like to draw attention to. Especially critical here is how the coal trade has led to the formation of a new indigenous elite who have been a key social force for land privatisation, increased inequality, exploitation of labourers, environmental destruction, and undemocratic governance. Coal is king, and money earned through coal has become the key source of political influence and, along with it, status in Meghalaya.

What we have here is a process similar to that which Taniya Murray Li (2014) accounts for in the case of cacao plantations in Sulewesi, Indonesia. Li writes,

> In these highlands, in contrast, capitalist relations emerged by stealth. No rapacious agribusiness corporation grabbed land from highlanders or obliged them to plant cacao. No government department evicted them. Nor was there a misguided development scheme that disrupted the old way of life. The non-commoditized social relations through which they previously accessed land, labor, and food were not destroyed by 'capitalism', envisaged as a force that arrives from outside. They eroded piecemeal, in a manner that was unexpected and unplanned.
>
> (Li 2014: 9)

Li is arguing against what she describes as a simplified, standard narrative within social movements literature always representing indigenous societies as victims of dispossession by outside forces of state and capital, and thereby missing the internal dynamic of capital accumulation and displacement that can be equally significant.

By unravelling the story of coal, we can also begin to understand why Meghalaya is stuck in the position of an extractive zone without any significant development of industries or other economic opportunities for the younger generation, who more than anything look for a life outside of subsistence agriculture. In the absence of such opportunities, many of the young instead migrate to the metropolis of the Indian mainland (see McDuie-Ra 2012; Karlsson and Kikon, manuscript under preparation).

Tribal mining

Besides the coal fields in Assam, one of the first coal deposits the British found was in Cherrapunjee, in the present state of Meghalaya. The difficulties of getting the coal down to the plains remained a major bottleneck, preventing this source from being exploited to the extent the British initially had expected (see Oldham 1984: 68–69). It would instead take another century or so for coal mining to pick up in these hill tracts. The story of coal in the hills is in many ways different from the dominant one that is linked to the large-scale operations under CIL. In the hills, the mineral resources as well as the extraction have remained in the hands of the local people, that is, the indigenous or tribal communities that constitute the majority of the population. The state – both on central and state levels – has to a large extent remained a bystander whose main role has been to try to tax the coal. The coal is mainly excavated by hand, with the simplest possible tools, and then loaded onto trucks for transport down to either coal deposits in Assam, for further transport by rail to customers all around India, or taken by trucks across the border, exported to buyers in Bangladesh.

Meghalaya like the other hill states in the region is under the Sixth Schedule of the Constitution through which so-called autonomous district councils are being established. In short, this was an arrangement to give a certain amount of self-rule to the tribal peoples in the hills and, as such, an attempt to appease or pre-empt secessionist aspirations that were building up after Independence. The autonomous district councils are under a kind of hybrid legal regime where national and state legislations co-exist with customary laws of the concerned community. Certain laws do not apply to Sixth Schedule areas, but it is not always clear which ones apply or not. In the case of land ownership and resource use, customary laws are supposed to prevail. But whether mineral extraction would fall under such customary jurisdiction is more uncertain. In practice, however, coal mining has been allowed to unfold in a kind of legal vacuum, often described as a 'cottage industry' that is part of traditional subsistence (Karlsson 2011: 232). It has basically been up to the landowners themselves to carry out mining according to their own interests or standards, without any interference of the state.

What started in a small-scale manner has during the last two decades become a major undertaking in Meghalaya. The mining business, as we will see, has evolved as a ruthless form of frontier capitalism, where profit maximising precedes all other concerns, be it human well-being or environmental sustainability. This was also the case with the logging boom that was going on until the Supreme Court intervened and put a ban on the felling of trees in the late 1990s (Karlsson 2011: 226–234). The 'timber ban' was violently opposed by many local interest groups, said to be an imposition on indigenous self-determination granted by the Indian Constitution and leaving people bleeding without any other means of subsistence. The undeniable fact, however, was that the forests were quickly disappearing and within a few years there would have been no trees left to cut anyway. More or less the same story seems to be unfolding now with coal, that is, uncontrolled extraction that eventually brought about an intervention from the outside.

In the name of the environment

In April 2014, the National Green Tribunal intervened and put a stop to all coal mining activities in Meghalaya. An appeal by All Dimasa Students' Union in Assam claimed that the unregulated rathole coal mining up-streams in Jaintia Hills polluted a river they depended on for drinking water and fishing. There had been several news reports pointing out that rivers and other water bodies had turned acidic due to the toxic wastes discharged from the coal mines, which again was an effect of the especially high sulphur content of the Meghalaya coal. In this particular case, the Dimasa Students' Union stated that acidity also caused problems for the hydro-electric project in the Kapili River, with severe corrosion in under-water parts (which also caused a temporary closure of the power-station).[7]

The Dimasa Students' Union appeal was later also joined by one from Impulse – an NGO in Shillong dealing with child rights – that pointed to the widespread use of child labourers in the Meghalaya coal mines. Even though, as the tribunal stated, labour issues were not directly within their mandate, it was nevertheless felt that 'human working conditions' and 'safety' had to be addressed as well.[8] The appalling situation for mining labourers and particularly the use of child labour in the rathole mines had also been subject to national as well as international attention and media reporting, which arguably added to the rather swift intervention of the tribunal. In its original ruling, the Tribunal also used a straight-forward language stating that the unregulated and 'illegal' mining is 'neither benefitting the Government nor the people of the country', but only the 'coal mafias'. To support the ruling the tribunal referred to the work by Professor O.P. Singh of the North-Eastern Hill University in Shillong. A longer quote from a report by Singh is included in the ruling, where the 'primitive' method of rathole mining is described and that it constitutes a major source of water, air, and soil pollution.[9]

The intervention by the tribunal was, as mentioned, not particularly welcomed in the state. Large-scale protests have being organised against the ban on coal mining. The protesters do not completely dismiss that there are environmental and labour issues to consider in the mining sector, but point to the enormous economic and social consequences of the abrupt and total ban on mining in the state. Thousands of people are being deprived of their livelihoods and the plight of the poor is especially highlighted by the opponents of the ban. For example, on the Facebook Forum 'NGT Ban Impact and Consequences' a member of the Jaintia Hills Autonomous District Council reports that a man recently committed suicide because of the ban. The writer argued that protection of the environment is indeed important, but he condemned the tribunal for not seeing the suffering of the people.[10] In an appeal to the Indian president, Meghalaya MP (and major coal trader) Vincent H. Pala states that the situation has become so bad that some of the mining labourers 'have even started selling their children due to distress'.[11] Critics of the tribunal also point to the suddenness of the ban and that the intervention came out of the blue, leaving them without time to prepare. The legality of the intervention has further also been questioned, arguing that it violates the Sixth Schedule. There are also recent attempts by the Meghalaya government to seek legal exemption for this type of small-scale mining, said to be based on customary practices.[12] The tribunal has so far dismissed the claim about mining being a 'customary activity' that should be tolerated since it has been carried out for a long period of time, stating that it must be carried out in 'compliance with the laws in force'.[13]

To be sure, the halt of coal mining has indeed severely affected many people in the state, be it those that own the mines, carry out transport or export the coal, to labourers and all those who cater for the industry, some with small businesses like tea stalls and garages on the road sides. The cement factories, both the old state-owned Mawmluh Cherra Cement Ltd. and the new privately owned cement plants that have come up during last ten years, face difficulties in operating due to the shortage of coal, which is used as fuel.[14] The state is losing a major source of revenue[15] and the different rebel groups active in the state are similarly suffering financial blows as they have been surviving on the seasonal taxation of the coal business. The mining, however, was an environmental and social catastrophe that was screaming for some kind of state intervention. The Meghalaya government knew this and had for almost a decade been trying to come up with a mining regulation or policy. But with the coal industry being the most powerful lobby group in the state, and with the coal interest within the government itself, such attempts have constantly been obstructed.

MP Vincent H. Pala is a case in point. Pala made a fortune from coal before joining politics. Another example is the newly elected Congress candidate Dikkanchi D. Shira, wife of chief minister Mukul Sangma, and wealthy coal mine owner. The most affluent of them all is party colleague Mr Ngaitlang Dhar, owning more than 100 coal trucks and with a declared fortune of about INR230 *crore*.[16] Dhar was also recently brought into the present Congress government under chief minister Mukul Sangma. So when the tribunal identified the 'coal mafia' as the sole benefactor of the unregulated rathole mining, one has to bear in mind that this does not refer to any rag-tag band of criminals, but to people who have been elected to govern the state and to represent it in the Indian parliament, the Lok Sabha.

However, in 2012 the state legislative assembly did pass a mining regulation called Meghalaya Mines and Minerals Policy. The policy is rather lame, mainly containing general formulations about using the mineral wealth in a sustainable manner, but there are some critical formulations that if put in force would bring about major changes to the mining sector. For example, it points to the need for adopting modern methods of mining instead of the 'antiquated and outdated method of manual extraction' (para 1.6), and in more direct terms it is stated that no mining should be allowed near rivers and streams to avoid pollution (para 8.1.4) and, most importantly, an elaborate system of granting mining concessions is to be introduced, including clearance from the pollution control board, the state forest and environment department, consultations with traditional governing bodies as well as the district council and with final permissions granted by the state government with approval from the central government when required (para 10). This is light years away from the present mining practices, which also explains why there have been no real attempts to implement the policy prior to the intervention by the National Green Tribunal. Now, however, the policy has regained political relevance, evoked also by the coal lobby as a way out of the ban.

Despite the environmental destruction, the most appalling aspect of coal mining is the widespread use of child labour. Children even under the age of ten are being sent down deep underground to dig out coal by hand in narrow mine shafts. The technique used is, as mentioned above, called 'rathole mining', which refers to the many small tunnels reaching out in different directions to reach the coal seam. The tunnels are sometimes no more than half a metre in height, which is why children are particularly suitable for carrying out this, the most dangerous underground work. To get to the tunnels the labourers have to climb down steep and often slippery bamboo ladders, in some cases the pits are as deep as 30 to 40 m. Fatal accidents with people falling down or accidents with primitive elevators that bring coal and labourers up and down the mines are common. The poorly supported shafts easily become death traps when the roof caves in. Visual images from the coal fields speaks about the most horrible working conditions for these child-labourers. Impulse, the child rights NGO, estimates that as many as 70,000 children might be working in the Meghalaya coal fields (2011). Most of these children hail from the neighbouring states of Assam and Nagaland, usually sent to the mining areas by their parents to help support their families. But many are believed to be victims of trafficking, brought from central India or the neighbouring countries, Nepal and Bangladesh. Some of these children do not receive any payment and Impulse suggests that there are reasons to investigate further whether this could actually be a form of slavery (2011: 26).

Labour safety more generally is, as mentioned, also a concern for the National Green Tribunal. An accident in 2012, in South Garo Hills, where 15 labourers were trapped in a mine tunnel and allegedly died there, was also transferred to the tribunal. The tribunal pointed to the lack of formal investigation into the case that reveals a most cynical attitude where the fate of human beings is reduced to that of 'cattle'.[17] The mine where the fatal accident took place is said to have been 'dug 80 ft vertically and 180 ft diagonally with several parallel rathole channels and sub-channels'.[18] The mine was owned by the *nokma*, the headman, of that particular village but was leased out to a non-tribal contractor who, against the usual practice, was pushing the workers to continue the extraction during the monsoon months. The accident happened in July in the midst of heavy rains. Rescue operations are obviously highly hazardous and unlikely to be successful under such conditions.[19] The tribunal seeks to establish what exactly happened and how the authorities responded or failed to do so.

Despite their precarious situation, the plight of mine labourers seldom becomes a public concern in Meghalaya. If they figure in the media it is mainly in relation to some campaign or rally against the influx of non-indigenous outsiders. The migrant coal labourers might also figure in relation to discussions about social ills like prostitution, gambling, excessive alcohol consumption, and general rowdiness, said to be prevalent in the mining areas. When ethnic sentiments run high in the state, it is not unusual that the mine labourers are targeted. But again, as few local people work in the coal fields, the mining sector would not be able to function without the migrant workers. The labourers also keep a low profile; they remain unorganised and tend to stick to their fellow ethnic brethren in the mining camps. Despite horrible living conditions and the hazardous work in the mines, some of the migrant workers do indeed earn enough during a season to make it worthwhile to come back year after year.[20]

Empowerment

Coal mining might have come to a standstill, but most likely it will re-emerge in some form or another. It does not take a lot to realise that there will be major environmental impacts from coal mining even if it is brought under a regulatory framework and is carried out in a 'scientific way'. Coal India's operations in Margherita and elsewhere in India speak about this (see Lahiri-Dutt 2014 and this volume). The situation is also more complicated in Meghalaya; the coal deposits are distributed over a large area, it is a hilly, rough, terrain that is difficult to access via roads and there are no railways in the state to date, and further complicating factors are the high levels of rainfall[21] as well as the seismic activities in the region, with high risks for earthquakes. In these conditions, it is hard to envision the large-scale mechanised mining that seems to be the ideal against which the practice of rathole mining is being assessed. For labour safety, one would imagine that open cast mines would be the only possibility and here one of the major problems is the enormous quantities of over-burden that have to be removed to reach the coal seam.

The only case of large-scale, open pit mining in Meghalaya is the controversial limestone mining carried out by the transnational firm Lafarge. The mine or extraction zone is located in the southern foothills of Khasi Hills, just on the border to Bangladesh, and huge quantities of limestone are excavated and transported on a 17-km long conveyor belt to its cement plant in Bangladesh. This naturally requires massive investments, capital that cannot be mobilised within the state. Lafarge has ended up in a series of legal battles concerning the mining area, illegal felling of trees, pollution, the noise from the frequent blasts, and, above all, compensation to the local landowners (Karlsson 2011: 219–226).

One would think that if one of the largest cement producers in the world has such problems pulling off a large-scale mining operation in Meghalaya, other private companies would certainly think twice before investing in such projects. For better or for worse, the complicated customary land-owning system, state laws preventing alienation of tribal land, and a hybrid, multi-layered, governance structure all work to debar entry of outside Indian or foreign investors. This has also worked to the advantage of the indigenous elite, who in the case of coal has been able to control much of the extraction, transport, and export of the mineral. In this way a number of people in Meghalaya have managed to earn a lot of money from coal. Such fortunes, however, seem to have had little positive impact on the economy at large. Much of the money has gone into buying land and real estate or building luxurious private houses, and other forms of 'conspicuous consumption' (Das 2014: 85).

Most importantly the positive empowering aspects of coal – where labourers have been able to negotiate better social and economic conditions due to their control over the supply of coal – that Mitchell identifies for Western Europe and North America at the turn of the twentieth century is largely missing in Meghalaya. In view of the overall concern for ethnic self-determination and rights of the indigenous tribal groups in the state, the labour force that mainly consists of migrant workers has had almost no political leverage or power to push for higher salaries and improved working conditions. Their position as 'illegal' has made it easy for the mine owners to control the labour force (Das 2014: 85). Shortage of labour does not seem to have been an issue. The coal lobby has also infiltrated the inner circles of political power in the state, using this to keep the mining sectors outside societal interference. For some time, they apparently even got away with the use of child labour. The small-scale nature of the mining and the wide geographical distributions of the coal deposits have also contributed to the difficulties for labours to organise collectively and put pressure on the mine owners by disrupting or cutting off the supply. Such actions would only become a local affair without any larger economic impact or social significance. As the different insurgent groups or ethnic militias active in Meghalaya also feed on taxing the coal business, migrant labourers cannot expect any support from them. The underground Khasi organisation Hynniewtrep National Liberation Council (HNLC) has strongly condemned the intervention of the National Green Tribunal, pointing to the severe effects the mining ban has on the poor in the state. One would assume that also includes the mine workers. But considering that the main cause of HNLC is sovereignty, which also was stressed in their critique of the ban,[22] the plight of the labour force that mainly consists of migrants will not be a major concern to them.

While coal extraction is a major undertaking in Meghalaya, it still makes a rather meagre contribution to the national supply of coal; an estimated five million tonnes, which is about 1 per cent of India's total annual production. Disrupting the extraction and transport chain of the Meghalaya coal does not have any serious repercussions outside the state. In fact one could even argue that this itself explains the bold action of the centre, inserting a complete 'ban' on the coal trade and while doing so acting over the heads of the elected bodies of the hill state. It is highly unlikely that the National Green Tribunal or any other state institution would act so heavy-handedly against the coal industry more generally, not least against CIL which still controls as much as 85 per cent of the coal production (Lahiri-Dutt 2014: xvi). As pointed out earlier, coal mining in India more generally is anything but a legally, socially, and environmentally 'clean' undertaking.

Here it is instructive to compare with hydro-power, which, under the present global regime of climate change, has re-emerged as the environmentally sustainable alternative (Huber and Joshi 2015). Northeast India has a special place in the larger order of things as it holds as much as 43 per cent of India's assessed hydropower potential. Tapping this source of energy is projected by the centre as a win–win proposition with electricity to the country and development to the local communities and the region as a whole. Large numbers of hydel-projects are in the pipeline or are already under construction, many by private companies (Baruah 2012). Despite the enormous difference between coal and hydro-power, it is interesting to note the emergence of a similar extractive regime in the hands of an indigenous elite, leading to the privatisation of land, loss of community control over the resource base as well as major environmental consequences. But what stands out most starkly in the case of hydro is the democratic deficit. As Neeraj Vagholikar and Partha J. Das argue – in an overview of the recent hydropower development in Northeast India – with the involvement of private players, a new modus operandi has emerged where huge monetary advances are being paid upfront by the company to the Arunachal Pradesh government at the time of signing a MoU. This has led to undemocratic pressures to set aside public consultations as well as the process of environmental and other forms of mandatory clearances. The central government is facilitating the development and has proactively granted various clearances to these projects, ignoring important concerns (Vagholikar and Das 2010: 3).

Decisions and control of the energy source is hence commonly lifted above the heads of individuals and the communities, and the indigenous elite seems to act more as brokers selling out to outside interests than to act as elected leaders with at least some concern for the public good. This again is a one-time decision, once the dam is built, land flooded, and people displaced, the matter is settled. The small-scale and low-tech nature of coal mining comes with better democratic possibilities to the extent that control remains with individual landowners and to some extent kin groups and villages, who can decide whether to mine, lease out or sell the land, or alternatively to allow the coal to remain in the ground. Dolly Kikon, who is working on resource extraction in the Assam-Nagaland foothills, mentions that she encountered two college students who had taken a short-term lease of a single coal cave and in March when the coal season was coming to a close had managed to extract 50 truck-loads of coal[23] (2014: 300–325). But there were also larger deals, for example, a landowner who was leasing out an entire mountain to a company in Assam who carried out the mining (ibid.: 226–319). As Kikon puts it, 'there were hundreds of such deals between Naga villages inside the jurisdiction of Nagaland state and companies from Assam' (ibid.: 220).

Like Mitchell, Kikon speaks about oil and coal – how oil is enclaved and under state corporate management, whereas coal is disbursed and in the hands of people themselves – but rather than stressing the different social legacies of the two, she points instead to how both coal and oil conjure male aspirations and fantasies about wealth generated from carbon extractions. Women are excluded from this hyper-masculine sphere of resource extraction – a veritable 'carbon cult' (Kikon 2014: 286–329). Like in the Assam-Nagaland foothills, the world of coal mining is a gendered, violent space in Meghalaya. The difference is that as the indigenous communities in Meghalaya are matrilineal and that land is inherited through the female line, women also participate in the coal trade and several of the prominent coal barons in the state are women. Coal mining in Meghalaya has been brought to the attention of both national and international media, which arguably pushed the centre to act and impose a moratorium. With more or less the same conditions, coal mining in Nagaland and elsewhere in Northeast India has interestingly not been subject to any such interventions.

Towards a conclusion

So then what does all this tell us? To begin with, one could say that it is a story that speaks about the absence of industrial development. Why is this the case when Meghalaya, like other parts of Northeast India, is rich in natural resources like coal, oil, and hydro power that could provide the energy required for manufacturing or other forms of industrial production? Such production could avail raw materials like bamboo, wood, and other forest produce that are plentiful in the region. The labour force is also relatively well educated, not least in terms of the high level of fluency in English. Again why, then, is this not happening?

A popular line of enquiry is to follow the 'resource curse theory' and point to the negative relationship between abundance of natural resources and overall economic and political development of a country (see Auty 1993). Oil is usually the case in point, and to escape the curse, several prominent economists argue, (for example Jeffrey Sachs 2007), that strong institutions have to be put in place. This, however, is easier said than done once you are in the vicious circle of corruption, inefficiency, and conflict, spurred by the scramble for oil revenues. Since everyone is busy getting a piece of the resource pie, no one thinks ahead and seeks to diversify the economy, increase productivity and develop new industries. Countries without valuable natural resources, paradoxically enough, are better off in this regard, forced to promote 'competitive industrialisation', as put by Richard Auty, a leading scholar in this field (2004: 34).

As I have noted, the wealth from coal has not gone into productive investments, but mainly into buying land and property. There are many who seek to get a piece of the coal spoils, not least within the state bureaucracy, the law enforcement and within the ethnic insurgent groups. Coal profits have further been converted into political power that obviously has been used to prevent societal control or accountability of the mining sector. When the coal trade came to a sudden close, it was clear that nothing new in terms of economic diversification had been created. People seem as poor as ever, or in fact, even worse off as land and rivers in the mining areas have been polluted and no longer can sustain subsistence agriculture. Coal does in many ways appear as a curse.

In the opening of *Carbon Democracy* Mitchell refers to the resource curse argument, saying that the Arab spring in 2011 seems to suggest the relevance of such thinking. In countries that produced less oil, one saw a more widespread readiness to join the democratic struggles. But he then goes on to offer a completely different reading that dismisses the resource curse argument, above all for isolating the social maladies within the countries of production, failing to see how for example undemocratic structures have been put in place by powerful outside actors – oil companies and Western states – that are part of a wider energy network (Mitchell 2011: 5). As Mitchell argues, it is not enough to look at how governments handle oil revenues, but one has to follow the resource itself, and look at 'the nature of oil and how it is produced, distributed and used' (ibid.: 1).

In this chapter, I have begun to unravel some aspects of the energopolitics of coal in the hill state of Meghalaya. The coal that is produced is transported by trucks out of the state. Only smaller quantities are used within the state itself, part of it for the production of cement, which is one of the few thriving industries in Meghalaya. As I argued, coal has changed the social fabric not least through intensified privatisation and commodification of land and nature, consolidating the extractive capitalist economy that was first established under the British. It is hard to see a way out; an alternative that could bring about a more sustainable and equitable future. However painful, the moratorium imposed by the National Green Tribunal might offer a moment of collective reflection that eventually might break the powerful spell of coal.

Notes

1 The edited volume *The Coal Nation: Histories, Ecologies and Politics of Coal in India* (Lahiri-Dutt 2014) also contains chapters of particular relevance for this chapter, dealing with colonial Assam (Saikia 2014), Northeast India in general (Fernandes and Bharali 2014), and the state of Meghalaya (Das 2014).

2 I am paraphrasing the CSE Citizens' Report titled 'Rich Lands Poor People: Is "Sustainable" Mining Possible' (Bhushan and Zeya Hazra 2008).

3 The central argument was also presented in an earlier essay (Mitchell 2009).

4 Such ideas are, for example, presented in the much discussed government plan for Northeast India from 2008 called Vision 2020 (online, available at: www.indian-chamber.org/northeast/Vision2020.pdf).

5 There is a coal museum in Margherita that provides glimpses of the history of coal in Assam. The photo collection exhibited at the museum is particularly interesting. See also Sakia (2014).

6 See David Rose's essay 'Why India is Captured by Carbon' in *Guardian*, 27 May 2015.

7 See 'Two Units of Assam's Kopili Hydel Project Shut Down', *Business Standard*, 19 June 2013, and '"Black Gold" Kills Rivers, Stains State Poll Canvas' by Rahul Karmakar in *Hindustan Times*, 22 February 2013.

8 National Green Tribunal, Circuit Bench at High Court, Shillong, Original Application No. 13 of 2014, and Original Application No 73 of 2014, Impulse Network and All Dimasa Students' Union Dima Hasao Distr. Committee vs State of Meghalaya, page 9.

9 Before the National Green Tribunal, Principal Bench, New Delhi, Original Application No. 73 of 2014, All Dimasa Students Union Dima Hasao Dist. Committee vs State of Meghalaya and others, pages 2–3.

10 See statement by Mr. Phazmon IongLoor, online, available at: www.facebook.com/NGTBanImpact (accessed 1 June 2015).

11 See the article 'Intervene in Coal Mining Ban, Meghlaya Leaders to President', *Business Standard*, 7 August 2014. Pala also gave this example in a speech in the Indian Parliament, 14 July 2014 – online, available at: www.youtube.com/watch?v=aig4LpiE8JY (accessed 2 June 2015).

12 See for example article on TNT website, online, available at: http://thenortheast today.com/meghalaya-house-approves-govt-resolution-on-coal-mining/ (accessed 23 March 2015).

13 Before the National Green Tribunal, Circuit Bench at High Court of Meghalaya, Shillong, Original Application No. 13 of 2014 and Original Application No. 73 of 2014 and M.A. No. 174 of 2014, M.A. No. 294 of 2014, M.A. No. 300 of 2014, M.A.

No. 317 of 2014, M.A. No. 352/2014, M.A. No. 371/2014 and M.A. No. 318 of 2014, In Original Application No. 73 of 2014 In The Matter Of: Impulse NGO Network Vs. State of Meghalaya and Ors. and All Dimasa Students Union Dima Hasao Dist. Committee vs. State of Meghalaya and Ors., page 5 (online, available at: http://librarylegal.com/documentdetail/All%20Dimasa%20Student%20Vs%20%20State%20of%20Meghalay.aspx?hc=0xF7A7E2F10C95A9B8B1A561E349113A2B) (accessed 3 March 2016).

14 See, for example, 'NGT Ban Effect: Cement Cos in Dire Straits', *Shillong Times*, 20 January 2015, and 'Meghalaya: MCCL's Employees Rues the Govt's Failure to Pay their Pending Salaries', *Northeast Today*, 11 June 2015.

15 Meghalaya was during the last decade annually collecting around INR10,000 *crore* in revenue from coal (Meghalaya State Development Report 2009: 55, table 3.14).

16 See myneta.info website, online, available at: http://myneta.info/meghalaya2013/candidate.php?candidate_id=177 (accessed 20 February 2016).

17 See, Before the National Green Tribunal, Circuit Bench at High Court of Meghalaya, Shillong. Original Application No. 110 (T HC) of 2012. Threat to Life Arising Out of Coal Mining in South Garo Hills District vs. State of Meghalaya and Ors (online, available at: www.indiaenvironmentportal.org.in/files/coal%20mining%20NGT%2024Jan2014.pdf) (accessed 19 May 2015).

18 'Deaths Continue in Mines of Meghalaya', by Andrew W. Lyngdoh. *Telegraph*, 18 March 2013.

19 'Hopes of Saving Miners Dim', *Telegraph*, 20 July 2012.

20 A research team under Professor Tanka B. Subba, Sikkim University, is carrying out work on the effects of remittances by Nepali migrant labourers in the Meghalaya coal fields (online, available at: www.nepalonthemove.dk/InformationFiles/Information_4/Files_en/Sub%20studies%20for%20web.pdf). With the ban, many of the migrant workers now return home. See, for example, the short but instructive film 'Broken Landscape', by Michael T. Miller (online, available at: www.theatlantic.com/video/index/389607/the-horrors-of-rat-hole-mining/).

21 Cherrapunjee in the Khasi Hills is famous for being the wettest place on earth and most of the mining areas are exposed to extreme levels of annual rainfall.

22 See, for example, 'HNLC Clamps Two-Day Shutdown against Coal Ban', *Telegraph*, 11 August 2014.

23 One truck-load of coal could, in 2010, be sold to Assamese traders for about INR5,000–5,500 (Kikon 2014).

References

Appel, Hannah C. (2012). 'Walls and White Elephants: Oil Extraction, Responsibility and Infrastructural Violence in Equatorial Guinea'. *Ethnography* 13(4): 439–465.

Auty, Richard (1993). *Sustaining Development in Mineral Economies: The Resource Curse Thesis*. London: Routledge.

Auty, Richard (2004). 'Natural Resources and Civil Strife: A Two Stage Process'. *Geopolitics* 9(1): 29–49.

Baruah, Sanjib (2012). 'Whose River is it Anyway? Political Economy of Hydropower in Eastern Himalayas'. *Economic and Political Weekly* 47(29): 41–52.

Bhushan, Chandra and Monali Zeya Hazra (2008). *Rich Lands Poor People: Is 'Sustainable' Mining Possible?* New Delhi: Centre for Science and Environment.

Boyer, Dominic (2011). 'Energopolitics and the Anthropology of Energy'. *Anthropology News* 52(5): 5–7.

Das, Debojyoti (2014). 'Border Mining: State Politics, Migrant Labour and Land Relations along the India–Bangladesh Borderlands'. In: Kuntala Lahiri-Dutt (ed.).

The Coal Nation: Histories, Ecologies and Politics of Coal in India, Farnham: Ashgate, pp. 79–104.

Ferguson, James (2006). Global Shadows: Africa in the Neoliberal World Order. Durham: Duke University Press.

Fernandes, Walter and Gita Bharali (2014). 'Coal Mining in Northeastern India in the Age of Globalisation'. In: Kuntala Lahiri-Dutt (ed.). The Coal Nation: Histories, Ecologies and Politics of Coal in India, Farnham: Ashgate, pp. 183–196.

Huber, Amelie and Deepa Joshi (2015). 'Hydropower, Anti-Politics, and the Opening of New Political Spaces in Eastern Himalayas'. World Development 73: 13–25.

Impulse (2011). 'An Exploratory Study of Children Engaged in Rat Hole Mining in the Coal Mines of Jaintia Hills, Meghalaya'. Shillong: Impulse NGO Network.

Karlsson, Bengt G. (2011). Unruly Hills: A Political Ecology of India's Northeast. Oxford: Berghahn Books.

Karlsson, Bengt G. and Dolly Kikon (eds). Leaving the Land: Indigenous Migration from the Resource Frontier to the Urban Sprawl in India. Manuscript under preparation.

Kikon, Dolly (2014). 'Disturbed Area Acts: Intimacy, Anxiety and the State in Northeast India'. Unpublished PhD dissertation, Stanford University.

Lahiri-Dutt, Kuntala (ed.) (2014). The Coal Nation: Histories, Ecologies and Politics of Coal in India. Farnham: Ashgate.

Li, Tanya Murray (2014). Land's End: Capitalist Relations on an Indigenous Frontier. Durham: Duke University Press.

McDuie-Ra, Duncan (2012). Northeast Migrants in Delhi: Race, Refuge, Retail. Amsterdam: Amsterdam University Press.

Meghalaya Government (2009). 'Meghalaya State Development Report'. Shillong: Meghalaya Government, Planning Department.

Mitchell, Timothy (2009). 'Carbon Democracy'. Economy and Society (3): 399–432.

Mitchell, Timothy (2011). Carbon Democracy: Political Power on the Age of Oil. London: Verso.

Oldham, Thomas (1984 [1854]). Geology, Meteorology and Ethnology of Meghalaya. New Delhi: Mittal.

Padel, Felix and Samarendra Das (2010). Out of This Earth: East India Adivasis and the Aluminium Cartel. New Delhi: Orient Blackswan.

Sachs, Jeffrey D (2007). 'How to Handle the Macroeconomics of Oil Wealth'. In: Marcatan Humphreys, Jeffrey D. Sachs, and Joseph E. Stieglitz (eds). Escaping the Resource Curse, New York: Columbia University Press, pp. 173–193.

Sakia, Arupjyoti (2014). 'Coal in Colonial Assam: Exploration, Trade and Environmental Consequences'. In: Kuntala Lahiri-Dutt (ed.). The Coal Nation: Histories, Ecologies and Politics of Coal in India, Farnham: Ashgate, pp. 63–78.

Vagholikar, Neeraj and Partha J. Das (2010). 'Damming Northeast India: Juggernaut of Hydropower Projects Threatens Social and Environmental Security of Region'. Briefing paper. Pune/Guwahati/New Delhi: Kalpavriksh, Aaranyak and Action Aid India.

Watts, Michael J (2005). 'Righteous Oil? Human Rights, the Oil Complex and Corporate Social Responsibility'. Annual Reviews in Advance 30(9): 1–35.

The nature of bauxite mining and
Adivasi livelihoods in the
industrialisation of Eastern India

Patrik Oskarsson

In post-liberalisation India mining has come to take on a key role in controversies over land and forests in Adivasi[1] Eastern India. Despite mining taking place in many varied forms, from the massive, open cast coal mines of public sector Coal India to small-scale, and often informal, stone and gem quarries, bauxite mining perhaps more than any other form of mining has received public attention as an indicator of the incompatibility of modern India's aggressive approach to industrialisation and economic growth, and the constitutional commitment to support sustainable, indigenous groups. The bauxite mines planned for hilltops on Adivasi lands of the states of Odisha and Andhra Pradesh appear as green, sustainable havens of indigenous groups, and yet private companies collaborate with the government to generate profits with little benefit returning to the communities.

The crucial role of the Indian state in enabling land transactions has long been debated. When bauxite mining is proposed, however, it becomes excruciatingly clear that active government involvement takes place for the monetary gain of a few rather than national development, and at the cost of already marginalised people in the mineral-bearing areas. The result is to decisively change the terms of the debate, resulting in decades-long controversy playing out in courts, the media, and at the proposed sites. Mining projects have become part of intense government lobbying leading to a highly polarised environment around mineral-based industrialisation and its implications for resource-dependent groups like Adivasis, where the meaning of development and the nature of resources to serve marginalised groups, as well as the nation, are crucial and highly controversial ingredients (Oskarsson 2010).

As bauxite mining[2] projects have remained virtually 'deadlocked' (Oskarsson and Nielsen 2014) in conflict over the past decade, and in some cases longer, as the latest in a long history of controversies over Adivasi land, contestation has irrevocably come to rely on widely different interpretations of what such operations actually imply to local environments and societies. The nature of bauxite mining has come to be key in informing policy, public opinion, movement protests, court judgements, and the media on how scarce natural resources on and around particular hills in Eastern India should best be put to use and who should be allowed to make decisions on resource use (Oskarsson 2010). Despite the production of countless government and civil society reports, court judgements, detailed investigations by various experts and media reports into some aspect of the complex controversies around bauxite mining, little to no shared understanding has been established of the social and environmental implications of bauxite mining (Reddy 2006; Oskarsson 2010; Padel and Das 2010; Saxena *et al.* 2010).[3]

This chapter, based on in-depth studies at three proposed bauxite mining locations[4] is an attempt to look for comparative, empirical evidence in search of the nature of bauxite mining and social change in Eastern India. Given the common use of a certain set of technologies and arrangements for the extraction of bauxite ore in a relatively confined region, the related changes to land, water, and forests, and attendant livelihood changes to supposedly homogenous Adivasi populations, should open up for some degree of understanding.

After a review of the theory around constructions of nature with reference to mining in the next section, this chapter continues with an overview of what bauxite ore is, where it exists and how it is mined. After this the following sections discuss how mining will change land, forests, and water in the three examined study locations and how these relate to livelihoods. Finally, some overall conclusions are drawn.

In search of a nature of bauxite mining

Natural resource management on the lands of subaltern groups, particularly when involving indigenous peoples, is a highly complex affair in the international literature on mineral governance. When mining literally turns certain lands upside down, dramatic change to physical environments ,and thereby also to the lifeworlds of people in the area, are all but certain even when serious attempts are made to first mitigate negative consequences and later restore original natural and social values (Hilson 2002; Howitt 2001). To make sense of the socio-environmental changes that will occur if large-scale mining commences, we need to grapple with a wide range of inter-disciplinary questions, which involve an understanding of the existing social and environmental conditions, the technologies and resources employed in proposed mineral extraction, and the varying cultures and forms of governance that are in existence in particular locations (Bebbington *et al.* 2008). These are by no account easy to determine, as particularly cultural values depend on subjective positions of what is valuable and important.

In Indian bauxite mining, efforts to reach a broader understanding of what this form of extraction entails are particularly hampered by years of clandestine planning, as companies and governments have collaborated in a closed 'developmental alliance' (Kohli 2009) in which affected peoples have not been taken into confidence. Indications from a number of investigations in recent years also indicate that corruption is part of why projects are promoted rather than national development resulting in drastically reduced public trust in authorities (Oskarsson 2013a). Socio-environmental analysis must clearly be complemented by an understanding of wider political economy forces.

Opposition to bauxite mining in India has tended to focus on land use changes to protect local peoples from dispossession. Civil society organisations and local protest movements have stressed the importance of changes to forest cover and water availability when calling for mining plans to be stopped, due to concerns that people will not be able to cope with the ensuing changes (Amnesty International 2010; Padel and Das 2007; Patra and Murthy n.d.; Ramamurthy 1995; Reddy 2006). In certain cases environmental conservation has also played an important role in these protests (Mishra 1987). The possibilities of environmentally sound practices, remunerative employment, and a local share in the profits, which are important claims in the international literature,[5] have in Indian bauxite mining contestation been eschewed for a more conflictual path of opposition.

The reasons for the strong opposition to mining dispossession are not too difficult to see. Though exact numbers are not available, it seems clear that mining is the biggest source of displacement in India after dams, with victims potentially numbered in the millions. Of these, very few have been resettled, and the problem has been particularly common for those affected by mining. Even when resettlement has been agreed to, it has been found to be impossible to implement land for land compensation policies. One important explanation for the lack of compensation – and the even less common full rehabilitation – from mining is its strong connection to forest land owned by the government.[6] For tribal peoples the denied rights over forests have meant denied compensation when the forest has been converted into a mine. Denied compensation for land also means a denial of other potential compensation offers like jobs or education that could help people rebuild livelihoods (Fernandes 2009). Industrial land on the other hand tends to be acquired in flatter, agricultural landscapes with a larger share of formally recognised ownership. This has, however, not prevented controversy for the acquisition of this type of land either, often seen as being a choice between livelihoods and food security on the one hand and industrialisation (with more technical jobs) on the other (Fernandes 2007).

Internationally, the universalising tendencies of the natural sciences have come to be tempered by site-specific, best practices in environmental management, including the need to take social factors into account, preferably in cooperation with local people (Howitt 2001). In South Asia a lot of work has to date been carried out on participatory forms of forest governance (Nightingale and Ojha 2013; Ojha 2013) but, in practice even if not according to the letter of the law, almost none on minerals, which could at least offer some amount of local, democratic influence on mine planning and governance (Lahiri-Dutt 2014). The approach to governing the environment in India continues to be dominated by scientific interpretations dominated by expert scientists. This is particularly the case for core economic activities like industrialisation and mining, despite openings for public participation in managing local resources (Ferguson and Gupta 2002; Gupta 2012).

In contrast, anti-mining activists make use of ideas with universalising aspirations about Adivasi cultures and how mining affects indigenous people

(Oskarsson 2015b). When the more than 500 separate groups of people that the Indian Constitution define as Scheduled Tribes are identified as indigenous or Adivasi the result can be an inability to appreciate variations in, for example, language, customs, livelihoods, or land use (Shah 2007). The international experience of how indigenous people in many parts of the world end up on the losing side when mineral extraction is proposed appears in many cases relevant also in India, and yet the sheer variation of peoples and the difficulty of labelling some groups as more indigenous than others make such efforts difficult. Similarly to the universal approach to environmental management, the role of place-based specificities become important while not fully discarding the need for broader assessments.

This chapter combines the key documents and reports on bauxite mining projects internationally and in Eastern India with the author's own research.[7] Three proposed bauxite mines provide the empirical material for the case studies; Niyamgiri in Southern Odisha, Gandhamardhan in Western Odisha, and Araku, in northeastern Andhra Pradesh. The outcome of this analysis can admittedly not be seen as producing a definitive account of socio-environmental change from bauxite mining, if indeed such a thing is at all possible to write, but can hopefully serve as a starting point for a broader understanding of the links between Adivasi environments and mineral extraction.

Bauxite mining and the environment

The formation of bauxite ore in the Eastern Indian states of Odisha and Andhra Pradesh has taken place via weathering processes over millions of years when Khondalite[8] rock common to the area has been exposed to strong monsoon rains followed by hot sun. During this slow process various minerals are slowly washed away to leave bauxite ore as a hard rock filled with holes on the very top part of some hills. The thickness of the bauxite deposits range from about 1 m up to as much as 54 m while the areal spread can be several square kilometres, like the 3.55 km² Niyamgiri deposit, or much smaller, like the 0.95 km² Galikonda deposit of Araku. Since the weathering process also has removed most of the topsoil the vegetation tends to be limited. It is thus common to find the top portion of Indian bauxite hills, crucially including the ore body, largely without forest or other vegetation beyond grasses and shrubs. The hillsides on the other hand are often richly forested (Oskarsson 2010).

Influenced by these core physical characteristics of bauxite hills, two opposing discourses on the nature of bauxite mining have come to shape understandings of the socio-environmental consequences of mining. Those companies and governments in favour of mining see a rich bauxite ore deposit on bare hilltops with few habitations. Those against mining on the other hand see forested hills with springs flowing from the bauxite deposits and down the hillsides in support of sustainable, tribal livelihoods (Oskarsson 2015b).[9] The construction of bauxite mining spaces as uninhabited spaces lacking in environmental values, common in pro-mining plans in India (Lahiri-Dutt *et al.* 2012; Oskarsson 2015a), reverberate strongly in the literature on land grabs where similar approaches to frame land as available for investors have been all too common both internationally (White *et al.* 2012) and in India (Baka 2013). Anti-mining activists have, however, held on to the view that the ore cannot be removed without negatively affecting wider eco-systems and Adivasi cultures (Oskarsson 2010).

The interest in developing the east coast bauxite deposits increased dramatically in the 1990s after the opening of the Indian economy to private participation for export, mainly to cater to Chinese demand. Changes to the Indian economy coincided with the international trend of higher mineral prices, and the possibilities to import technology for the refining and smelting of aluminium. The end result was vastly changing circumstances in favour of bauxite projects. Privatisation and restructuring means that the Indian aluminium industry is at present concentrated in three companies: public sector Nalco, the private Hindalco (of the Birla Group), and Vedanta. A number of other Indian big business groups are vying to develop new deposits, while long-term controversies appear to have reduced interest among foreign investors, at least for the time being (Oskarsson 2010).

A key problem with general statements about how bauxite mining changes local environments is the variable composition and quality of the mineral. Gendron *et al.* explain that 'bauxite is a heterogeneous mineral that is difficult to define accurately. It occurs in many different forms, and its physical properties vary greatly, even within single ore beds' (2013: 1). It is thus likely that the variable nature of the mineral with additional interplay with other natural and social factors will produce a wide range of outcomes (Barham *et al.* 1994). What we do know, however, is that open cast mining with extensive land disruption is a given in India when the ore exists on top of hills with little overburden.[10] In Odisha the vast flat bauxite hills, which often stretch for several kilometres, make mining operations particularly straightforward technically since the mining can proceed on top of the same mountain for many years. In Andhra Pradesh the topography of the hills are steeper with smaller but thicker deposits.

The planned rate of mining is usually about three million tonnes per year in Indian bauxite mining operations in support of associated refineries of approximately one million tonnes of alumina per year. Depending on the size of the ore deposits, actual mining operations become very different, ranging from Galikonda of the Araku region, which would only last for 13 years, to the much larger Niyamgiri of 30 years (Ministry of Environment and Forests 2008). Initial steps in bauxite mining operations, other than the construction of transport infrastructure, will be to clear vegetation, wherever necessary, and to remove the overburden. Actual mining practices consist of dozer-rippers who can tear the solid rock apart, combined with blasting to remove the ore. Excavators and labourers will load trucks (or possibly a conveyor belt) for transport to a nearby railway station or directly to the refinery. Mining will proceed in smaller blocks of 20–30 ha and once mined out move on to a new block (Indian Council of Forestry Research and Education n.d.; Sterlite Industries (India) Limited 2003; Vimta Labs 2005). Steep hills naturally make the process more difficult as a great number of villages exist just below the proposed mountains and depend on the slopes for coffee (ibid.). Soil erosion and rock debris are significant hazards for those living below the mining hills.

Once mining in one segment has been completed it moves to the next while back-filling, and other land reclamation activities are supposed to start, including reforestation. EIAs on bauxite mining tend to recommend to plant trees to prevent landslides and soil erosion but give little detail of how, when, and where this will be done other than to recommend the use of indigenous species of trees and to identify the relevant state Forest Department responsible (Indian Council of Forestry Research and Education n.d.; Sterlite Industries (India) Limited 2003; Vimta Labs 2005). The first problem with this is that forest cover is likely to have been limited in the first place in the mining area and the planting of trees will represent a change of the ecology rather than a restoration. The second problem is related to what kind of forest should be planted. There are, as far as is known, no attempts at present to create natural forests in mined out areas in India, with little to no research having been carried out on the topic for any kind of mining. The following sections aims to contribute to an improved understanding of the nature of bauxite hills via an examination of its land resources, forests, and water sources.

Land-dependent rural livelihoods at the bauxite hills

> One of India's most remote tribes. A mountain they revere as a god. And a multinational mining company with its sights set on the mountain's sacred stone. The stage is set for a bitter struggle against the backdrop of Eastern India's dramatic landscapes. As the bulldozers draw closer what will one tribe do to save their forests, their mountains, and their god?
>
> (Survival International 2009)

This dramatic start to the Survival International documentary 'Mine – Story of a Sacred Mountain' emphasises the spiritual importance of the Niyamgiri Hill for the Donghria Kondh Adivasis, including the very rock the hill is made up of. The long-drawn struggle between the multinational mining company Vedanta, supported by the Indian state, and an anti-mining movement consisting of 'heterogeneous actors and participants, with diverse interests and capacities, from around the world' (Kumar 2014: 196) has come to take centre stage in the wider contestation over bauxite mining and Adivasi rights in India over the past decade. The impressive biodiversity and the marginalised tribe, which only lives on the hill with a close spiritual connection and livelihood dependency, have reverberated strongly domestically and internationally.

The question is, however, to what extent the lush Niyamgiri Hill with its Adivasis represents the uniform picture of all bauxite hills? The story of the lush hill and its tribe is of course more complicated than what appears in many of the statements that have been made over the years. Also at and around Niyamgiri are other groups whose interests should also be taken into account when mining and other forms of resource use are discussed. By the foot of the hill are Kutiya Kondh, together with the main Kondh Adivasi, as well as other groups of more recent settlers who practise settled agriculture. While it is well-known that the agricultural plains nowadays contain a very diverse population of tribes and non-tribes, a field visit to a village on top of Niyamgiri in 2007 made it clear that also here non-tribes have become residents. Dalits have become traders who market the various forest products, including medicinal plants collected by the Donghria Kondh of the village.

In the Araku area farmers are overwhelmingly Adivasi, a clear divergence from much of the rest of central India, including at Niyamgiri and Gandhamardhan, where land alienation to non-Adivasi groups has been significant. Among the Adivasi groups in Araku a great diversity exists, however, with Visakhapatnam District being inhabited by 14 officially recognised groups, most of them natively Telugu-speaking but a few with roots in Odisha or with their own languages (Oskarsson 2010). Gandhamardhan, being located outside of the Scheduled Areas, is a very mixed area socially. A survey carried out in six villages in Bargarh District indicated a very diverse social setting, with completely Adivasi villages, a Dalit village of recent immigrants, but most common were villages with a mix of tribes, Dalits and OBC (Other Backward Castes) groups. Many of these villages remained dominated by a traditional headman, known as Gauntia, who not only controlled village life but also a majority of the agricultural land (Oskarsson 2013b).

At Araku and at Gandhamardhan, villages are located at the foothills rather than on top of the hills since these areas provide better supply of water and flatter land more suitable for farming. Historical and present day conflicts with forest bureaucracies appear to have also influenced settlement patterns. Local farmers depend on hill streams for their small plots in areas without significant irrigation infrastructure. In Araku hilltop villages do exist, however (Oskarsson 2010, 2013b). The Donghria Kondh are thus unique in that they only live on the hill, while other Adivasi and non-Adivasi groups, like at Araku and Gandhamardhan, cultivate the flat valleys around the bauxite hills. The valleys surrounding Niyamgiri with flat, agricultural land are, like at Araku and Gandhamardhan, socially varied, with a number of different Adivasi as well as lower caste Hindu groups making a living off settled agriculture, pastoralism, and forest-related livelihoods.

On all the bauxite hills studied here cultivable land is scarce on or immediately next to the ore deposits. People have therefore tended to settle away from the hilltops either in more forested parts of the hills or, more commonly, below in valleys with flat land. Consequently direct displacement from people losing their homes to mining will be low if mining commences, at most a few villages of perhaps 30–50 households in total for a mine. Claims based on the displacement of farmers and immediate land use changes have thus been difficult to make, even for the Donghria Kondh, who only have Niyamgiri Hill as their home. Protests against bauxite mining have instead focused on wider area changes to forests and water.

Bauxite mining affecting forested hills?

While much of the past debate over mining and deforestation has been within the Indian state, particularly in the 1980s and 1990s, the strong wave towards community management of forests has come to influence mining debates recently with improved, though still limited, possibilities for communities to be heard. This was most apparent when the villages next to the Niyamgiri mine, based on Supreme Court intervention, were allowed to vote in 2012 on whether land use should be changed from forests to bauxite mining. All 12 villages voted against mining, leading to a cancellation of the proposal to mine. It remains unclear, however, whether voting will be allowed in other mining cases since the key issue at Niyamgiri was that community claims had not been settled according to the Forest Rights Act of 2006.

Differences in opinion over forest growth on bauxite hills have remained also within Indian governments. In recent years the development of forest compensation programmes and a story of deforested bauxite hilltops able to be mined without negative forest impact have created improved possibilities for mining companies to secure forest approvals. As recently as 2001 the Andhra Pradesh Forest Department refused to approve bauxite mining since 'the forest area is rich in flora and fauna'.[11] But just a few years later a high-level meeting of the Andhra Pradesh government concluded that there was no problem for mining to proceed since the 'bauxite capping is devoid of any forest' (GoAP, Industries and Commerce Department 2005: 4). The detailed reasons behind this change of opinion are not available. The changes do, however, appear connected to the forest compensation, which since 2009 provides large sums of money and new land for forest departments when mining is approved on forest lands (Kohli and Menon 2011).

The bauxite hills have come to be known for having biodiverse forests with Adivasi groups as their custodians. But not only is the demographic composition of the hills and their surroundings much more diverse than commonly thought, as could be seen in the previous section, there is also a wide variety of physical environments, including forest cover and forest quality. Biodiverse forests can be found particularly at Niyamgiri and Gandhamardhan, but a wider, comparative picture would tell us that some hills are barely forested at all, like the Baphlimali bauxite hill in Kashipur District of Odisha, or are plantations as part of coffee cultivation, as at Galikonda and Raktakonda hills in Araku. The variability of forests is likely to depend on a combination of human and environmental characteristics that have developed over long periods of time. For the purposes here it should be sufficient to notice that there is wide variability. In the case of Araku, the natural forest appears to have been lost at least for decades, and possibly even for generations (Oskarsson 2010).

Forests are not merely about biodiversity and livelihoods, however, given their strong spiritual association in Hindu as well as Adivasi beliefs. The spiritual side of the bauxite hills remains poorly investigated despite support in the Forest Rights Act for spiritual places including those of worship and burial to be recognised as community areas. It is for example well known that the Donghria Kondh celebrate certain festivals on top of Niyamgiri (see Ramesh, this volume). And a formal place of worship exists at Gandhamardhan less than 1 km from the hilltop where the Kappard Patra shrine is worshipped by local Adivasis. And the Hindu pilgrimage route between two temples at Gandhamardhan is used by thousands of pilgrims each year.

A key shared characteristic for all the Bauxite hills is, however, that the particular ore-bearing areas with high concentration of bauxite are not forested. This is since, as discussed above, the topsoil has been washed away in the processes that created the bauxite deposits in the first place. Over the years civil society environmentalists campaigning on the issue have come to diverge, and at times see the great forests down the hillsides as an indication of entirely forested hills. This is not particularly surprising given the poor planning documents and maps that have tended to be part of bauxite projects. Even if the hilltop is neither forested nor cultivated by settled agriculture it has never been properly investigated what environmental and social values actually exist in these unique locations with their grasslands.

A further complication in understanding forest outcomes relate to the practices of how mining is carried out, and if and how it is reforested once mining is finished. According to environmental regulations, new forest is supposed to be planted after a mine is closed since the land is still designated as forest (whether it was ever actually covered by trees or not). The first problem with this is, as we have seen, that there might not have been any forest in the first place and so planting new forest will represent a permanent change to the landscape. The second problem is related to what kind of forest should be planted along mine roads leading up to the hill where actual forest is likely to be lost, and relatedly who should control and benefit from this. Should forest be grown where none existed before? At the moment we know very little about the unique environmental features of the hilltops where the bauxite ore exists. It might just be that this unique environment with grasslands does not exist anywhere else and though scarce at first sight nevertheless contain species not found elsewhere.

If new forest is to be planted then what kind of forest? The few details of present reforestation plans indicate commercial plantations. At times these are to be mixed with what is referred to as native species. Nowhere has the stated goal of Australian bauxite mine reclamation[12] been used, that is to restore the ecology to what it was before mining commenced. Should mine reclamation strive to grow forests from which local communities, preferably even the same people, who were displaced or disrupted earlier, could benefit? If yes, then how should this forest programme be managed and who should decide? These questions remain uncertain, with contradictory support in law between the established Joint Forest Management and the more recent Forest Rights Act, which puts control solely in the hands of traditional forest-dwellers.

Water from bauxite hills sustaining livelihoods near and far?

When direct displacement has been low, and forest debates limited the mining zones to being framed as grasslands under the control of the Forest Department, water availability has taken on crucial importance in bauxite mining protests.

> If the flat-topped hills [containing bauxite ore] are destroyed, the forests that clothe them will be destroyed too. So will the rivers and streams that flow out of them and irrigate the plains below. So will the Dongria Kond. So will the hundreds of thousands of tribal people who live in the forested heart of India, and whose homeland is similarly under attack.
>
> (Roy 2010: xii)

A more detailed explanation of the connection between the ore and water availability is provided by Padel and Das who state that 'the layer of bauxite is like clay, holding moisture, letting it seep out gently throughout the year through streams which form all around the mountain's flank' (2010: 7). The theoretical basis for hydrological change from mining has been mainly set out by Ramamurthy, a rare geologist among mining activists in India. In his analysis it is the bauxite ore, with its porous structure created through the slow weathering process, which is key to a good water retention capacity compared to the underlying solid rock (Ramamurthy 1995). Removing the bauxite via mining in this interpretation means changing a crucial part of the hydrology of a water-stressed region, where most either directly depend on agricultural livelihoods or live in cities with frequent water shortages during hot summer months.

The idea that open caste bauxite mining on top of hills like Niyamgiri is likely to change both the availability and quality of the water in streams running down the hillside is quite straightforward, given the radical changes to the topography of the hill implied by this form of mining and the limited backfilling that is proposed. Dramatic effects from mining could be expected for farmers in villages within a few kilometres of the hills where no other sources of irrigation exist. The claims to water change from mining are, however, much larger than this insofar as the wider river systems that the local streams feed into, are also seen as being at risk. The water narrative has in recent years created strong concerns for regional water deficiency if mining commences based on the bauxite hills that are part of the watersheds of important regional and national rivers, including the Vamsadhara River, which floats from Niyamgiri in Odisha through Andhra Pradesh.

Detailed evidence to support the position that wider changes will occur to water availability if bauxite mining commences is not available. This is perhaps not surprising since activists lack the capacity to conduct either independent laboratory tests of rock geology, or large-scale and time-consuming investigations into the forestry, geology, and hydrology of bauxite hills and the effects of mining on the environmentally fragile region.[13] Counter-evidence denying the proposition that bauxite mining will hurt local and regional watersheds is similarly very scarce, being mainly based on a highly technical geological report by a government research institute (Central Mine Planning and Design Institute 2006).

Lacking evidence that is seen as scientifically valid, activists have pointed to how some of the best forests remaining in Eastern India are located at bauxite hills,[14] and that the same mountains act as important watersheds locally and for inter-state rivers. It has been noticed at Nalco's Panchpatmali mine that mining has caused hill streams to run dry (Patra and Murthy n.d.) and the same has happened due to other forms of open cast mining in Odisha (Kumar 2004). In-depth studies of local agri-ecological systems that would be able to inform the debate about similarities, and possible differences, in how agriculture and forestry is practised in the region, and how different geological and other characteristics shape water availability, remain scarce leaving a good amount of uncertainty as livelihoods and mining continue to be debated. Reports such as those cited above have been sufficient to convince civil society actors but not most government representatives, who are more inclined to natural science approaches.

An opposite explanation that mining has a beneficial effect on water availability comes from the MoEF. In 2008 the ministry stated that mining bauxite would actually help water retention of the mountain by developing cracks from mining blasts into which water could seep and remain stored (Ministry of Environment and Forests 2008). This imaginative interpretation seems to be based on a report by a central government research institute that concluded that bauxite ore did not possess very good capacity to retain water (measured in low porosity), nor was it able to transmit water to groundwater (measured in low permeability) (Central Mine Planning and Design Institute 2006). While slightly less certain due to strong local protests, environmental impact assessment reports (EIAs) on bauxite mining have come to favour the view that mining will improve water availability (Indian Council of Forestry Research and Education, n.d.: 121).

Environmental consultants preparing impact assessments on bauxite mines in India have instead identified risks related to water with regard to pollution from mine run-off and water use. Water quality may be affected by polluted run-off from the open cast mine unless proper drains are provided. Containing run-off during vigorous monsoons is likely to pose a serious challenge, with as much as 1,900 mm of annual rainfall. EIAs are typically certain that this can be accomplished and tend to simply state that '[garland] drains will be constructed around the dumps. Sump pits will … be dug to collect the silt material' (Indian Council of Forestry Research and Education, n.d.: 14). The water used for dust suppression and other mining activities will be taken from local streams. EIAs will detail this usage but not provide an analysis of other present users of the water, or even the availability of water throughout the year, despite admitting that water scarcity in summers is common (Amnesty International 2011; Oskarsson 2010).

Open cast mining on top of the bauxite hills imply a radical rearranging of nature and land use locally. Local streams have been found to be vital to livelihoods around Gandhamardhan and Niyamgiri in Odisha and across the hills of Araku valley in Andhra Pradesh (Amnesty International 2011; Oskarsson

2010, 2013b). The flow of water down hillside rivulets as well as possible water quality changes cannot be seen as clarified in available planning documents. Bauxite mining will remove a big 'chunk' of the mountain and this is likely to have some effect on the hydrology. Actual water retention is not very well studied in India, however, with available sources suggesting no particular capacity of bauxite to retain water (Central Mine Planning and Design Institute 2006; Tingay 2010). Internationally there is mention of hydrological concerns from Latin American bauxite mining, while it has been less discussed in Australia (Goodland 2009). Further studies are clearly much needed given the many concerns that have been voiced by communities and activists in India.

The importance of the small bauxite hill rivulets in local, rain-fed agricultural systems appears clear. And if mining commences it will use local water in competition with other uses, creating real concern for negative changes in already water-stressed villages in the immediate vicinity of the bauxite hills. Official responses in EIA reports to these local realities have not been serious enough to date and are in much need for improvement. The impact of bauxite mining on local water availability is real and needs to be better understood, not to mention much better addressed than is the case at present.

The suggested connection between bauxite mining and river flows appears much less certain, however. Certainly the rivers that form downstream of the bauxite hills are the main sources of fresh water in water-deficient north coastal Andhra Pradesh and in southern coastal Odisha, with water shortages causing serious consequences for farmers and city-dwellers alike. But when the local impact at the hills is extrapolated to a threat of disaster striking across an entire region, then clear exaggeration is in place. Mining that will take place in, at most, a few square kilometres cannot reasonably be expected to affect the entire Vamsadhara River (which originates at the proposed Niyamgiri mine) with its catchment area of 10,830 km² or the Sarada River (originating close to Araku) with its catchment area of 2,666 km² according to the Indian government's Central Water Commission (2006). The dramatic statements made by activists about regional water scarcity from bauxite mining thus need to be tempered, while government and company responses to mining's effect on local water use need to be significantly improved.

Conclusion

This chapter has examined statements about the nature of bauxite mining and Adivasi livelihoods in Eastern India to at least partially explain the strong resistance to such projects in recent decades. Drawing on previous research in three proposed bauxite mining locations, a certain nature does appear based on geological and climactic conditions that have worked over millions of years to leave certain hills with bauxite mineral in sufficiently high concentrations to attract investors. The strong rains that left bauxite ore in high concentration also washed away most of the topsoil, leaving the mineral-bearing zones with little, but therefore not necessarily less valuable, vegetation, including forest cover.

Other aspects of the physical environment and the social context of the bauxite hills were found to vary considerably between the three examined locations, however. Two out of three examined locations have people living on top of the hills (Araku and Niyamgiri), though in small numbers and not necessarily at the precise locations for mining.[15] Two out of three locations (Araku and Niyamgiri) are home exclusively to Adivasi populations. There can, however, be many tribes in one location, including as many as 14 in the Araku region. And in the surrounding areas of two locations (Gandhamardhan and Niyamgiri) are many different caste Hindu groups, indicating much greater social variation than is usually indicated.

In terms of the physical environment of the bauxite hills, two out of three have something approximating natural forests with good biodiversity (Niyamgiri and Gandhamardhan). Araku on the other hand has long been a location for coffee cultivation, with virtually no forest. And at least two of three locations suffer from severe droughts during summers, despite bauxite hills supposedly being able to store water (Araku and Gandhamardhan). In sum, none of the commonly brought forward ideas about the nature of bauxite hills can be uniformly supported by the evidence presented here. They are not uniformly the homes of Adivasis, they have variable forest cover, and are not naturally well-endowed in water sources.

These conclusions indicate a need for both pro- and anti-mining sides to revise their ideas about the nature of bauxite hills. A more varied picture is called for in which the geological factor of bauxite ore seems to influence outcomes less than place-specific social and environmental characteristics. While there are very good reasons to object to the at present poorly addressed environmental degradation and social implications of bauxite mining, this analysis shows that the variable nature and social composition of bauxite hills make generalisations difficult to make, for mine proponents and anti-mining activists alike. From a justice perspective, a better focus would instead seemingly be to debate the political economy of resource projects where mining and many other industries continue to be proposed without significant national or local benefits.

Notes

1 Adivasis, meaning the original inhabitants, are seen as people who inhabited the Indian sub-continent preceding the arrival of the Aryans. The official name in the Indian Constitution is Scheduled Tribes. They are also referred to as tribals.

2 Bauxite, an ore containing aluminium oxide, alumina, together with a range of other elements, is the only commercially used source of aluminium in the world: 95 per cent of bauxite ore is used to produce aluminium. Aluminium production is a three-stage process consisting of bauxite mining, alumina refining, and aluminium smelting, where the first two are usually carried out in the same location to reduce transportation costs.

3 See for example Amnesty International (2010), Bhargava and Reddy (2006), Central Mine Planning and Design Institute (2006), Concerned Scholars (n.d.), Saxena *et al.* (2010); Supreme Court of India (2008).

4 See Oskarsson (2010, 2013b).

5 See for example (Bebbington *et al.* 2008; Hilson 2002).
6 Though good forest cover is not necessarily present just because the land is officially settled as forest land, the Forest Survey of India has found that bauxite ore does tend to exist in areas of good forests (Forest Survey of India 1998).
7 See Oskarsson (2010, 2012, 2013a) and Oskarsson and Nielsen (2014).
8 Khondalite consists of quartz, feldspar, garnet, and sillimanite. The name derives from the Kondh, who live especially in southern Odisha but also in northern Andhra Pradesh where this rock formation was first described.
9 Indian Council of Forestry Research and Education (2008), BS Envi Tech (2008), Ministry of Environment and Forests (2008). Pattanaik *et al.* (2009) and Moody (2007) are in favour of forested bauxite hills.
10 Overburden is used in mining to describe material that lies above the area of economic interest, mainly soil, rocks, etc.
11 Letter from the Ministry of Environment and Forest rejecting clearance based on information from the AP Forest Department, 3/5 2001, cited in (GoAP, Industries and Commerce Department 2005: 3).
12 See (Gardner and Bell 2007; Koch 2007; Koch and Hobbs 2007) on ecosystem restoration from bauxite mining in Australia.
13 Such observations have found support by the government organisation Wildlife Institute of India (2006).
14 Despite the many decades of bauxite mining in India, no authoritative studies on how to best regenerate vegetation in mined out areas exist in the public domain. Research in India has instead tended to focus on matters of technical efficiency in production.
15 Poor quality maps in environmental and other planning documents make it impossible to understand exactly where mining is proposed.

References

Amnesty International (2010). 'Don't Mine Us Out of Existence: Bauxite Mine and Refinery Devastate Lives in India'. London: Amnesty International.

Amnesty International (2011). 'Generalisations, Omissions and Assumptions: The Failings of Vedanta's Environmental Impact Assessments for its Bauxite Mine and Alumina Refinery in India's State of Orissa'. London: Amnesty International UK.

Baka, Jennifer (2013). 'The Political Construction of Wasteland: Governmentality, Land Acquisition and Social Inequality in South India'. *Development and Change* 44(2): 409–428.

Barham, Brad, Stephen G. Bunker, and Denis O'Hearn (1994). *States, Firms, and Raw Materials: The World Economy and Ecology of Aluminum.* Madison, WI: University of Wisconsin Press.

Bebbington, Anthony, Denise H. Bebbington, Jeffrey Bury, Jeannet Lingan, Juan Pable Muñoz, and Martin Scurrah (2008). 'Mining and Social Movements: Struggles Over Livelihood and Rural Territorial Development in the Andes'. *World Development* 36(12): 2888–2905.

BS Envi Tech (2008). 'Draft Environmental Impact Assessment Report of Integrated Aluminium Complex by ANRAK Aluminium at Makavaripalemmandal, Visakhapatnam district, Andhra Pradesh'. Hyderabad: ANRAK Aluminium.

Central Mine Planning and Design Institute (2006). 'Interim Report on Hydrological Investigations Lanjigarh Bauxite Mines M/S Orissa Mining Corporation'. Ranchi: Central Mine Planning and Design Institute.

Central Water Commission (2006). *Integrated Hydrological Data Book*. New Delhi: Government of India.

Concerned Scholars (n.d.). 'Bharat Aluminium Company: Gandhamardan Hills and Peoples Agitation'. Sambalpur: Concerned Scholars.

Ferguson, James and Akhil Gupta (2002). 'Spatializing States: Toward an Ethnography of Neoliberal Governmentality'. *American Ethnologist* 29(4): 981–1002.

Fernandes, Walter (2007). 'Singur and the Displacement Scenario'. *Economic and Political Weekly* 42(3): 203–206.

Fernandes, Walter (2009). 'Displacement and Alienation from Common Property Resources'. In: L. Mehta (ed.). *Displaced by Development: Confronting Marginalisation and Gender Injustice*, New Delhi: Sage, pp. 105–132.

Forest Survey of India (1998). 'Report on Mining in Forest Areas'. Dehradun: Government of India. Online, available at: www.fsi.nic.in/fsi_projects/Report%20on%20Mining%20in%20Forest%20Areas.pdf (accessed 20 February 2016).

Gardner, John H. and David T. Bell (2007). 'Bauxite Mining Restoration by Alcoa World Alumina Australia in Western Australia: Social, Political, Historical, and Environmental Contexts'. *Restoration Ecology* 15: S3–S10.

Gendron, Robin S., Mats Ingulstad, and Espen Storli (2013). *Aluminum Ore: The Political Economy of the Global Bauxite Industry*. Vancouver: UBC Press.

GoAP, Industries and Commerce Department (2005). 'Minutes of the Meeting held on 2 July 2005 in the Chambers of the Hon'ble Minister for Revenue'. Hyderabad: Government of Andhra Pradesh.

Goodland, Robert (ed.) (2009). 'Suriname's Bakhuis Bauxite Mine: An Independent Review of SRK's Impact Assessment'. Paramaribo, Suriname: Vereniging van Inheemse Dorpshoofden in Suriname.

Gupta, Akhil (2012). *Red Tape: Bureaucracy, Structural Violence, and Poverty in India*. Durham: Duke University Press.

Hilson, Gavin (2002). 'An Overview of Land Use Conflicts in Mining Communities'. *Land Use Policy* 19(1): 65–73.

Howitt, Richard (2001). *Rethinking Resource Management: Justice, Sustainability and Indigenous Peoples*. London: Routledge.

Indian Council of Forestry Research and Education (2008). 'Draft Report on Environment Impact Assessment and Environment Management Plan for Jerrila Block I Bauxite Mines, Visakhapatnam District, Andhra Pradesh'. Dehradun, India: Indian Council of Forestry Research and Education.

Indian Council of Forestry Research and Education (n.d.). 'Environmental Impact Assessment with Detailed Ecological and Socio-Economic Studies for Proposed Galikonda Bauxite Mines Vishakhapatnam'. Dehradun, India: Indian Council of Forestry Research and Education.

Koch, John M. (2007). 'Alcoa's Mining and Restoration Process in South Western Australia'. *Restoration Ecology* 15: S11–S16.

Koch, John M. and Richard J. Hobbs (2007). 'Synthesis: Is Alcoa Successfully Restoring a Jarrah Forest Ecosystem after Bauxite Mining in Western Australia?' *Restoration Ecology* 15: S137–S144.

Kohli, Atul (2009). *Democracy and Development in India: From Socialism to Pro-Business*. Oxford: Oxford University Press.

Kohli, Kanchi and Manju Menon (2011). *Banking on Forests: Assets for Climate Cure*. Delhi: Heinrich Böll Foundation; Kalpavriksh.

Kumar, Kundan (2004). 'Dispossessed and Displaced: A Brief Paper on Tribal Issues in Orissa'. Online, available at: www.freewebs.com/epgorissa/Orissa%20mining%20 and%20industrialisation%20note.doc (accessed 20 February 2016).

Kumar, Kundan (2014). 'The Sacred Mountain: Confronting Global Capital at Niyamgiri'. *Geoforum* 54: 196–206.

Lahiri-Dutt, Kuntala (2007). 'Coal Mining Industry at the Crossroads: Towards a Coal Policy for Liberalising India'. ASARC Working Paper. Canberra: Australian National University.

Lahiri-Dutt, Kuntala (2014). 'Introduction to Coal in India: Energising the Nation'. In: Kuntala Lahiri-Dutt (ed.). *The Coal Nation: Histories, Cultures and Ecologies*, London: Ashgate, pp. 1–36.

Lahiri-Dutt, Kuntala, Radhika Krishnan and Nesar Ahmad (2012). 'Land Acquisition and Dispossession: Private Coal Companies in Jharkhand'. *Economic and Political Weekly* 47(6): 39–45.

Ministry of Environment and Forests (2008). 'Note on Bauxite Mining in Orissa: Report on Flora, Fauna, and Impact on Tribal Population'. New Delhi: Government of India.

Mishra, A.B. (1987). 'Mining a Hill and Undermining a Society: The Case of Gandhamardan'. In: Anil Agarwal, Darryl D'Monte, and Ujwala Samarth (eds). *The Fight for Survival: People's Action for Environment*, New Delhi: Centre for Science and Environment, pp. 125–144.

Moody, Roger (2007). 'The Base Alchemist'. In: R. Kalshian (ed.). *Caterpillar and the Mahua Flower: Tremors in India's Mining Fields*, New Delhi: Panos South Asia, pp. 83–102.

Nightingale, Andrea J. and Hemant R. Ojha (2013). 'Rethinking Power and Authority: Symbolic Violence and Subjectivity in Nepal's Terai Forests'. *Development and Change* 44(1): 29–51.

Ojha, Hemant (2013). 'Counteracting Hegemonic Powers in the Policy Process: Critical Action Research on Nepal's Forest Governance'. *Critical Policy Studies* 7(3): 242–262.

Oskarsson, Patrik (2010). 'The Law of the Land Contested: Bauxite Mining in Tribal, Central India in an Age of Economic Reform'. PhD dissertation, University of East Anglia, UK.

Oskarsson, Patrik (2012). 'AnRak Aluminium: Another Vedanta in the Making'. *Economic and Political Weekly* 47(52): 29–33.

Oskarsson, Patrik (2013a). 'Dispossession by Confusion from Mineral-Rich Lands in Central India'. *South Asia: Journal of South Asian Studies* 36(2): 199–212.

Oskarsson, Patrik (2013b). *Visualising Resources on Gandhamardhan Hill: Mapping Revenue and Forest Land in Bargarh District of Western Odisha*. Hyderabad: Centre for Economic and Social Studies.

Oskarsson, Patrik (2015a). 'Governing India's Bauxite Mineral Expansion: Caught between Facilitating Investment and Mediating Social Concerns'. *Extractive Industries and Society* 2/3(2): 426–433.

Oskarsson, Patrik (2015b). 'Diverging Discourses on Bauxite Mining in Eastern India: Life-supporting Hills for Adivasis or National Treasure Chests on Barren Lands?' Paper presented at the SASNET International Conference on the Structural Transformation of South Asia, in Lund, Sweden, 20–22 May.

Oskarsson, Patrik and Kenneth Bo Nielsen (2014). 'Development Deadlock: Aborted Industrialization and Blocked Land Restitution in West Bengal and Andhra Pradesh, India'. *Development Studies Research* 1(1): 267–278.

Padel, Felix and Samarendra Das (2007). 'Agya, What Do You Mean by Development?' In: R. Kalshian (ed.). *Caterpillar and the Mahua Flower: Tremors in India's Mining Fields*, New Delhi: Panos South Asia, pp. 24–46.

Padel, Felix and Samarendra Das (2010). *Out of this Earth: East India Adivasis and the Aluminium Cartel*. New Delhi: Orient Black Swan.

Patra, S. Himansu and Aruna Murthy (n.d.). 'Fact Finding Report of Nalco. Bhubaneswar: Vasundhara'. Online, available at: www.freewebs.com/epgorissa/NALCO%20Report%5B2%5D-1.pdf (accessed 20 February 2016).

Pattanaik, Chiranjibi, S. Narendra Prasad, and C. Sudhakar Reddy (2009). 'Need for Conservation of Biodiversity in Araku Valley, Andhra Pradesh'. *Current Science* 96(1): 11–12.

Ramamurthy, Sreedhar (1995). *Impacts of Bauxite Mining and Aluminium Industry in India*. New Delhi: Academy for Mountain Environics.

Reddy, Shravanti (2006). 'Kashipur: An Enquiry into Mining and Human Rights Violations in Kashipur, Orissa'. Mumbai: Indian People's Tribunal on Environment and Human Rights.

Roy, Arundhati (2010). 'Foreword'. In: Felix Padel and Samarendra Das (eds). *Out of This Earth: East India Adivasis and the Aluminium Cartel*, New Delhi: Orient Black Swan, pp. xi–xiii.

Saxena, Naresh C., S. Parasuraman, Promode Kant, and Amita Baviskar (2010). 'Report of the Four Member Committee for Investigation into the Proposal Submitted by the Orissa Mining Company for Bauxite Mining in Niyamgiri'. New Delhi: Ministry of Environment and Forests.

Shah, Alpa (2007). 'The Dark Side of Indigeneity? Indigenous People, Rights and Development in India'. *History Compass* 5(6): 1806–1832.

Sterlite Industries (India) Limited (2003). 'Revised Executive Summary of Rapid EIA Report for Lanjigarh Bauxite Mining Project, Kalahandi'. Bhubaneshwar: Sterlite Industries.

Supreme Court of India (2008). 'Final Judgement in the Case of Forest Diversion for Niyamgiri Bauxite Mine, I.A. No. 2134 of 2007'. Delhi: Supreme Court of India.

Survival International (2009). '"Mine": Story of a Sacred Mountain with Joanna Lumley (short version)'. Online, available at: http://vimeo.com/3938756 (accessed 20 February 2016).

Tingay, Alan (2010). 'Comments on the Environmental Impact Assessments for Proposed Lanjigarh Bauxite Mine, Alumina Refinery and the Refinery Expansion'. Unpublished document.

Vimta Labs (2005). 'Rapid Environmental Impact Assessment for the Proposed Bauxite Mines (3110 mtpa) at Lanjigarh, Kalahandi District, Orissa'. Hyderabad: Vimta Labs.

White, Ben, Saturnino M. Borras Jr., Ruth Hall, Ian Scoones, and Wendy Wolford (2012). 'The New Enclosures: Critical Perspectives on Corporate Land Deals'. *Journal of Peasant Studies* 39(3/4): 619–647.

Wildlife Institute of India (2006). 'Studies on Impact of Proposed Lanjigarh Bauxite Mining on Biodiversity Including Wildlife and its Habitat'. Dehradun, India: Wildlife Institute of India.

8 Resource extraction in Jharkhand's West Singhbhum

The continuing marginalisation of Adivasi livelihoods despite decentralisation

Siddharth Sareen

Decentralisation reforms have proceeded apace alongside rapid industrialisation over the past three to four decades in many developing countries, particularly in Asia, and India is no exception. Whether these reforms have sought to democratise, deconcentrate, or delegate power and control over resources can be debated (Agrawal and Ribot 1999; Bose 2012); but what is evident is that they have rarely managed to address the problem of rapid industrialisation failing to direct sufficient benefits from rich regional natural resource bases towards local populations in order to bring the inhabitants out of chronic poverty and vulnerability (Colfer and Capistrano 2005; Larson and Ribot 2005). The concept of a 'resource curse' has been amply critiqued (Lahiri-Dutt 2006; Wright and Czelusta 2003; Karlsson this volume), but the institutional and political factors that lead to resource rent being captured elsewhere without regional development (Basedau 2005; Mehlum *et al.* 2006; Watts 2004) remain abundant despite attempts by governments to decentralise control over resources. To realise the objectives of increasing inclusion, equity, and efficiency by devolving power and control over resources to local levels that inform decentralisation reforms (Ribot 2011), the way these reforms are situated within particular historical-institutional contexts of industrialisation must be understood (Arts and Buizer 2009; Stuligross 2008).

This chapter documents how decentralisation reforms have failed to achieve regional development in one of India's most resource-rich and conflict-affected districts, namely West Singhbhum, in the federal state of Jharkhand which was formed out of the southern part of Bihar state in 2000. Focussing on indigenous communities of the Ho, a people recognised as a Scheduled Tribe by the Indian Constitution and thus afforded numerous legal safeguards and privileges, it probes how the nature of development in recent decades has systemically failed to enable sustainable local livelihoods for these forest-dwelling subsistence farmers through decentralised governance. Instead, natural resource extraction aimed at driving India's economic growth in the same period has compounded the vulnerabilities of this marginalised group rather than bringing empowerment. Resource expropriation coupled with the dearth of alternative local livelihoods in the rural hinterland due to jobless growth forces peoples like the Ho to illegally sell their most important natural resource, namely wood, without being allowed to self-determine their local development trajectory; meanwhile, mining companies are permitted to drastically alter vast tracts of forest through resource extraction.

Over a decade ago, summing up the first comprehensive volume on Jharkhand by Corbridge *et al.* (2004), Robbins (2005: 902) put forward this observation and question:

> Newly formed in 2000 by carving out the historically poorest and [most] marginalised parts of the state of Bihar (itself historically poor and marginal), Jharkhand appears as the fruition of a century of struggle over the rights of 'tribal' communities and disenfranchised groups under colonial and postcolonial authority.... Has attending to the situation of women, Adivasis ('tribals'), and local communities reinvented or simply reinstated the global development machine?

'Attending to the situation' of local communities has taken place through decentralisation and extractive industrialisation, which can be seen as two juxtaposing forces. This chapter shows how the everyday lives of the Adivasi Ho people answer Robbins' query by indicating that development is better characterised by reinstatement rather than reinvention over the past several decades in this region, i.e. by continuing resource extraction rather than the devolution of decision-making over resources to local levels. Its first part traces the history of natural resource governance in West Singhbhum from 1976 onwards, at the beginning of a period of pronounced state–community conflict prompted by extractive industrial activity without local benefits, while recounting parallel national-level legislative developments based on secondary research. The second part picks up the state-level narrative in this regard from 15 November 2000 onwards, when Jharkhand was created as a federal Indian state out of the resource-rich southern part of Bihar in response to a complex, long-standing political movement, again drawing on existing literature to provide an overview of the regional institutional and political context with regard to natural resource governance. The third part of the chapter maintains this focus in present-day West Singhbhum, based on six months of primary research carried out subsequent to the state-wide elections conducted in 2010. These long-due elections operationalised local self-governance through the three-tier institutions referred to as *panchayati raj institutions* (PRIs) at the district, block, and village-cluster level, as well as through the *gram sabha* (village assembly) as a deliberative institution for collective decision-making at the community level. The fourth and final part pulls together the argument running through the earlier sections, concluding that attempts at decentralised natural resource governance in recent decades have been unable to establish Ho people's control over resources and their own development trajectory or to safeguard their means of sustainable local livelihoods, as Jharkhand's political economy has continued to be characterised by entrenched patterns of industrial production based on resource exploitation by outsiders. It argues that this trend is reinforced in contemporary

Jharkhand despite new state creation, suggesting that future state-building efforts must focus on local livelihoods through more substantive decentralised natural resource governance in order to ensure political stability and pro-population development in this volatile region.

India and West Singhbhum 1976–2000: from the 'forest felling movement' to industrialisation with decentralisation

Resource extraction has a long history in West Singhbhum running through India's colonial and postcolonial periods into present times. It has not only taken its toll by intervening in and altering traditional Adivasi forms of resource governance, but has also framed historical and current uses of land and forests in ways that enable benefits from these resources to accumulate to outsiders (Damodaran 2006; Prakash 1999; Streumer 2003). Continuing colonial trends in terms of expropriating resources from marginalised forest inhabitants, forest governance in post-Independence India predominantly took the form of industrial production of timber by the Forest Department, the largest controller of forests in the country, while neglecting village commons (Guha 2001). The Forest Department conducted operations and amassed profits through the subsequent sale of timber and an abundance of other valuable forest products, as well as through commercial leasing of forest plots to private contractors, employing forest reservation policies that criminalised traditional usufruct activities (Corbridge and Jewitt 1997). In 1976, the National Commission on Agriculture began providing 'more funds for social and farm forestry on non-forest and private lands to meet people's demands' while continuing commercial forestry 'with greater vigour on forest lands' (RRI 2012: 81).

West Singhbhum district with its rich '*shorea robusta*' or sal forests was no exception to such 'ecological subordination' (Parajuli 1996), and for decades the Forest Department was as powerful an entity as any in the region. It operated forest felling series, replacing sal, which favoured biodiversity and fulfilled forest inhabitants' requirements, with stands of commercially valuable monocultures of teak, until its oppressive control over forests flew in the face of local inhabitants' traditional forest-dependent practices and livelihoods (Areeparampil 1992). Villagers increasingly came to regard the Forest Department's operations as primarily benefitting itself and timber contractors, while they only received low wages for manual labour in forestry operations, and no share of the revenue generated by cropping valuable timber. Compounded by factors such as regional famine and local political mobilisation based on struggles for an autonomous territorial 'Jharkhand' or 'forest area' (Corbridge and Jewitt 1997; Paty 2007), 1978 saw the emergence of a '*jangal katai andolan*' or 'forest felling movement' demanding local autonomy over the forest, and arguing for people's right to decide how to use it and to benefit from it. Using the slogan 'sal means Jharkhand, teak means Bihar', inhabitants uprooted teak trees in favour of species geared to benefit their local economy rather than the government coffers of then-Bihar (PUDR 1982).

As unrest grew, violent incidents of conflict began to take place, and in much of West Singhbhum, forestry officials were driven out of the villages and the Forest Department's bungalows were destroyed. The ensuing state–community conflict, which lasted till the mid-1980s, turned violent on multiple occasions (Areeparampil 1992; Das 2008). Villagers were hardly the prime movers in this, with powerful private players and political groups benefitting from unregulated access to wood at fire-sale prices or for free as 4,000 acres of forest were logged (Damodaran 2006). Local political groups saw an opportunity to mobilise support around a popular cause. According to current Ho forest inhabitants, these groups raised funds by way of small but regular contributions from many village households, encouraging them to clear the forest around them and assuring them that their financial contributions would be used to gain formal recognition of inhabitants' claims to this land. The word '*jharkhandi*' is derived from 'of the forest area' (as opposed to outsiders) and resonates well with the Mundari word '*khuntkatti*' (the Ho language belongs to the Mundari school), which in turn refers to the 'original clearer of forest' as the village founder and head of his clan in Ho society (Upadhya 2005). Despite a regional act (Chotanagpur Tenancy Act 1908) that safeguards Scheduled Tribes' agricultural and habitational land tenure against appropriation by non-Scheduled Tribes, the growing population's need for clearing and claiming forest land as their own to cultivate gave this movement popular appeal in the aftermath of oppressive Forest Department regulation, which had labelled many villagers as being in breach of rules for exercising traditional usufruct rights. Communities' own access to the forest, while freed from the overbearing regulation of the Forest Department, nevertheless suffered due to vastly diminished wood stock and the absence of any alternative local livelihoods comparable to selling wood (Jewitt 2008).

In 1988, the National Forest Policy tried to move things in a different direction, legislating greater community rights over forests (RRI 2012). Forest governance in India being largely in the hands of its federal states, this policy change was necessarily ponderous, leading to slow uptake across Indian states, which operationalised it to varying extents. Moreover, Forest Departments have access to different degrees of funds and manpower in each state, as broached for Jharkhand in the next section. In any case, from 1990 onwards this government initiative began taking shape as Joint Forest Management, which changed the discourse around natural resource governance to a partnership with local communities (Kumar 2002). On its own, this programme might not have changed much, but a series of legislative reforms towards decentralisation in the 1990s ensured that more substantial changes became possible. The seventy-third Constitutional Amendment of 1992 instituted a decentralised system of local self-government called *panchayati raj*, and the Panchayat (Extension to Scheduled Areas) Act, 1996 (PESA), further empowered these institutions in Scheduled Areas (constitutionally-specified regions populated by Scheduled Tribes) such as the whole of West Singhbhum district (Sundar 2009).

Simultaneously, the New Economic Policy of 1991 and subsequent National Mineral Policy, 1993, as well as a number of amendments to the Mines and

Mineral (Development and Regulation) Act, 1957, sought to engender a land concession regime to attract private sector investment. These enabled private players to move into mining minerals, an economic sector that had hitherto been dominated by the public sector with only a few large business houses able to participate, due to high barriers for entry such as bureaucratic procedures associated with procuring licences. In iron ore rich West Singhbhum, this led to an explosion of interest in land concessions for large-scale mining with 20-year leases (Areeparampil 1996). The decentralisation reforms ushered in concurrently during this period were critical in preventing an outright ouster of forest inhabitants in favour of extractive industrial activity, since they afforded inhabitants some say in their development trajectory, recognising their right to decide collectively based on democratic principles (Gregersen *et al.* 2004: 53–56).

Even so, mining activities, which public companies had already conducted for decades, proliferated during this era, with unregulated mining rampant and officials willing to turn a blind eye in return for kickbacks (Gupta 2014; Shah Commission 2013). Thus, two-pronged industrial activity continued to thrive, if less in terms of timber production then more in terms of mineral extraction, expanding its reach and depth as well as outsiders' ability to accumulate wealth away from the mineral-bearing areas, while continuing to prevent local benefits for forest inhabitants. While not the only reason (Basu 2012), a strong part of the basis behind demands for a new state independent of chronically underdeveloped, corrupt Bihar was the argument that a smaller state carved out of Bihar's resource-rich southern part would benefit from exploiting its resources optimally and ensuring regional development to benefit its population (Prakash 2011; Stuligross 2008). Alongside a host of political factors such as the regional wheeling and dealing of India's national political parties, this belief in a more democratically functioning state responsive to the demands of its many varied population groups led to the federal Indian state of Jharkhand being formed on 15 November 2000 (Tillin 2011).

Jharkhand and West Singhbhum 2000–2010: from new state formation to contradictory legislation on local governance

In some respects, things went from bad to worse with the formation of Jharkhand. Not a single state government managed to complete a full term in office, with 13 changes in the span of one and a half decades. Researchers claimed that state formation diverted attention at the national level away from whether or not substantive changes in governance, particularly of natural resources, had indeed taken place in Jharkhand, despite the population still lacking a government responsive to its numerous and nuanced needs (Shah 2010; Sundar 2009; Tillin 2011). The micro-politics of natural resources still remained uncaptured and unresolved, not receiving requisite attention at sufficiently disaggregated levels. Instead of a government that could bring about stability and democratic governance in a newly-formed state, Jharkhand began to experience a continuation and intensification of a patronage state (Corbridge 2002; Corbridge *et al.* 2003), with various political elites vying for access to newfound authority while privileged private actors went about seeking preferential resource access in a clientelist manner or through sheer power within the context of a highly chaotic state. This chaos was amplified by frequent violent clashes between insurgent Maoist groups and the police, as well as *bandhs* or curfews imposed by these groups, who themselves had substantial interests in Jharkhand's natural resources (Shah 2006).

Since India's federal structure requires its national constitutional mandates to be operationalised by each federal state, Jharkhand was expected to put in place state-level legislation to bring about the PRIs and village assembly as local self-governance institutions (Johnson *et al.* 2005). This duly happened with the Jharkhand Panchayat Raj Act, 2001 (JPRA). This legislation, however, deviated to a large extent from the constitutional mandate of PESA, diluting the power and resources devolved to institutions of self-governance, and adding ambiguous clauses like 'Subject to the rules as may be prescribed by the State from time to time and availability of funds' (GoJ 2001) that rendered the PRIs and village assembly dependent on undefined state legislation (PRIA 2004). Whereas PESA stated that the village assembly could 'safeguard and preserve ... community resources and the customary mode of dispute resolution' (GoI 1996, clause 4d), the JPRA assigned many of the village assembly's powers to higher-level PRIs. For instance, the JPRA did not mention the village assembly's right to be consulted before land acquisition by the government, and assigned rights to prevent or contest unlawful land alienation to the district-level PRI rather than to the village assembly as suggested by PESA (GoJ 2001; for a comprehensive tabulation, see ELDF 2012b and PRIA 2004: 31–35). The reluctance of agencies like the Forest Department to devolve control over natural resources like forest has been aided by the fact that 'the modern state and its legal apparatus do not recognise the customary ownership rights of land' (PRMF 2010: 82). This has effectively negated much of the relations of downward authority that form part of the basis for substantive democratic reforms (Dandekar and Choudhury 2009).

As in most Indian states with Scheduled Areas, PESA rules have not yet been passed in Jharkhand. Yet with the passage of JPRA in 2001, the constitutionally-mandated PESA became operational to some extent – albeit in the limited form described – shortly after the formation of Jharkhand. A number of roadblocks, however, continued to prevent state-wide elections to the PRIs and the operationalisation of village assemblies from taking place in the politically volatile state. Reasons officially cited for the postponement ranged from 'delimitation of constituencies, reservation, revision of voter's list, rain, drought and even festivals' (PRIA 2004: 21) to the administrative demands of organising elections for the national and state governments. Another factor holding back local elections was the incompatibility of the JPRA with the Indian Constitution's Article 243(d) on reservation policy, which was resolved by amending the JPRA accordingly in 2010, to reserve quotas for marginalised categories such as Scheduled Tribes as representatives in PRIs (GoI 2010: 5). Given the predominance of ethnic minorities in Jharkhand, such quotas have been a contentious issue even after state formation (Rycroft and Dasgupta 2011).

Thus, it was only in 2010 that local elections to PRIs in Jharkhand were finally held (GoI 2010). The last time local elections took place in this region was in 1978 when it was part of Bihar, before local institutions had been defined in a consistent manner at the national level. Thus, essentially for the first time ever in Jharkhand in 2010, local councillors and other functionaries were elected to the district, sub-district, and village-cluster level institutions, which are *zila parishads, panchayat samiti* and *gram panchayat* respectively. With the PRIs functional, the village assembly, comprising all adult inhabitants of a village community, gained definitive formal recognition as well. In this sense, at the close of its first decade, Jharkhand's rural population was institutionally equipped to self-govern its resources down to the very local level. Major minerals like iron and coal remained outside this purview, but despite contradictory national- and state-level legislation, the PRIs and village assembly arguably held the right to self-determine local development consistent with their traditions, meaning their decisions potentially had a bearing on whether and how resources could be exploited (GoI 1996; Shah 2010). This development, in addition to the land tenure safeguards provided by the Chotanagpur Tenancy Act against non-Scheduled Tribes appropriating land (Sundar 2009), seemed to offer some protection to rural forest inhabitants of West Singhbhum.

Yet, due to a historical quirk linked with West Singhbhum, a set of traditional authorities based on customary law rather than democratic principles came to be recognised parallel to the PRIs and village assembly. Part of West Singhbhum was categorised as the Kolhan Government Estate during British rule, and a direct administration system based on Wilkinson's Rule from 1837 provided for the customary laws of the Ho people who inhabit this area to be upheld without interference (Upadhya 2005). This in turn was legitimised through PESA in 1996, as operationalised through JPRA in 2001, in effect according governmental recognition to the authority of traditional Ho village chiefs (called *mundas* in the Ho language) and paramount chiefs (called *mankis*) who preside over traditional village clusters known as *pirs* (Sundar 2005). In keeping with this pre-Independence rule, an official known as the Kolhan Superintendent continues to have an office within the West Singhbhum district collectorate complex in the district headquarter town of Chaibasa, appointed as the government officer responsible for matters administrated by the *mundas* and *mankis*. The extent to which this officer plays a role in land and forest governance is addressed later on.

Thus, in 2010 all Ho villages in the Kolhan Government Estate portion of West Singhbhum came to have the PRIs and village assembly as democratic self-governance institutions on the one hand, and the *manki-munda* system as customary local governance institutions on the other. There was considerable interest amongst indigenous studies and local governance scholars and practitioners as to whether this would result in conflict between these parallel local institutions due to overlapping domains of authority or whether the Ho would draw on each set of institutions for different functions, the former to govern natural resources and implement government schemes and the latter to conduct traditional community functions and settle minor conflicts (Kumar 2014; Puthumattathil 2014). The passage of more national legislation shortly prior to this, namely the Scheduled Tribes and Other Traditional Forest Dwellers (Recognition of Forest Rights) Act, 2006 (known as FRA), further strengthened the village assembly's legal basis for governing village forest and agricultural land, empowering it to function as the first authority in adjudicating long-term inhabitants' land tenure, subject to operationalisation by Jharkhand's government (ELDF 2012a). It is in this historical-institutional context that an empirical study of natural resource governance in West Singhbhum was conducted, which the next section explains and elaborates upon.

West Singhbhum 2010–2015: from institutional overlaps to mining iron ore and logging wood

This section is based on six months of empirical work conducted between January 2013 and January 2015 across 20 villages predominantly populated by Ho people in West Singhbhum district. A variety of qualitative methods were employed, including hundreds of semi-structured and structured interviews, and 49 key informant interviews with traditional village chiefs, elected local councillors, government officials at district and sub-district levels in government line agencies, including the Forest Department, local and regional traders in non-wood forest products (NWFPs), staff members of civil society organisations, regional researchers, and project contractors.

The findings are presented and drawn on in terms of the role of the following institutions in decision-making over natural resource governance and local development: (i) the customary *manki-munda* system; (ii) the formally democratic village assembly and PRIs; and (iii) the government line agencies in charge of natural resource governance, namely the Forest Department for forests and higher-level government institutions for mineral and land resources.

The manki-munda *system*

Villagers associated their village *munda* with executing four main functions: Collecting nominal amounts as historically established rent on land holdings (known as '*maal-guzari*') from all village households based on an official village map and depositing them with the land revenue department (a colonial-era practice continued based on Wilkinson's Rule with varying degrees of regularity across Ho villages); resolving minor intra-community conflicts, such as over inter-household land boundaries, and allocating use of village commons based on customary law; conducting traditional village functions such as religious rituals along with the traditional village priest or *deuri*; and certifying documents for village inhabitants to access particular services, such as validating their residential address to open bank accounts or verifying their eligibility for pension schemes and housing subsidies.

The views of inhabitants from different villages varied in terms of the extent to which *mundas* executed these tasks: For instance, *mundas* of some villages appeared to be more regular at collecting *maal-guzari* than others, and the same held true of their usefulness in resolving intra-community conflict and maintaining village traditions. One village woman stated: 'They just want to be fed and watered [i.e. bribed], that's how it has always been.... Before the local elections it was the *munda-manki*, now there are also the *mukhiya-pradhan* (local councillors), but nothing has changed'. A woman in another village, however, maintained that the *munda* 'makes rules for the village ... forms different committees ... the system is transparent. [His] father was fairer. It is a hereditary system. The current *munda* tends to give in to pressure. But there is no bribery'. Triangulating the responses of interviewees from within and across villages made it possible to gauge how active the *munda* was in executing his duties in each village, to what extent villagers regarded him as having the authority to do so, and how helpful his role was for village inhabitants.

Mundas and *mankis* met once a month to discuss issues of concern to Ho people and discuss any unresolved problems. This forum was useful for relatively inexperienced *mundas* who had been appointed to their post after the death of an ascendant to gain an understanding of their role and power, as one such stated when interviewed. Due to this network and their privileged position as traditional village leaders, *mundas* also served as valuable sources of information about government schemes and practical matters that many villagers were unacquainted with, since the latter were often illiterate, untraveled outside their district, and not very conversant in Hindi, the language of the district administration.

All in all, these traditional chiefs were not involved in decision-making over natural resource governance or local development besides maintaining demarcated property relations within the village, and hence clashed neither with local self-governance institutions nor with government line agencies due to overlapping domains. Their main relevance in these regards was their role in resolving the conflicts that arose concerning land or particular governance arrangements, in which case inhabitants looked to them as being best equipped to discuss the applicable rules and make decisions. Hence they functioned as facilitators of the other institutions authorised to act on these matters, being able to resolve minor disagreements based on village maps, customary laws, and their discretion over the allocation of village commons. As mentioned, however, this role depended on how capable the particular individuals who served as *mundas* were regarded to be by the inhabitants in their village, which tended to vary.

PRIs and the village assembly

A village-cluster typically included 10–12 spread-out villages. Village sizes varied from less than 100 households with two hamlets to more than 500 households with eight hamlets, with the lowest-level PRI, called the *gram panchayat*, located in the head village of a village-cluster. Inhabitants of other villages within the cluster said they were not included in village-cluster council meetings. Elected local councillors headed the *panchayat samiti* or block council; similarly, elected representatives comprised the *zila parishad* or district council. While these institutions held meetings and their representatives engaged with government officials at the block and district levels, villagers did not refer to these institutions as having any bearing on natural resource governance. To quote one villager: 'The *mukhiya* [local councillor] brings government schemes to the village. The village assembly does not decide which schemes. When funds come they are usually tied to a purpose, and we are asked whether we want it'. Thus, the PRIs were primarily involved in implementing rural development schemes offered by government line agencies in a largely top-down manner, without each village being able to exercise its demands through the village assembly using a bottom-up process. However, this was a more decentralised arrangement than before, as a village assembly president explained thus:

> Now the funds come to the local councillor, to the village-cluster council [*gram panchayat* level], for various development works. Funds are distributed by a village-level contractor now, not at the block level [*panchayat samiti* level] like before the local elections.

The village assembly, on the other hand, did play a role in natural resource governance, albeit to a rather different extent in different study villages. In the non-forest villages, inhabitants did not see it as being relevant in this regard, as their villages did not have any forest areas, and matters concerning the village commons were seen as the domain of the *munda* as explained in the preceding sub-section. In forest villages, however, inhabitants did consider the village assembly pertinent for undertaking forest governance, while it was not involved in land governance in any of the study villages: In the only observed case where a generation-old village in the forest tried to use the FRA to have its land claim over the forest land recognised, it tried (unsuccessfully) to file a claim through various offices at the district collectorate without any village assembly being involved. During the data collection period, the forest village assemblies were active to very different extents in regulating access to their village forest. Their success or failure seemed to depend on factors such as how proactive the *munda* and other influential inhabitants were at involving inhabitants in protecting the village forest against outsiders coming to chop and sell wood, and the degree of social cohesion and agreement amongst inhabitants about the necessity and feasibility of this task (Sareen and Nathan forthcoming).

Outcomes ranged between two extremes: (i) village assemblies organising patrol groups in the village forest, defining and enforcing fines on offenders caught logging and breaking the rules, and generating funds through contributions from each village household for their operations, and (ii) village assemblies that were entirely dysfunctional, with inhabitants jeering at the inability of their *munda* and other inhabitants to regulate access to the forest, and insisting that this was an unfeasible task in their village even if possible somewhere else. Many village assemblies experienced mixed results, with inhabitants agreeing that their wood stock was being diminished due to unregulated logging that posed problems for their future, but finding themselves unable to organise sufficiently through their village assembly to prevent loggers from accessing their forest. One villager summed up this difficult situation thus: 'We cannot tell people [not to log wood] in our own village ourselves. People will retort asking what they will eat and where money will come from'. Another, however, explained a neighbouring village assembly's success saying: 'People there are more united and there is a good leader, so the village assembly works'. This particular village assembly's success was acknowledged far and wide, as one that regulated access to its forest and found various means to raise funds from forestry activities as well. Thus, while the three-tier PRIs did not play a role in natural resource governance, the community-level village assembly did to a highly variable extent, particularly with regard to forest access.

The Ho also collected several NWFPs from their village forest and from forest controlled by the Forest Department, selling products such as *kendu* leaves, *mahua* flowers and sal leaves during the late winter, spring, and early summer to generate important income during the farming off-season. These were most often traded at weekly village *haats*, or markets, with local agents and regional traders benefitting from large profit margins, while village inhabitants secured very low returns as primary collectors. In general, none of the formal democratic institutions managed to govern this trade in natural resources to secure more favourable terms for the forest inhabitants.

Line agencies and higher-level government institutions

The Forest Department was heavily under-staffed. For instance, one of West Singhbhum's four forest divisions, Sadar Chaibasa, had only four forest guards against a required capacity of 78, which the divisional forest officer (DFO) stated would still have been insufficient to conduct scientific forestry operations. Villagers from both forest and non-forest villages logged wood in forests controlled by the Forest Department and sold it illegally as fuel and timber to soap factories and urban households on the outskirts of Chaibasa. Hundreds of bicycle loads of wood were logged every day from the forests both in and around the study villages while the Forest Department with its small group of foresters turned a blind eye, unwilling to risk a major riot if it tried preventing villagers from earning through this main local livelihood. Besides funding occasional forest road construction and forestation projects, the Forest Department did not undertake large-scale forestry projects or regulate forest access at the ground level, instead dealing largely with paperwork. The frequent presence of suited men with folders tucked under their arms, confident of being able to meet officials, was in stark contrast to villagers waiting for several hours, occasionally asking a clerk when an official might be expected to arrive, only to be asked to keep waiting a bit longer.

In the absence of transparent answers from the officials concerned, one can only conjecture at what the selective activities of the Forest Department pertained to: There are a few likely explanations. One possibility is that forest dwellers were filing land claims to establish tenure over forest land they had inhabited long-term, which requires the Forest Department's verification as part of a multi-step process. However, the District Welfare Officer stated that only 2,800 such claims had been made in the entire district of West Singhbhum since the FRA commenced – a small number over the past decade for a district of 1.5 million people. Both he and the Kolhan superintendent said the Forest Department seemed disinterested in verifying the claims that did come in, as it had a conflict of interest in recognising forest dwellers' rights over forest that was still under its control. Another possibility is that, as two divisional forest officers stated, officials were still required to do a lot of work such as making ten-year working plans, going through the motions despite knowing they lacked the resources to implement much by way of large forestry projects. A third possibility is that the Forest Department was kept busy processing environmental clearance applications for mining leases, West Singhbhum boasting one of India's richest iron ore reserves. As a recent report shows (Shah Commission 2013), 42 large-scale mining leases were active and a further 19 pending in its Saranda forest division alone, all of which required environmental clearance from the Forest Department as one stage of the process of obtaining mineral concessions.

However, in recent years this clearance requirement has been substituted through numerous means, including the Cabinet Committee on Investment's top-down approval of mining projects since its formation in New Delhi in 2012, and the Ministry of the Environment and Forests' fast-tracked clearance to dozens of mining concessions, most notably 70 projects across India in a span of 20 days during one minister's short term, followed by 240 out of 325 pending projects within three months of the current minister assuming office (Kothari 2014; Chauhan 2014). Through these actions, the ministry imposed its own top-down decisions with scant respect for the roles of PRIs and village assemblies whose authority these actions effectively contradicted and nullified. Thus, high-stakes decisions on natural resource governance were executed through higher-level government institutions, completely side-stepping local self-governance institutions and the constitutionally mandated democratic process of collective local decision-making over development by communities (GoI 1996), as observed elsewhere in India (Jenkins *et al.* 2014; Nielsen 2010).

This tendency is backed by local observations as well: When the term of the previous Kolhan Superintendent ended, no official was brought in as a replacement. Instead, from 2014 onwards this post was temporarily assigned to the Land Reform Deputy Collector, who was also the District Land Acquisition Officer. The very government official Ho chiefs were to turn to regarding (often land-related) local self-governance matters was also the bureaucrat in charge of land acquisition *and* land reform in a district where companies were flocking to get mining concessions, an arrangement that seemed to have high potential for conflict of interest. In one instance, where inhabitants from a distant Ho village brought a grievance about illegal road-building on their land to this officer, he was observed as being initially dismissive and then delaying their case; when questioned afterwards, the villagers stated that their concerns had remained unaddressed and they felt helpless.

Village inhabitants, when asked for their views on leasing land for industrial mining, said they were willing to consider it if it provided them with livelihoods. However, field observations suggested that the nature of iron ore mining does not generate a sustained demand for unskilled manual labourers, while drastically damaging the landscape in ways that damage water sources and future farming prospects for the Ho's staple crop of rice. Some of the study villages were close to mines that had been shut down around 1980. They complained about overflow of waste into farmland due to lack of adherence to norms for closing the mines after extraction ended. Elderly inhabitants said mining had provided livelihoods while the mines operated, but only selectively, and working conditions had been tough, requiring hard labour. According to some interviewees, workers had migrated in from other regions, only to be left without jobs or much arable land once the mines closed. Thus, mining was a complex social issue for villagers, involving the possibility of temporary local livelihoods, alongside concerns about the downward accountability of companies and the impact on the landscape in the long run.

A linked issue on which there was universal concern among village inhabitants, however, is regional militarisation due to counter-insurgency operations by the Indian government. These interventions have been targeted against Maoist or Naxalite insurgent groups with a long-running presence in West Singhbhum, particularly its thickly-forested, iron-rich Saranda forest division. The Indian government has repeatedly highlighted its US$41 million 'Saranda Action Plan' as bringing security and development to this region (MoRD 2011). The development the government has brought, however, is the commercial leasing of thousands of hectares of West Singhbhum's reserved forest land to companies for mineral extraction (Shah Commission 2013). Inhabitants in several study villages complained about military units encroaching on tribal lands in the district, and about military personnel entering their villages as part of combing operations and taking away their chicken and grain or making the women feel uncomfortable. They said insurgents occasionally visited them and demanded food while camping overnight, but did not mistreat them; it was certainly not villagers' interests that militarisation was securing. The government's approach to natural resource governance, then, made these village inhabitants feel neither secure nor included in resource governance and development; rather, its strengthening of military presence secured and helped enable industrial mining operations, as repeatedly suggested in the national media.

Conclusion: the continuing marginalisation of livelihoods through resource extraction despite decentralisation

From the 1970s to current times, much has changed in West Singhbhum: The transition from outright conflict between the Forest Department and forest communities to a state-building context, the strengthening of progressive policies through decentralisation reforms, the formation of the new state of Jharkhand, and the institutionalisation of local self-governance. Yet, as shown, the biggest change has been that of opening up the district's natural resources for exploitation through twin industrial activities: (i) wood and NWFPs from its forests for indiscriminate sale without implementing a number of formal policies due to lack of both institutional capacity and political will, and (ii) land itself for mining iron ore with the approval of higher-level institutions, not allowing local inhabitants to self-determine their desired mode of local development, nor enabling collective decision-making on natural resource governance. Various decentralisation reforms notwithstanding, both these regional processes linked with industrialisation are degrading the natural resource base that Ho people depend on for their way of life and very survival, and extracting valuable resources while destroying the productive capacity of their land, without sharing the considerable revenue generated through iron ore mining or ensuring the provision of sustainable local livelihoods to inhabitants. Despite the policy advances, then, the local population today hardly seems better off in terms of natural resource governance than during its conflicts with an oppressive Forest Department in the 1970s.

Tracing the recent evolution of natural resource governance in the context of the ongoing effects of industrialisation in West Singhbhum by attending to the trends in national policies from four decades ago, their operationalisation subsequent to the formation of the federal state of Jharkhand in 2000, and the impact of the creation of local self-governance institutions after the 2010 elections underscores the importance of several factors at multiple levels for realising the objectives of decentralisation reforms. They are argued here in a manner that situates them within existing literature on natural resource governance in this and similar resource-rich, state-building contexts.

First, while national policies in India have come a long way in recent decades, its federal nature leaves a great deal of the operationalisation in the hands of state governments, whose interests are often opposed to the intent that informs decentralisation reforms. Decentralisation reforms are typically characterised as being concerned with democratising power and control over resources to local populations (Crook and Manor 1998; Larson and Ribot 2005). Addressing the outcomes of decentralisation, then, requires politicising democracy by attending to factors in sub-national regions such as states and districts (Harriss *et al.* 2004; Sud 2014). Not ensuring that national-level policies such as PESA and FRA are fully translated into state-level legislation such as JPRA in letter and spirit fails to address the potential for perverse institutional incentives and to safeguard against the lack of downward accountability in implementing decentralisation reforms (Agrawal and Ribot 1999; Evans 2004; Webster *et al.* 2009).

Second, the recognition of parallel, overlapping institutions creates confusion and potential for conflict at the local level (Sundar 2009; Upadhya 2005), with the institutions that govern natural resources operating in a 'grey zone between legality and illegality' (Vasan 2005). For decentralisation reforms to work past the dangers of natural resource governance being co-opted by 'twilight institutions' (Lund 2007) and patronage politics (Corbridge *et al.* 2003; Suykens 2010), contradictory legislation needs to be addressed, ensuring that 'bureaucratic' institutions are socially and culturally 'embedded' in order to enable democratic decision-making over natural resources (Cleaver 2012). While the customary institution of *mankis* and *mundas* does not seem to interfere with the village assembly's attempts at natural resource governance in Jharkhand, interventions by government line agencies and higher-level institutions influence the process far more than local democratic institutions for self-governance. These negate the expression of local agency through village assemblies and have not allowed PRIs to become established forums for decision-making over natural resources, despite their formation over half a decade ago, perpetuating top-down and unaccountable natural resource governance in the study district.

Finally, due to the nature of governance being determined through locked-in practices such as the Forest Department's and national-level institutions' de facto control over environmental and forest clearances in a context of overlapping legislation on the one hand, and through new interventions such as regional militarisation being justified by national-level discourse on the other, the development needs of local inhabitants in West Singhbhum continue to be neglected (Basu 2012; Shah 2010; Tillin 2011). The impact of natural resource governance being driven by the top-down prioritisation of resource extraction in West Singhbhum threatens the continued way of life of local communities like the Ho. As demonstrated, it has not only led to runaway mining, but to the widespread logging of wood without systemic support to the local regulation of access to forests. For communities that have traditionally been highly dependent on their natural resource base as subsistence farmers who also forage from the forest, this failure to enable constitutionally mandated democratic natural resource governance has the potential, as in the 1970s, to breed conflict and deep disillusionment with the state. In short, decentralisation reforms have not yielded substantial change in West Singhbhum; despite decision-making having come at least a bit closer to local inhabitants, resource extraction driven by top-down concerns of industrialisation continues to steadily marginalise Adivasi livelihoods.

References

Agrawal, Arun and Jesse Ribot (1999). 'Accountability in Decentralization: A Framework with South Asian and West African Cases'. *Journal of Developing Areas* 33(4): 473–502.

Areeparampil, Mathew (1992). 'Forest Andolan in Singhbhum'. In: S. Narayan (ed.). *Jharkhand Movement: Origin and Evolution*, New Delhi: Inter-India, pp. 144–188.

Areeparampil, Mathew (1996). 'Displacement Due to Mining in Jharkhand'. *Economic and Political Weekly* 31(24): 1524–1528.

Arts, Bas and Marleen Buizer (2009). 'Forests, Discourses, Institutions'. *Forest Policy and Economics* 11(5/6): 340–347.

Basedau, Matthias (2005). 'Context Matters: Rethinking the Resource Curse in Sub-Saharan Africa'. Working Papers in Global and Area Studies. Hamburg: German Overseas Institute.

Basu, Ipshita (2012). 'The Politics of Recognition and Redistribution: Development, Tribal Identity Politics and Distributive Justice in India's Jharkhand'. *Development and Change* 43(6): 1291–1312.

Bose, Purabi (2012). 'Forest Rights: The Micro-politics of Decentralisation and Forest Tenure Reform in Tribal Indian'. Unpublished PhD dissertation. Netherlands: Wageningen University.

Chauhan, Chetan (2014). 'Prakash Javadekar Clears 240 Projects in 3 Months'. *Hindustan Times*, 11 September. Online, available at: www.hindustantimes.com/india/prakash-javadekar-clears-240-projects-in-3-months/story-WCrxd2rhSxQ3ozpOBZ7YiN.html (accessed 6 March 2016).

Cleaver, Frances (2012). *Development through Bricolage: Rethinking Institutions for Natural Resource Management*. Abingdon: Routledge.

Colfer, Carol J.P. and Doris Capistrano (2005). *The Politics of Decentralization: Forests, People and Power*. London: Earthscan.

Corbridge, Stuart (2002). 'The Continuing Struggle for India's Jharkhand: Democracy, Decentralisation and the Politics of Names and Numbers'. *Commonwealth and Comparative Politics* 40(3): 55–71.

Corbridge, Stuart and Sarah Jewitt (1997). 'From Forest Struggles to Forest Citizens? Joint Forest Management in the Unquiet Woods of India's Jharkhand'. *Environment and Planning A* 29(12): 2145–2164.

Corbridge, Stuart, Sarah Jewitt, and Sanjay Kumar (2004). *Jharkhand: Environment, Development, Ethnicity*. New Delhi: Oxford University Press.

Corbridge, Stuart, Glyn Williams, Manoj Srivastava, and Rène Veron (2003). 'Making Social Science Matter – I: How the Local State Works in Rural Bihar, Jharkhand and West Bengal'. *Economic and Political Weekly* 38(24): 2377–2389.

Crook, Richard C. and James Manor (1998). *Democracy and Decentralisation in South Asia and West Africa: Participation, Accountability and Performance*. Cambridge: Cambridge University Press.

Damodaran, Vinita (2006). 'The Politics of Marginality and the Construction of Indigeneity in Chotanagpur'. *Postcolonial Studies* 9(2): 179–196.

Dandekar, Ajay and Chitrangada Choudhury (2009). *PESA, Left-Wing Extremism and Governance: Concerns and Challenges in India's Tribal Districts*. Anand: Institute of Rural Management.

Das, Ashis K. (2008). 'Behind Bow and Arrow: A Look into the Tribal Unrest on Forest Movement of East and West Singhbhum, Jharkhand'. In: Deepak K. Behera and Georg Pfeffer (eds). *Contemporary Society Tribal Studies VII: Identity, Intervention and Ideology in Tribal India and Beyond*, New Delhi: Concept Publishing Company.

ELDF (Environment Law and Development Foundation) (2012a). *Towards Better Forest Governance in India: A Comprehensive Manual on Forest Rights Act and PESA Jharkhand*. New Delhi: ELDF.

ELDF (2012b). *PESA Implementation – Some Essential Prerequisites and Suggestions for the State of Jharkhand*. New Delhi: ELDF.

Evans, Peter (2004). 'Development as Institutional Change: The Pitfalls of Monocropping and the Potentials of Deliberation'. *Studies in Comparative International Development* 38(4): 30–52.

GoI (Government of India) (1996). *Panchayat Extension to Scheduled Areas Act, 1996*. New Delhi: GoI.

GoI (2010). *The Jharkhand Panchayat Raj Amendment Bill, 2010*. New Delhi: GoI.

GoJ (Government of Jharkhand) (2001). *The Jharkhand Panchayat Raj Act, 2001*. Ranchi: GoJ.

Gregersen, Hans, Arnoldo Contreras-Hermosilla, Andy White, and Lauren Phillips (2004). *Forest Governance in Federal Systems: An Overview of Experiences and Implications for Decentralization*. Jakarta: CIFOR.

Guha, Ramachandra (2001). 'The Prehistory of Community Forestry in India'. *Environmental History* 6(2): 213–238.

Gupta, Bashabi (2014). 'Marginalisation and Social Capital: Dialectics of Tribal Space in Jharkhand'. Unpublished PhD dissertation, Jawaharlal Nehru University.

Harriss, John, Kristian Stokke, and Olle Törnquist (2004). 'Introduction: The New Local Politics of Democratization'. In: John Harriss, Kristian Stokke, and Olle Törnquist (eds). *Politicizing Democracy: The New Local Politics of Democratization*, Basingstoke: Palgrave Macmillan, pp. 1–28.

Jenkins, Rob, Loraine Kennedy, and Partha Mukhopadhyay (eds) (2014). *Power, Policy, and Protest: The Politics of India's Special Economic Zones*. New Delhi: Oxford University Press.

Jewitt, Sarah (2008). 'Political Ecology of Jharkhand Conflicts'. *Asia Pacific Viewpoint* 49(1): 68–82.

Johnson, Craig, Priya Deshingkar, and Daniel Start (2005). 'Grounding the State: Devolution and Development in India's Panchayats'. *Journal of Development Studies* 41(6): 937–970.

Kothari, Ashish (2014). 'A Hundred Days Closer to Ecological and Social Suicide'. *Economic and Political Weekly* 49(39): 11.

Kumar, Sanjay (2002). 'Does "Participation" in Common Pool Resource Management Help the Poor? A Social Cost–Benefit Analysis of Joint Forest Management in Jharkhand, India'. *World Development* 30(5): 763–782.

Kumar, Sujit (2014). 'Interrogating "Integration" in Adivasi Discourse: Customary vs. Democratic Institutions in West Singbhum'. *Journal of Adivasi and Indigenous Studies* 1(1): 62–75.

Lahiri-Dutt, Kuntala (2006). '"May God Give Us Chaos, So That We Can Plunder": A Critique of "Resource Curse" and Conflict Theories'. *Development* 49(3): 14–21.

Larson, Anne and Jesse Ribot (2005). 'Democratic Decentralisation Through a Natural Resource Lens: An Introduction'. In: Jesse Ribot and Anne Larson (eds). *Democratic Decentralization through a Natural Resource Lens: Experience from Africa, Asia and Latin America*, London: Routledge, pp. 1–25.

Lund, Christian (ed.) (2007). *Twilight Institutions: Public Authority and Local Politics in Africa*. Oxford: Blackwell.

Mehlum, Halvor, Karl Moene, and Ragnar Torvik (2006). 'Cursed by Resources or Institutions?' *World Economy* 29(8): 1117–1131.

MoRD (Ministry of Rural Development, Government of India) (2011). *Saranda Action Plan*. New Delhi: MoRD.

Nielsen, Kenneth Bo (2010). 'Contesting India's Development? Industrialisation, Land Acquisition and Protest in West Bengal'. *Forum for Development Studies* 37(2): 145–170.

Parajuli, Pramod (1996). 'Ecological Ethnicity in the Making: Developmentalist Hegemonies and Emergent Identities in India'. *Identities* 3(1/2): 15–59.

Paty, Chittaranjan K. (2007). *Forest, Government, and Tribe*. New Delhi: Concept Publishing Company.

Prakash, Amit (1999). 'Contested Discourses: Politics of Ethnic Identity and Autonomy in the Jharkhand Region of India'. *Alternatives* 24(4): 461–496.

Prakash, Amit (2011). 'Politics, Development and Identity: Jharkhand, 1991–2009'. In: Daniel J. Rycroft and Sangeeta Dasgupta (eds). *The Politics of Belonging in India: Becoming Adivasi*, Abingdon: Routledge, pp. 175–189.

PRIA (Participatory Research in Asia) (2004). *Tribal Self-rule Law: Implications of Panchayat Laws in Scheduled Areas of Jharkhand*. New Delhi: PRIA.

PRMF (PR Memorial Foundation) (2010). 'A Report on Status of Panchayat Extension to Scheduled Areas PESA Act 1996 in the States of Andhra Pradesh, Orissa, Jharkhand, Gujarat and Chhattisgarh'. New Delhi: Planning Commission, Government of India.

PUDR (People's Union for Democratic Rights) (1982). *Undeclared Civil War: A Critique of the Forest Policy*. New Delhi: PUDR.

Puthumattathil, Antony (2014). 'Colonialism and Racism Uninterrupted: Evidence from India with Special Reference to the Hos of Jharkhand'. Unpublished PhD dissertation, Belgium: Ghent University.

Ribot, Jesse C. (2011). *Choice, Recognition and the Democracy Effects of Decentralization*. Visby: ICLD.

Robbins, Paul (2005). 'Review of "Jharkhand: Environment, Development, Ethnicity", by Stuart Corbridge, Sarah Jewitt and Sanjay Kumar'. *Annals of the Association of American Geographers* 95(4): 902–903.

RRI (Rights and Resources Initiative) (2012). *Deeper Roots of Historical Injustice: Trends and Challenges in the Forests of India*. Washington, DC: RRI.

Rycroft, Daniel J. and Sangeeta Dasgupta (eds) (2011). *The Politics of Belonging in India: Becoming Adivasi*. Abingdon: Routledge.

Sareen, Siddharth and Iben Nathan. (Forthcoming). Nurturing Democratic Practice through Local Deliberative Institutions: Ho Village Assemblies in Jharkhand.

Shah Commission (2013). 'First Report on Illegal Mining of Iron and Manganese Ores in the State of Jharkhand, Vol. IV'. New Delhi: Ministry of Mines.

Shah, Alpa (2006). 'Markets of Protection'. *Critique of Anthropology* 26(3), 297–314.

Shah, Alpa (2010). *In the Shadows of the State: Indigenous Politics, Environmentalism, and Insurgency in Jharkhand, India*. Durham: Duke University Press.

Streumer, Paul (2003). 'Those Smiling Villages – An Inter-Disciplinary Study of British Imperialism and Nation Building: The Case of the Ho People in Eastern India, 1767–1875'. Unpublished PhD dissertation, Netherlands: University of Leiden.

Stuligross, David (2008). 'Resources, Representation, and Authority in Jharkhand, India'. *Asia Pacific Viewpoint* 49(1): 83–97.

Sud, Nikita (2014). 'The State in the Era of India's Sub-national Regions: Liberalization and Land in Gujarat. *Geoforum* 51: 233–242.

Sundar, Nandini (2005). '"Custom" and "Democracy" in Jharkhand'. *Economic and Political Weekly* 40(41): 4430–4434.

Sundar, Nandini (ed.) (2009). *Legal Grounds: Natural Resources, Identity, and the Law in Jharkhand*. New Delhi: Oxford University Press.

Suykens, Bert (2010). 'Diffuse Authority in the Beedi Commodity Chain: Naxalite and State Governance in Tribal Telangana, India'. *Development and Change* 41(1): 153–178.

Tillin, Louise (2011). 'Questioning Borders: Social Movements, Political Parties and the Creation of New States in India'. *Pacific Affairs* 84(1): 67–87.

Upadhya, Carol (2005). 'Community Rights in Land in Jharkhand'. *Economic and Political Weekly* 40(41): 4435–4438.

Vasan, Sudha (2005). 'In the Name of Law: Legality, Illegality and Practice in Jharkhand Forests'. *Economic and Political Weekly* 40(41): 4447–4450.

Watts, Michael (2004). 'Resource Curse? Governmentality, Oil and Power in the Niger Delta, Nigeria'. *Geopolitics* 91: 50–80.

Webster, Neil, Kristian Stokke and Olle Törnquist (2009). 'From Research to Practice: Towards the Democratic Institutionalisation of Nodes for Improved Representation'. In: Olle Törnquist, Kristian Stokke, and Neil Webster (eds). *Rethinking Popular Representation*, New York: Palgrave Macmillan, pp. 223–234.

Wright, Gavin and Jesse Czelusta (2003). *The Myth of the Resource Curse*. Stanford: Stanford University.

Part IV
The ambiguity of resistance

9 Rural industry, the Forest Rights Act, and the performance(s) of proof

Prakruti Ramesh

The story of the forest-dwelling peoples of central and eastern India, through successive colonial and postcolonial regimes, is a story of their marginality, and their dependence on the largesse of the forest bureaucracy, which still effectively controls the 23 per cent of Indian land legally designated as 'forest' (Guha 2012: 10). Though the grid of forest laws devised in the twentieth century – including the Indian Forest Act, 1927, the Wildlife Protection Act, 1972, and the Forest Conservation Act, 1980 – differ in their priorities and approaches, they have worked largely towards further disinheriting tribals[1] and other poor forest-dwelling communities of their rights to reside in and access forests (Guha 1994; Dreze 2005). Asher and Agarwal (2007: 12), for example, describe how the cumulative effect of the Wildlife Protection Act and the Forest Conservation Act has been to try to create 'human-free wilderness zones', and to ostensibly obstruct the conversion of forest land to 'non-forest uses', even as they both provide clauses for such conversion. Both laws have therefore been instrumental in casting forest dwellers as 'encroachers' on forest land (Ramnath 2008: 38).

Guha (1983) contends that though the impact of colonial and postcolonial forest legislation on forest dwellers and their life-support systems has been 'uniform', the social imperatives behind forest policy have changed. While in the colonial period it was the strategic interests of imperialism – and relatedly, the need to construct and maintain the Indian railways – that informed forest policy, in the postcolonial period forest policy has largely been subservient to the interests of a mercantile and industrial bourgeoisie. A major implication of this is that in many areas, tribal people and other forest dwellers are 'facing harassment and threats of eviction from forest lands and forced relocation or displacement from the areas proposed for development projects without settlement of their rights' (MoTA 2012: 2).

State control of forests in India has thus been an organising principle of their management since the inception of an official Forest Department in 1864 (Hazra 2002). With a few exceptions, like the Joint Forest Management programme of the 1990s, state intervention in forest areas has been characterised by a 'centralising and exclusionary thrust' (Guha 1994: 2194; see also Sundar 2000). This principle of state control and management of forests may be said to derive from the assumption that lands which are common property tend to be overused and left to degenerate, an argument that Garrett Hardin in 1968 pithily encapsulated as 'the tragedy of the commons'.[2] The 1970s and 1980s were decades during which, however, new assumptions about the importance of community control over natural resources began to be formulated (Kumar 2014b), deriving at least in part from the work of Elinor Ostrom and her contemporaries who advocated participatory forms of resource governance.

The Recognition of Forest Rights Act, 2006 (hereafter referred to as the RFRA) is an Indian law that took birth in the twin contexts of the increasing alienation of tribals from their lands, and the heightening pitch of activism associated with such alienation. It was envisioned originally as a law that would protect poor and forest-dependent people from arbitrary eviction and displacement by the Forest Department (Kumar and Kerr 2012: 753). While the law has been used for this purpose on numerous occasions, it has also been invoked, in a far more visible and high-profile way, to stymie the proposed activities of extractive rural industries. Speaking especially of the cases of large capital investment[3] by POSCO in Jagatsinghpur, Odisha, and Vedanta Aluminium in Lanjigarh, Odisha (on which, more will be said later in this chapter), it is evident that the RFRA has the potential to challenge, if not significantly curtail, the handing over of forest land for industrial purposes without the settlement of rights of people laying prior claim to that land. That said, the continued existence of earlier laws has left uncertainty regarding which law takes precedence – this despite the fact that the RFRA claims to vest forest rights in forest-dwelling Scheduled Tribes and other traditional forest dwellers, 'notwithstanding anything contained in any other law for the time being in force' (RFRA 2006: sec 4 (1)).

This chapter is about the challenges of providing proof under the RFRA's 'habitat right', a form of community right (as opposed to individual right) available to pre-agricultural communities and to Particularly Vulnerable Tribal Groups (PVTGs). While there is growing awareness among forest-dwellers about habitat rights, the definition provided in the Act and accompanying rules is so vaguely enunciated, and the procedures for filing for the same so conspicuously absent, that the right suggests a realm of imaginative (if not exasperating) possibility to forest dwelling communities who aim for insurance against the loss of their territory to state or industrial ventures. With reference to a case study in Niyamgiri, Odisha, I propose that establishing claims over land under the habitat right are accompanied by curious productions and demonstrations of proof of indigeneity that have come to include the performance of identity.

The layout of this chapter is as follows: First, it considers the provenance and history of formation of the RFRA. It then discusses aspects of the text and context of the RFRA and highlights some ways in which it attempts to negotiate between the recognition of indigenous custom, and the integration of bearers of that custom within a system of technocratic proof-production. While acknowledging that the law is progressive in many respects, this chapter contends that the RFRA imparts a legacy of inconsistencies and elisions that could seriously affect its implementation on the ground. Finally, it considers the application of the RFRA in a context of proposed extractive rural industrialisation in the

Niyamgiri Hills of Odisha. It shows, in conclusion, and with reference to findings from my fieldwork, that the obligation to furnish proof to register their eligibility under the RFRA has led to some curious cultural innovations among communities living in the Niyamgiri Hills. These innovations suggest not only, in somewhat simple fashion, that laws interact with and leave their impress upon cultures, but also that the ambiguities of proof-production under their dispensation lead to new pressures to 'perform' certain state-endorsed categories of belonging.

A short history of the RFRA

One of the triggers for the introduction of the RFRA was the order in 2002, by the Ministry for Environment and Forests, to evict all 'forest encroachers' within a period of six months. It was estimated that about 300,000 families were displaced as a result. This led to an outcry from civil society organisations across the country, which began to express the need for a national forum to redress forest rights violations. A coalition of over 200 organisations came together under the banner of Campaign for Survival and Dignity (CSD), presenting thousands of tribal men and women with the opportunity not only to report evictions and human rights violations, but also to have their accounts heard and affirmed (Kumar and Kerr 2012).

Kumar and Kerr show how the campaign for the introduction of the RFRA relied on an innovative politics of networking across scales, so that it was able to invoke local concerns at regional and national platforms, while simultaneously involving forest dwellers and grassroots organisations in voicing a demand for the new law. Describing it as an instance of 'democratic assertion', they show how mobilisation for the law derived impetus from the fact that existing legislations like the Forest Conservation Act, 1980, and the Wildlife Protection Act, 1972, were being used systematically to displace forest-dwellers from their land and criminalise their livelihoods.

Kumar and Kerr emphasise that the campaign sought to frame the demand for the RFRA as a measure to counteract historical injustices perpetrated against tribal people. The draft bill that members of the specially constituted Technical Support Group drew up in 2005, under the auspices of the UPA(I) government,[4] challenged wildlife conservationists opposed to the giving over of forest land for human habitation with the argument that forest dwellers are an integral component of the forest ecosystem. Displacing traditional forest dwellers, they suggested, could disrupt ecosystem services that are vital to the sustainable management of forests. Initial drafts of the bill made it clear that forest occupancy and user rights ought to be granted to all traditional forest dwellers, irrespective of their status as Scheduled Tribe or Scheduled Caste. However, the Prime Minister's Office objected to the inclusion of non-tribal forest dwellers, and indicated that the law should apply only to those forest-dwelling Scheduled Tribes who were resident in forests before 1980. It also recommended that sanctuaries and national parks be excluded from the ambit of the law.

Continuing pressure from CSD representatives, however, along with the participation of approximately a quarter of a million forest dwellers and tribals in public demonstrations, led the government to create a joint parliamentary committee composed mostly of tribal MPs from all parties (Kumar and Kerr 2012: 757). In 2006, the committee endorsed the CSD position, and recommended the inclusion of non-tribal forest dwellers, as well as the extension of the cut-off date to 2005. Later in the same year, the RFRA was tabled and passed in parliament, mostly through the initiative of a network of civil society organisations and forest dwellers who coordinated the expression of their demands and employed discursive strategies that successfully challenged narratives promoting the use of forests for wildlife conservation or, indeed, for industry. Kumar and Kerr (ibid.: 756) suggest that this successful campaign of the CSD owed at least as much to political opportunism on the part of the Congress government to secure a tribal 'vote bank' in advance of the 2004 general elections, as to the tenacity of its proponents. Another likely catalyst for the tabling and passage of the RFRA was the presumed link between the evictions of forest dwellers and the growing support for extremist leftist activity (Maoism) in the forests of central and eastern India (Sarin et al. 2010: 30). Nevertheless, opposition to the RFRA, especially from the conservationists' lobby, continued even after the bill became a law, and ensured that its implementation was effectively delayed until its rules were published in the year 2008.

The RFRA has been heralded as a 'landmark legislation' (Sarin et al. 2010: 4) and as a 'decisive political shift' (Asher and Agarwal 2007: 5) towards democratising forest management and governance. This has to do with the fact that the framing of the law, as indicated in this section, was undertaken by subaltern groups in concert with activist organisations and NGOs. The RFRA is a promising document for those forest dwelling and forest dependent communities in India who have been historically marginalised. The following sections look into the text of the law, analysing it for the vision it implicitly espouses.

Content of the Recognition of Forest Rights Act (and rules)

The founding justification for the RFRA was that extensive historical injustices have been done against traditional forest dwellers – both when state forests were being consolidated under colonial rule, and since Independence. The law must be seen as one in a series of interventions about forest use in India; indeed the RFRA is inter-textual, clearly and self-consciously in negotiation with a matrix of preceding laws like the Biological Diversity Act, 2002, the Wild Life (Protection) Act, 1972, and the Forest Conservation Act, 1980. The RFRA departs from existing forest laws in its view that traditional forest dwellers are not external to the forest eco-system, but an essential part of it. It departs also from the Joint Forest Management reforms in that forest dwelling communities and not the forest department are regarded as the final custodians of the forest.

The Scheduled Tribes and Other Traditional Forest Dwellers (Recognition of Forest Rights) Act has a two-part statement of intent:

1   To recognise and vest the forest rights and occupation in forest land in forest dwelling Scheduled Tribes and other traditional forest dwellers who have been residing in such forests for generations but whose rights could not be recorded;

2   To provide for a framework for recording the forest rights so vested and the nature of evidence required for such recognition in respect of forest land.

(RFRA 2006: 1)

The RFRA simultaneously affirms the need to safeguard the country's natural and cultural heritage, and sees traditional forest dwellers as customarily achieving this. It emphasises decentralised and transparent governance, and advocates the right of forest dwellers to collectively determine how their land is used. In this, it derives much force from the Panchayats (Extension to Scheduled Areas) Act, 1996.

Following from this, the RFRA makes it clear that the rights of use and occupation of forest land are annexed to 'responsibilities and authority for sustainable use, conservation of biodiversity and maintenance of ecological balance' (RFRA 2006: 1). To this end, it would be interesting to consider the RFRA as a normative, even moralistic, text. It affirms the rights to customary use of the forest, but its description of such customary use is clearly that of sustainable management rather than of opportunistic or commercial extraction. In other words, the traditional forest dweller it envisages as its key beneficiary is one who lives in harmonious interrelationship with his or her environment.

In a draft paper about the history of stigma against shifting cultivation in Odisha, Kundan Kumar says that state efforts to convert land into 'legal forests' tend to delegitimise practices of shifting cultivation (n.d.: 21). The rendering illegal of traditional swidden practices has led effectively to a disjunction between *de jure* and de facto land tenure. Forest dwellers in Odisha have continued to illegally practise shifting cultivation; however, Kumar notes, the periods during which land is left fallow (and allowed to regenerate its nutrients) have shrunk. In addition, many shifting cultivators no longer see sense in investing in the land they use, since they have no legal title to it and may be evicted from it at any time. Paradoxically, therefore, attempts by the state to stop shifting cultivation in the name of restoring the environment have culminated in the deepening degradation of forest land. By confirming the legality of their claims to forest land, the RFRA has the potential to constitute (or renew) an indigenous conservation regime (Kumar notes, however, that the RFRA makes no explicit mention of the right to shifting cultivation, and therefore its applicability to this particular issue is moot). But in whose hands would such an inclusive and decentralised conservation regime lie?

The RFRA's beneficiaries: Scheduled Tribes and other traditional forest dwellers

The RFRA distinguishes between two kinds of beneficiaries at the same time as it seeks to give them comparable entitlements. In their early negotiations, when the law was still in the draft stage, members of the CSD were emphatic about the inclusion not only of forest-dwelling Scheduled Tribes, but also of other poor, vulnerable groups who were resident in forest land and dependent on its produce. The CSD sought to make the RFRA applicable to all forest-dwellers, in keeping with the observation that the placing of people in categories like Scheduled Tribe and Scheduled Caste is often arbitrary, non-thorough and politically motivated. The CSD's version of the bill was passed in spite of opposition from the government.

It is important to note, however, that although both Scheduled Tribes and other traditional forest dwellers are included, in principle, under the scope of the law, the procedure for filing claims to land is different for the two sets of people. If the claimant is categorised as a Scheduled Tribe living in an area where he or she is scheduled, it is sufficient to attach a copy of the Scheduled Tribe certificate to the claim. If the claimant is not a Scheduled Tribe living in his or her Scheduled Area, however, proof is to be attached that the claimant's family has been resident in the area for three generations (or 75 years). The regime of proof applicable to Scheduled Tribes is therefore markedly different than that applicable to Other Traditional Forest Dwellers.

In this context it is pertinent to look into whether this difference in the letter of the law translates into serious handicaps for those who are not Scheduled Tribes. How, for instance, has the introduction of the RFRA worked to consolidate certain identities, or deepened rifts between communities that may previously have shared forest space and resources? Matthew Shutzer (2013) presents case studies from Kalahandi, Odisha, which indicate that the decentralisation of resource governance among target communities can create unequal beneficiaries. His case studies show further that the beneficiaries of legislations like the RFRA, although conceived of as sharing similar economic and material circumstances, may in fact be quite heterogeneous. The Kutia Kondhs of Lanjigarh, Kalahandi, a PVTG, for instance, have differential access to jobs and urban amenities, depending on whether they live in the plains, at medium elevation, or at a high altitude. Their relative dependence on or distance from the privileges conferred by the RFRA thus also varies. It is therefore necessary to ask how the RFRA, which aims to redress historic inequities, in turn generates new exclusions. Shutzer suggests that through the implementation of the RFRA, 'indigenous spaces' have been mapped and re-mapped in ways that codify relations between indigenous peoples and 'the abstract space of forest resources' (2013: 3), as well as between indigenous peoples and other communities who are defined as non-indigenous. Further, in light of the normative dimensions of the RFRA earlier discussed, Shutzer asks how the RFRA reifies and reassembles 'a conception of customary indigenous practices that define the criteria for how indigenous communities are intended to act upon the environment' (ibid.).

Arpitha Kodiveri (2016) refers to the RFRA as containing a 'technical and evidentiary bias' towards Scheduled Tribes. She discusses the case of members of the Pano Scheduled Caste in the Kandhamal District of Odisha, and the pressures against their inclusion in the process of filing claims under the RFRA. She also shows how the intervention of a local NGO, the Vanvasi Kalyan Ashram, closely linked with the Rashtriya Swayamsevak Sangh (RSS) and other organisations under the *sangh parivar*, worked to entrench the idea that the Kondh Adivasis had a 'prior claim' to forest land over their Pano counterparts. She calls for a greater attentiveness to the intersection between untouchability and the RFRA, especially in places like Kandhamal where 'caste-based atrocities are practised by the local Adivasi population' (ibid.: 56). The architects of the RFRA intended to create a legislation that would assist and empower all 'traditional' forest dwellers, independent of their inclusion as Scheduled Tribes. Yet, the law in practice creates a more significant hurdle of proof for non-Scheduled Tribe people seeking to establish their occupancy of forest land, and, as Kodiveri argues, possibly makes room for the perpetuation of caste-based exclusions.

A typology of rights: individual and community claims under the RFRA

The RFRA provides forest-dwellers with the option of applying for individual and community tenure over forest land (RFRA 2006: 3). Sections 3(1) (a), 4(3) and 4(6) of the Act state that individual claimants will only receive rights to 'land under their occupation' since prior to 13 December 2005 up to a ceiling of 4 ha (RFRA 2006: 6). Any claim to land exceeding this 4-ha limit would need to be filed by a community for shared access to land that they can prove they have been customarily using for livelihood or spiritual needs, including burials or places of worship.

Community rights include a special right to community tenure over the customary habitat (territory) of tribal groups categorised as pre-agricultural communities and PVTGs, a sub-group within the tribal category for whom special support programmes have been developed. This is called the 'habitat right' and it applies to tribes like the Baigas of Madhya Pradesh and Chhattisgarh and the Dongria and Kutia Kondhs of Odisha. The exact points of difference between the community right and the habitat right are not enunciated in the Act or the rules. However, from correspondence with researchers of the RFRA,[5] and in consultation with the FAQ issued by the Ministry of Tribal Affairs, it seems that a 'habitat' pertains to 'customary territories used by the PVTG for habitation, livelihoods, social, economic, spiritual, cultural and other purposes' (MoTA 2015: 1). In some cases the habitats of PVTGs may overlap with forests and other rights of other people/communities. Whereas a claim to a community forest right might originate in one village *gram sabha*, the habitat right could encompass claims by multiple *gram sabhas* that might even span more than one district.

The RFRA sees forests as spaces of shared use, and institutionalised community access based on local democracy as a means to creating a conservation regime that also achieves an equitable distribution of resources. Of the 13 rights listed in the Act, five explicitly contain mention of the word 'community' while only one contains the word 'individual'. Though it could be argued that all the rights listed imply both individual and community access, the more frequent appearance of 'community' than 'individual' could indicate that the RFRA wishes a greater emphasis on the former, or at least that it vests individual rights in community tenure.

Using comparative case studies, Tania Li (2010) studies the rationale behind ideas of collective tenure in British and Dutch colonies in Asia and Africa, showing how vestiges of that rationale continued after colonial rule ended. Officials across colonies, she says, saw segments of the native population as sequestered from mainstream culture, and believed that these segments were especially vulnerable to capitalist exploitation. The colonial government devised measures to protect (or incarcerate – Li suggests that this could be the other side of the coin) these communities by issuing collective titles to land. Doing this, it was thought, would help to stave off market solicitors and make forest land less amenable to piecemeal dissipation. The assumption underwriting community tenure was that the community would be made guarantor of forest land, and that this would lessen its opportunistic sale.

Li disputes the idea that collective tenure arrangements are an 'essential' component of pre-capitalist societies. She suggests that the argument for collective tenure and the implicit association of such tenurial rights with indigenous peoples arose as a defensive reaction to situations of increasing land scarcity. According to Li (2012: 385):

> Collective landholding is sometimes imposed by local groups on their own members as they act to defend their livelihoods and communities. More often, however, it has been imposed from outside, first by paternalistic officials of the colonial period and now by a new set of experts and advocates who assume responsibility for deciding who should and who should not be exposed to the risks and opportunities of market engagement.

Nevertheless, she argues, individuals in rural communities do for many reasons wish to sell their land – either because of the perceived benefits that accompany living in an urban centre, or because of compulsions like debt. They often fail, therefore, to conform to the assumptions embedded in programmes designed for their protection.

A recent assessment of claims filed under the RFRA indicates that only 2 per cent of the total claims filed are for community forest rights (*New Indian Express* 2014). All the rest are individual claims. Amita Baviskar suggests that the RFRA's 'provision for making communal claims to manage forests has not been pursued as vigorously as the provision for private land ownership' (cited in Li 2010: 405), primarily, it would seem, because of a lack of awareness among

Scheduled Tribes and other traditional forest dwellers about its existence (Tatpati 2015: 89), but also because community claims are actively contested by the forest bureaucracy because they cover larger areas of land and go well into actual forests.

In Bhubaneswar, the capital city of Odisha, I met with the director of an NGO called Vasundhara, which works on issues of forest conservation and sustainable livelihoods. He spoke of the democratic provenance and potential of the RFRA. Citing words from the Act's preamble, he mentioned that it is framed in the manner of an apology for historical and continuing wrongs committed by the state against forest-dwelling people.[6] In its implementation, however, there were problems that he did not foresee from reading the letter of the law. One of these was that individual and community titles circumscribe customary use of the forest, making it easy for forest officials to characterise activity occurring outside of these limits as unlawful. In his words, 'land is given with one hand and taken away with the other'. At the time of my visit, the NGO Vasundhara was on a mandate from the Ministry of Tribal Affairs to clarify the definition of 'habitat rights'.

The rules accompanying the RFRA specify with some clarity how to file a claim for individual and community rights to forest land. The Act attempts to provide a definition of what constitutes a 'habitat' in Sections 2 (h) and 3 (1) e, but procedures for filing for the same are conspicuously absent. An employee of the NGO Vasundhara said to me, 'no one knows what a habitat is. We think of it in connection with wildlife'. By virtue of its ambiguity, the habitat right embodies the potential to reimagine the boundaries not only of tenurial status, but also of community and belonging. To presage a discussion that will be held in a later part of this chapter, and in connection with circumstances in Niyamgiri, Odisha, I suggest that the equivocation and ambivalence surrounding applications under the habitat right are likely to lead not only to problems of proof, but also to new and innovative ways of surmounting such problems and establishing credible linkages with land.

Issues of implementation: the problem of proof

According to the RFRA, individual or community claims to forest land need to be accompanied by proof that the area has been under occupation by the claimant(s). The parameters of proof include:

1   Statements by elders of the village, *reduced to writing and signed by them*, preferably in the form of an affidavit;
2   Photographs and a map of the land being claimed, showing physical structures like bunds, burial stones, wells, check dams, etc.
3   *Any previous documents* referring to the land or to structures on it, like *pattas*, leases, grants, house tax receipts, etc. or published documents like Gazetteers.

(Campaign for Survival and Dignity, n.d., emphases mine)

This makes it pertinent to explore the ways in which effective implementation of the RFRA depends on the intervention of certain technologies such as writing, photography, and maps, in places where such technologies could be difficult to access.

In her assessment of 'tribal rights issues' with regard to the diversion of forest land in the Kalahandi and Rayagada districts of Odisha, Usha Ramanathan *et al.* (2010) refer to technological impediments to the filing of claims under the RFRA. They say that claimants in the region were turned away because they did not append a photograph of themselves to their application – even though no such requirement is stated in the RFRA rules. Ramanathan here points to bureaucratic malfeasance – but more generally, the reliance on certain kinds of technology to furnish proof under the RFRA could lead to specific problems (and, perhaps, to specific innovative solutions).

Nevertheless, the RFRA presents a curious blend of assumptions. It recognises the rights of forest dwellers to the customary usage of forest space. It envisions traditional forest dwellers as people who live in harmony with their environment, and thereby sets a discursive standard for this relationship, 'empowering them' to manage and conserve the forests they inhabit. In order to be entitled to forest land, therefore, forest dwellers must refashion themselves as conservationists, even as they access and use forest products the way they have 'traditionally'. Candidates applying for forest land under the RFRA, further, have to furnish proof of occupation that is legible to a technocratic state (maps, photographs, written statements). The application for titles to land under the RFRA therefore hinges, de facto, on the applicant's literacy in the languages in which claims are accepted, and/or his or her familiarity with the use of photography and maps.

A clear expectation of this law is that the Scheduled Tribe candidate applying for recognition of land-rights has been through a system of schooling. Education levels among Scheduled Tribes and Scheduled Castes in India are, however, abysmal. The Census of 2011 indicates that a mere 58.9 per cent of the Scheduled Tribe population in India is literate (MoTA 2013: 13). This has significantly to do with the language used in schools. According to news reports about Odisha, for example, approximately 70 to 90 per cent of tribal students in the state are monolingual, and speak only the tribal language that they grew up with (*Economic Times* 2015), thus leading students to drop out of primary schooling institutions, where they are confronted with textbooks and instruction that are primarily in the Odia language.

Application of the RFRA in an industrial context: the case of the Niyamgiri Hills and bauxite mining

The Niyamgiri Hills of Odisha, part of the longer, discontinuous Eastern Ghats range, hold rich reserves of bauxite, the ore from which aluminium is produced. The hills are thickly forested and are the natural habitat of several species of fauna and flora. They are also home to indigenous and forest-dwelling communities, prominent among whom are the Dòngria Kondh, a PVTG, whose distinctive ethnic appearance makes them the regular, if decontextualised, stars of advertisements about Odisha's 'tribal development' programmes, but also of global, anti-mining campaigns such as those by the UK-based NGO Survival International.

In the year 2003, a London-based mining and metals corporation called Vedanta Aluminium signed a Memorandum of Understanding (MoU) with the state-owned Orissa Mining Corporation. According to the MoU, Vedanta Aluminium would set up an alumina refinery in close proximity to a site that was claimed would render 73 million tonnes of minable bauxite ore. It would then proceed to mine this ore. The Proposed Mining Lease (PML) site was located on a mountain that tribal communities in Niyamgiri call the Niyam Dongar (Mountain of Law). To the Dongria Kondh, this mountain is the seat of an ambulatory god called the Niyam Raja.

For more than a decade, communities in the Niyamgiri Hills – in concert with a host of regional, national and international actors – have resisted what they define as state–corporate collusion. Their struggle, viewed retrospectively, has been fought on several platforms (Kumar 2014a). Different kinds of arguments have been leveraged, including the Dongria Kondhs' right to their religion, culture, and livelihood. It was further argued that mining would result in unprecedented levels of pollution, disrupting several ecological processes (the Niyamgiri Hills are close to the Karlapat Wildlife Sanctuary and together these constitute an elephant corridor in the region).

Several actors have used the provisions of the RFRA to fight off corporate claims on the Niyamgiri Hills. The two 'expert' reports[7] commissioned by the Ministry of Environment and Forests about the sustainability of a mining venture in the Niyamgiri Hills refer extensively to violations of the RFRA by Vedanta Aluminium and the Orissa Mining Corporation, such as the breaching of the tribals' rights to be consulted in a democratic and transparent way about appropriations of their land. Although other laws pertaining to wildlife and environment conservation were also in danger of being contravened, the reports place unequivocal emphasis on the RFRA.

Invoking the RFRA in August 2013, the apex court of India declared that there would be a referendum among villages in the Niyamgiri Hills on the issue of whether mining should occur. The villages were unanimous in their decision to prevent mining from occurring, and this 'movement' has since constituted, in however provisional and contingent[8] a way, a successful expression of power by a large cross-section of civil society, and an important precedent in judicial rulings about tribal autonomy in Fifth Schedule areas.

Habitat rights in Niyamgiri and the 'other' problem of proof

Among the two rights available under the RFRA's dispensation, the habitat right (which, as mentioned before, is a special case of the community right) was of foremost relevance to those Dongria Kondh inhabitants of the Niyamgiri

Hills who wished for security against Vedanta Aluminium. This was because it was not a parcel of land, or even the precincts of a village that were under threat, but potentially an entire range of hills over which the Dongria and Kutia Kondh communities reside, practice shifting cultivation (*podu chasa*), grazing, and the collection of medicinal plants, and therefore wish to establish a claim. During my visit to Niyamgiri, and my conversations with activists from the Dongria Kondh communities, it became apparent that the habitat right was seen increasingly as an intervention against what was perceived as the inanity of individual titles. 'What do these *pattas* mean when the entire Niyamgiri is ours?' I was asked. Meenal Tatpati *et al.* (2015) have also written about the 'puzzling' fact that Dongria Kondh villages rejected individual and community rights that were offered to them by the government. Dongria Kondh members are beginning to see the habitat right as a way of guaranteeing that there will be no encroachment on the area by the forest department or by industry.

In the absence of clarity about how to apply for habitat rights, the Dongria Kondh appear to be establishing their right of 'habitat' over the Niyamgiri Hills in an innovative way. Together with their many organised and unorganised supporters, they have been paying tribute to their god Niyam Raja on Vedanta Aluminium's Proposed Mining Lease site. Every February since the year 2007, members of this community (across over 100 Dongria Kondh villages in Niyamgiri) have gathered there to celebrate and display their cohesiveness and to mark and sacralise the PML site. While tributes to Niyam Raja had earlier occurred in a more dispersed fashion in individual villages (Hardenberg 2005), it was only in 2007 that it began to take this more public, political form, amounting to a photographable spectacle. This 'festival' could be seen as a statement of their claim to the Niyam Dongar Mountain. It could also be seen as an assertion of their collective tribal identity, and of the 'otherness' that makes their practices *seem* tribal to the state.

According to the Usha Ramanathan *et al.* and N.C. Saxena reports of 2010, the PML site, located at the crest of the Niyam Dongar, was not used by the Dongria Kondh and other forest-dwelling communities for cultivation or the collection of forest produce. It was also not used ostensibly as a site for prayer. Nor were there villages located on it. Thus, in this instance, the RFRA would offer the forest dwellers the relative vagueness of protection but not the precision of immunity, as there were no outward indications that the site was used for habitation, self-cultivation, or for social or religious purposes. The embellishment (if not the invention)[9] of tradition, and the amplification that this received in national and regional news media, can be interpreted as a kind of proof-making directed at establishing a more conclusive claim to the PML site. I argue, in other words, that the Dongria Kondhs' 'tribal-ness' has to be iteratively and collectively performed for them to appear before the law as a PVTG: The Dongria Kondh are *classified* as a PVTG and are therefore entitled to apply for the habitat right, but that should not make us blind to the rhetorical and performative apparatus that was instrumental in giving unprecedented visibility to the vulnerability of the Dongria Kondhs and their fragile environs.[10]

It is arguable, for instance, that the RFRA was effectively leveraged at least in part because the Dongria Kondhs conform, in their audio-visual representations, to stereotypes about tribal communities. The film *Mine*, made by the international NGO Survival International, spread a message about Vedanta Aluminium's predatory incursions into sacred, virgin forest-land, and showed the Dongria Kondh as a haplessly endangered community living off the forest. It thus made explicit parallels between the story of Niyamgiri and the story of James Cameron's Hollywood blockbuster *Avatar*.[11] The film depicts the Dongria Kondhs as fierce and exotic savages: Climbing trees, tapping toddy, brandishing axes when threatened, and speaking in a strange tongue whose meanings are nevertheless easily rendered into English. *Mine* paints 'in' the Dongria Kondhs, as if the entire Niyamgiri Hills were their *sole* property, as if the Niyamgiri Hills existed in isolation from nodes of urban and peri-urban access, as if the Dongria Kondhs lived in a self-sufficient, untroubled and bountiful natural bliss with no desire, for example, to visit a city, to have their children engage with world history, or to learn some kinds of scientific forestry to better harness the forest produce they routinely use.

The simplistic, even reductionist (although, arguably, 'strategically essentialist'), vision of the Dongria Kondhs that the film conjures is part of a wider net of imagery and associations that are current about tribal peoples, associations that are understood within 'vocabularies of contrast' (Rycroft and Dasgupta 2011: 4). It is in conjunction with this, I suggest, that the Dongria Kondhs find they have to perform their marginality, their vulnerability, and, ultimately, their Otherness, in order to qualify as candidates before the RFRA and its accompanying discourses of tribal empowerment and security.

The case discussed demonstrates the use of the RFRA in defence of the rights of tribals against the demands of the state and of industry. Given this successful application of the RFRA, it may not be too whimsical to say that this law is likely to be invoked more and more frequently in conflicts between industries and peasants over the right to land. This has partly to do with the RFRA's relative newness, and its consequent ambiguities and ellipses. It provides a vision for action, but leaves to local agents the implementation (and so, redefinition) of this vision.

Under the RFRA, members of the Dongria Kondh community are enjoined to participate as modern citizens in the acquisition of proof that they are Scheduled Tribe people, and in deliberations about what should be done with their land. They are simultaneously rewarded when they are 'tribal', traditional, and 'outside' the 'mainstream'. A long-term condition of their participation as modern citizens is that they be educated. However, many members of the Dongria Kondh community evince dissatisfaction with, and distrust of, the schooling system. In my conversations with Kondh members of the Niyamgiri Surakhya Samiti (Committee for the Protection of Niyamgiri), it was clear that their dissatisfaction with schools derives principally from the fact that classroom instruction is carried out in Odia rather than in their own language, Kui. This has the effect of making them feel excluded. In a study of schools across six

Indian states, authors Vimala Ramachandran and Taramani Naorem (2013) discuss dropout rates among Scheduled Caste and Scheduled Tribe students in Odisha, and draw attention inter alia to 'language as a site of exclusion'.

Likewise, distrust of school environments among the Dongria Kondhs is kindled by the belief that their children will learn to 'sell out' to companies like Vedanta Aluminium in much the same way as the somewhat infamous – and now ostracised – Jeetu Jakesika, a prominent leader of the anti-mining movement in Niyamgiri, who was 'co-opted' by Vedanta Aluminium when the corporation allegedly offered to sponsor his higher education (Chaki 2010). Dongria Kondh leaders are increasingly afraid that education will splinter the community on the issue of whether mining should occur. They are also concerned that their children will be taught to devalue their forests and ancestors, as well as their cultural identity. To many members of the Dongria Kondh community, getting educated is a risky prospect. It involves exposure to new wants and new notions of belonging that imperil their collective identity, in an environment where the government and industry are only too willing to poach on divisions between them.

A consequence of the Dongria Kondhs' dissatisfaction with the schooling system is that dropout rates among children of a school-going age are high. Therefore, members of the community continue to depend on a host of unreliable 'outside' interlocutors[12] to understand and protect their rights. Many of these interlocutors are themselves, however, barely literate, and many have divergent notions of what constitute the tribals' best interests. The 'true' interests (and there may well be many) of the Dongria Kondh are thus refracted through the many lenses of their exchanges with these interlocutors. The Dongria Kondhs' ability to protect their own rights depends crucially on the faculties and intentions of these mediators.

The RFRA, in sum, was envisaged as a law that would protect the rights of tribals against transgressions by the state and by industry. In order to avail of the protections offered by this law, tribals are encouraged to become educated at the same time as they are rewarded for their continued practice of custom and tradition. These two expectations are not easily reconciled, given the current system of schooling among rural tribal students in Odisha. Consequent upon the industry's claims on the Niyamgiri Hills and the threats to their rights, the Dongria Kondhs must remain united, and therefore tribal, if they are to retain possession of their lands. As the present education system is perceived to threaten such unity and cultural identity, tribal children are dropping out. In the long term this trend could make the tribals vulnerable to exploitation by other interlocutors. This could compromise their rights, in spite of the existence of the RFRA.

Conclusion: proof-making in a context of illiteracy

K. Balagopal (2007) tells a story of how educated young tribals in the West Godavari district of Andhra Pradesh approached the courts, seeking a reconsideration of land claims that had been settled in favour of non-tribals. The

West Godavari district falls in part within the Schedule V areas of India.[13] The tribals asked that the land claims be re-evaluated in light of the fact that they had been settled at a time when the people of their community had been uneducated, and therefore unable to effectively understand or lobby for their rights. Balagopal's account is interesting in that it shows that although progressive laws in India are in no short supply, the capacity to call upon such laws when in need, and to have them implemented in one's favour, hinge crucially on the ability to read and write in dominant or ascendant languages patronised by the state.

In the case of the Dongria Kondh and other marginal forest dwelling communities in southwest Odisha, it is apparent that most of their members lack the capabilities to, for example, access written information, make or read maps, or verify their own land records (if they have any) for authenticity. This is not to suggest that the RFRA does not represent an important intervention in conflicts over the use of land, something that is certainly the case in contexts of rural development/industrial ventures, which appropriate land at an unprecedented scale, thus displacing and immiserating populations who are not skilled in ways that allow them to benefit from such development. What I have attempted in this chapter, however, has been to elucidate the imagination of the RFRA, i.e. its intended beneficiaries, its parameters of proof, and its effects, as well, on the imaginations and practices of forest-dwelling groups and activists. I have shown that the RFRA, in spite of being a relatively new and plastic legislation, upholds two clear, if not explicit, standards for its beneficiaries. It expects them, on the one hand, to be integrated into modern government enough to be able to prove their occupancy of the land they want title to, while on the other hand, it expects them to 'be tribal' – either by state classification or by the fact of their marginality and dependence on forests for subsistence needs. The tribals who seek to benefit under the dispensation of the RFRA's 'individual' claims are compelled to furnish proof that is legible to a technocratic state. In the case of the habitat right, however, and in the absence of clarity about how to apply for such rights, PVTGs find they have to perform their 'particular vulnerability' in order to qualify as genuine-seeming candidates before the law.

Notes

1 Scholars like Xaxa (2005) have argued that the category 'tribe' is a colonial construction originally devised for administrative expediency. The terms 'tribe' and 'tribal' refer to and subsume a vast variety of people, who differ from one another on the basis of language, region, demographic size and access to developmental services like healthcare and education. In addition, these are terms that are increasingly seen as having too many pejorative connotations to use in thoughtful academic language, connotations that include backwardness and primitivity. I choose the word 'tribal' over the alternative 'Adivasi' in this chapter, however, because the Indian Constitution's sustained use of the term 'Tribe' has sanctioned its validity even among subaltern groups who desist from identifying completely with the label. In order to make demands on the state, subaltern activists often have to first accept state-ordained identity even as they seek to be recognised and understood differently from it.

2 The 'tragedy of the commons' argument also characterises critiques of the Recognition of Forest Rights Act (RFRA), 2006. A study of the failure to manage the 'commons' of the state's forests by The Energy and Resources Institute (TERI) claims that nearly 100,000 ha of forest land were lost to RFRA claims.

3 POSCO's steel plant in Jagatsinghpur is reported to have been undertaken at an investment of GBP5.4 billion; Vedanta Aluminium's total investment in Lanjigarh is reportedly GBP5.2 billion.

4 The UPA (I) was a coalition of centre–left political parties in India formed after the 2004 general election. One of the most prominent members of the UPA is the Indian National Congress, whose president Sonia Gandhi was also the chairperson of the UPA.

5 Primarily, this has comprised correspondence with the independent researcher and activist C.R. Bijoy as well as Subrat Kumar Nayak of the NGO Vasundhara in Odisha.

6 On page 1 of the Act it says:

> The forest rights on ancestral lands and their habitat were not adequately recognised in the consolidation of State forests during the colonial period as well as in independent India resulting in historical injustice to the forest-dwelling Scheduled Tribes and other traditional forest dwellers who are integral to the very survival and sustainability of the forest ecosystem.

7 The Usha Ramanathan et al. report, 2010 and the N.C. Saxena report, 2010.

8 The issue of whether to mine the Niyamgiri Hills has allegedly (as of October, 2015) been reopened. As per some reports in the media, the state government is planning to reconvene (or circumvent) *gram sabhas* in the Niyamgiri region with an aim to get permission for bauxite mining. Activist groups are reorienting themselves to this new ground situation.

9 It is not that no relationship with the PML site existed before the threat of mining. Rather, the relationship did not have this concrete ritual form.

10 Most news reports about the issue mention Dongria Kondhs to the exclusion of other forest dwelling communities. This is in spite of the fact that both the Usha Ramanathan et al. report and the N.C. Saxena report assert that many forest dwelling and forest dependent communities would be affected by the proposed mine (e.g. the Dombos/Panos and the Kutia Kondhs).

11 See for instance, 'Real "Avatar" Tribe Deals Fatal Blow to Vedanta Mine', online, available at: www.survivalinternational.org/news/9478 and 'Indian Tribe's Avatar-like Battle against Mining Firm reaches Supreme Court' *Guardian*, online, available at: www.theguardian.com/world/2012/apr/08/indian-tribe-avatar-supreme-court (accessed 6 March 2016).

12 From my field experience, interlocutors for the Dongria Kondh community have included NGO spokespersons, activists affiliated to regional political parties like the Samajwadi Jan Parishad, the Lok Shakti Abhiyan and the CPI(ML) New Democracy, and literate members of the Kutia Kondh community, a PVTG residing in the lower elevations of the Niyamgiri Hills.

13 As per the Indian Constitution, land under possession by tribals in Scheduled V Areas cannot be transferred to non-tribals. This measure has been undertaken to 'protect' tribals from alienation from their lands although its implementation varies significantly between states due to different land laws and highly varying implementation of such laws.

References

Asher, Manshi and Nidhi Agarwal (2005). *Recognising the Historical Injustice: Campaign for Forest Rights Act*. Pune: National Centre for Advocacy Studies.

Balagopal, K. (2007). 'Land Unrest in Andhra Pradesh-III: Illegal Acquisition in Tribal Areas'. *Economic and Political Weekly* 42(40): 4029–4034.

Campaign for Survival and Dignity (n.d.). *A Guide to the Forest Rights Act*. New Delhi: Campaign for Survival and Dignity. Online, available at: www.forestrightsact.com/resources-for-activists (accessed 6 March 2016).

Chaki, Bijay (2010). 'A Different Tune on Vedanta'. *New Indian Express*, 2 October. Online, available at: www.newindianexpress.com/magazine/article286554.ece?service=print (accessed 6 March 2016).

Dreze, Jean (2005). *Tribal Evictions from Forest Lands*. New Delhi: National Advisory Committee.

Economic Times (2015). 'Tribal Language Books Introduced to Check Dropout in Odisha'. 12 August. Online, available at: http://articles.economictimes.indiatimes.com/2015-08-12/news/65490059_1_tribal-students-dropout-rate-odia (accessed 6 March 2016).

Guha, Ramachandra (2012). 'The Past and Future of Indian Forestry'. In: *Deeper Roots of Historical Injustice: Trends and Challenges in the Forests of India*. Washington, DC: Rights and Resources Initiative.

Guha, Ramachandra (1983). 'Forestry in British and Post-British India: A Historical Analysis'. *Economic and Political Weekly* 18(44): 1882–1896.

Guha, Ramachandra (1994). 'Forestry Debate and Draft Forest Act: Who Wins, Who Loses?' *Economic and Political Weekly* 29(34): 2192–2196.

Hardenberg, Roland (2005). 'Children of the Earth Goddess: Society, Marriage and Sacrifice in the Highlands of Orissa'. Unpublished Habilitation Thesis, Westfälischen Wilhelms-Universität Münster.

Hazra, Arnab Kumar (2002). *History of Conflict over Forests in India: A Market Based Resolution*. New Delhi: Liberty Institute.

Kalpavriksh and Vasundhara (2015). 'Citizens' Report 2015: Community Forest Rights under the Forest Rights Act'. Washington, DC Rights and Resources Initiative.

Kodiveri, Arpitha (2016). 'Narratives of Dalit Inclusion and Exclusion in Formulating and Implementing the Forest Rights Act, 2006. Policy Report No. 17'. New Delhi: Hindu Centre for Politics and Public Policy.

Kumar, Kundan (n.d.). 'Erasing the Swiddens: Shifting Cultivation, Land, and Forest Rights in Odisha'. Draft Paper. Online, available at: www.academia.edu/3249705/Erasing_the_Swiddens_Shifting_Cultivation_Land_and_Forest_Rights_in_Odisha (accessed 6 March 2016).

Kumar, Kundan (2014a). 'The Sacred Mountain: Confronting Global Capital at Niyamgiri'. *Geoforum* 54: 196–206.

Kumar, Kundan (2014b). 'Decentralisation and Democratic Forest Reforms in India: Moving to a Rights-based Approach'. *Forest Policy and Economics* 51: 1–8.

Kumar, Kundan and John M. Kerr (2012). 'Democratic Assertions: The Making of India's Recognition of Forest Rights Act'. *Development and Change* 43(3): 751–771.

Li, Tania Murray (2010). 'Indigeneity, Capitalism, and the Management of Dispossession'. *Current Anthropology* 51(3): 385–414.

MoTA, Government of India (2012). 'Guidelines on the Implementation of the Scheduled Tribes and Other Traditional Forest Dwellers (Recognition of Forest Rights) Act 2006'. Online, available at: http://tribal.nic.in/content/forestrightactotherlinks.aspx (accessed 6 March 2016).

MoTA, Government of India (2013). 'Statistical Profile of Scheduled Tribes in India'. Noida: Ministry of Tribal Affairs Statistics Division.

MoTA, Government of India (2015). 'Clarification Pertaining to Recognition of Habitat rights under Scheduled Tribes and Other Traditional Forest Dwellers (Recognition of Forest Rights) Act, 2006 (FRA)'. Online, available at: http://tribal.nic.in/WriteRead Data/CMS/Documents/201504230254287991144clarification.pdf (accessed 11 March 2016).

New Indian Express (2014). 'Guidelines Sought for Forest Area Conversion'. 8 January. Online, available at: www.newindianexpress.com/states/odisha/Guidelines-Sought-for-Forest-Area-Conversion/2014/01/08/article1989144.ece (accessed 6 March 2016).

Ramachandran, Vimala and Taramani Naorem (2013). 'What it Means to Be a Dalit or Tribal Child in Our Schools'. Economic and Political Weekly 48(44): 43–52.

Ramanathan, Usha, Vinod Rishi, and J.K. Tewari (2010). 'Site Inspection Report'. Online, available at: www.moef.nic.in/downloads/public-information/rpt_usha.pdf (accessed 6 March 2016).

Ramnath, Madhu (2008). 'Surviving the Forest Rights Act: Between Scylla and Charybdis'. Economic and Political Weekly 43(9): 37–42.

Rycroft, Daniel and Sangeeta Dasgupta (2011). The Politics of Belonging in India: Becoming Adivasi. New York: Routledge.

Sarin, Madhu and Oliver Springate-Baginski (2010). 'India's Forest Rights Act: The Anatomy of a Necessary but Not Sufficient Institutional Reform'. IPPG Discussion Paper Series No. 45. Manchester: University of Manchester.

Saxena, N.C., S. Parasuraman, P. Kant, and A. Baviskar (2010). 'Report of the Four Member Committee for Investigation into the Proposal Submitted by the Orissa Mining Company for Bauxite Mining in Niyamgiri'. New Delhi: Ministry of Environment and Forests.

Shutzer, Matthew (2013). 'The Practice of Custom in India's Recognition of Forest Rights Act: Case Studies from Kalahandi, Odisha'. South Asia Multidisciplinary Academic Journal. Online, available at: http://samaj.revues.org/3623 (accessed 6 March 2016).

Sundar, Nandini (2000). 'Unpacking the "Joint" in Joint Forest Management'. Development and Change 31(1): 255–279.

Tatpati, Meenal (ed.) (2015). 'Citizens' Report 2015: Community Forest Rights under the Forest Rights Act'. Pune, Bhubaneshwar and New Delhi: Kalpavriksh and Vasundhara, in Collaboration with Oxfam India on Behalf of Community Forest Rights Learning and Advocacy Process.

Tatpati, Meenal, Rashi Mishra, and Subrat Kumar Nayak (2015). 'Securing Tribal Rights means Understanding them First'. India Together. Online, available at: http://india together.org/articles/dongria-kondh-securing-tribal-rights-human-rights (accessed 6 March 2016).

Xaxa, Virginius (2005). 'Politics of Language, Religion and Identity: Tribes in India'. Economic and Political Weekly 40(13): 1363–1370.

10 'We will need a passport to enter the site'

Envisioning land, industrialisation, and the state in Goa

Heather Plumridge Bedi

> If you go inside [the Special Economic Zone] you need a passport, a visa. It is our village area and if we need passport and visa to enter then how will it work?
>
> (Interview, 18 December 2008)

Passports and visas permit entry, but may also limit entry or the assertion of rights. Passports and visas symbolically and simultaneously represent the ability *and* inability for citizens to enter particular territories. Passports and visas open borders, but without them individual abilities to assert rights to space and movement may be compromised and even undermined. In the context of the promotion of Special Economic Zones (SEZs) in the Indian state of Goa, fenceline community members – including the Goan villager quoted above – symbolically evoked passports, visas, and rights as they expressed their opposition to the setting up of SEZs in their state – and even in their own backyard. These sentiments were articulated by many other affected Goan citizens and, as I show in this chapter, a major social movement opposing SEZs, the SEZ Virodhi Manch (SVM), soon emerged to articulate such governance and land uncertainties that were widely perceived to accompany this particular form of industrialisation. The movement was ultimately successful in forcing the state government to halt the SEZ policy in Goa.

As envisioned and planned in Goa, the SEZ model would allow the state to create spatial exceptions to normal governance and, in turn, reconfigure power, place, sovereignty, and territory. Geographically and spatially, such industrial zones are perceived – and in some cases actualised – as quite distinct from the places they border. Introduced in India through national legislation in 2005, SEZs are emblematic of the growing pains associated with economic growth, loss of agricultural land, and urbanisation facing the liberalising nation (Bedi and Tillin 2015). Perhaps because of its successful campaign, the SEZ resistance in Goa has generated a scholarly literature that has analysed the striking irregularities in approving SEZ applications and allotting land to developers (Da Silva 2014); on land inequalities (Sampat 2015); on the framing of the SEZ resistance around local contexts (Bedi 2013); and on the judicialisation of the SEZ struggle following state inaction (Bedi 2015). However, the governance and land implications for fenceline communities as articulated individually and collectively via the social movement remain unexplored dimensions. The aim of the chapter is therefore to explore how the proposal of SEZs alters how fenceline communities – and the general public – envision the state in relation to land governance and sovereignty.

The chapter draws on one year of ethnographic fieldwork in Goa and five follow-up visits of shorter duration to provide the empirical basis for this exploration. Based on 140 in-depth interviews with fenceline communities with SEZs proposed in or adjacent to their villages, activists, social movement participants, journalists, corporate representatives, government officials, and citizens, the chapter shows how directly affected villagers and other Goans perceived the SEZs as exceptional entities that would negatively alter local land governance. The spatial and sovereign exceptions, or 'variegated sovereignties' in Ong's (2006) terminology, made to accommodate industrial SEZs were seen as exclusionary and incompatible with local visions of sovereignty and land governance, and prompted fears that SEZs were in fact a mechanism to subvert the powers of the decentralised local government and, in effect, promote state retreat. These sentiments were most forcefully articulated through the idea that fenceline communities would require a passport or visa to enter these fortified zones, often located in their own back yard and commonly demarcated by high, electrified fences, and guards.

To contextualise the analysis that follows I review ideas of citizen agency and visions of the Indian state. Here, SEZs serve as a vehicle to understand how everyday expectations and engagements between citizens and the state are shifting in liberalising India. I also examine how economic enclaves are theorised more generally in relation to sovereignty. I then move on to analyse conceptualisations of the state and sovereignty in Goa in the context of rapid industrial development through SEZ promotion. I argue that the micro-politics of Goan SEZs elucidate enduring expectations in relation to an imperfect but present state.

Citizen agency and the state

Scholarship on India (and beyond) catalogues the agency of citizens vis-à-vis the state, and the everyday ways that they experience and engage with the state. In a seminal contribution to the debate on the state in India, Fuller and Harriss (2001) critique an influential stream in the literature on state–society relations in India that holds that 'the state-idea' is not part of 'ordinary Indians' understanding', arguing instead that the state is neither an entity incompatible with, nor is it incomprehensible to, Indian society. Rather, empirical research 'consistently shows an everyday understanding of the workings of the state and its administrative procedures among ordinary people which could hardly exist if there was a profound incompatibility'. This awareness creates an environment where people engage with the state as citizens or groups with legal or political rights (Corbridge et al. 2005: 18).

Other scholars focus on the multifaceted nature of the Indian state. Hansen (2001a), for example, notes the duality of the state in the public imaginary, arguing that the state is co-constituted by both 'profane' and 'sublime' qualities. To fully appreciate this complexity, Hansen (ibid.: 226) suggests that we see:

> The imagination of the state as marked by a deep and constitutive split. On the one hand its 'profane' dimensions: The incoherence, brutality, partiality, and the banality of the technical sides of government, as the rough-and-tumble of negotiation, compromise, and naked self-interest displayed in local politics. On the other hand, the 'sublime' qualities imputed to a more distant state: The opacity of the secrets and knowledge of the higher echelons of the state, its hidden resources, designs and immense power, and the illusions of higher forms of rationality or justice believed to prevail there.

The public imagination of the state as detailed in this chapter illustrates how Hansen's notion of the simultaneity of profane and sublime qualities of the state are articulated in practice. As demonstrated later, citizens are highly critical of the state's role in facilitating irregular land transactions to set up SEZs; and yet they prefer the existing state they know to the unknown governance practices associated with SEZs. Governance in the Goan setting, I argue, is imagined predominantly in relation to local governing institutions, and to the SVM, governance implied a present and active local government, and not an abdicating state.

While encounters with the state are framed by governance expectations among citizens, people's expectations of the state will, in turn, transform with economic, social, political, and environmental changes. Importantly, the increased power that accrues to corporations in liberalising India is likely to impact and change citizen perceptions and sightings of the state. As Partha Chatterjee (2011: 33) argues, 'with the continuing rapid growth of the Indian economy, the hegemonic hold of corporate capital over the domain of civil society is likely to continue'. While Chatterjee highlights primitive accumulation and marginalisation as one important outcome of this process, it is, for the purpose of the present analysis, useful to emphasise that the rise of corporate capital also manifests a governance transition, although one that is often contested. Such contestations are strikingly visible in the area of land and industrialisation, where the state now occupies an unusual perch as it simultaneously attempts to attract and regulate investment in land-intensive projects in a context in which land resources are limited and available at a premium, while also acknowledging the claims of popular movements contesting the loss of agricultural, forest, common, or other important lands (Bedi and Tillin 2015). The introduction of SEZ legislation epitomises these contradictions and provides an important avenue for exploring new, reinterpreted visions of the Indian state.

The state, SEZs, and exceptional sovereignties

As the editors point out in their introduction to this volume, it is debatable whether the transformations that have occurred in the Indian state over the past decades can be summarised as unequivocally neoliberal in character. Yet the adoption of the SEZ policy can arguably be seen as being in conformity with some of the basic tenets of neoliberalism, such as the increased use of market mechanisms. Ong (2006: 3) explains neoliberalism as a political tool that is, 'reconfiguring relationships between governing, and the governed, power and knowledge, and sovereignty and territoriality'. Neoliberalism can be a malleable tool that specifically enables regimes to create spatial exceptions to normal governing (Ong 2006: 100). Ong proposes the term 'graduated sovereignty' to explain permutations in normal governance patterns to create space for the free promotion of capital, without adhering to the usual governance requirements of the enclave's host nation. Graduated sovereignty thus refers to new governance patterns that maintain flexibility to adjust to the needs of global capital (Ong 2006: 78) – it is a mechanism to enhance a nation's global competitiveness by giving preferential treatment to those entities engaging in the global market. The resulting shift of power away from the state may well lead to an increase in corporate power as the state may willingly cede power to stimulate economic growth, something which, in turn, 'fragments citizenship' (Ong 2006: 84). In a comparable, yet slightly different vein, Jenkins sees the introduction of SEZs as a mechanism to dodge political constraints and contradictions in India. To Jenkins, 'SEZs represent an attractive way, politically speaking, of introducing reforms from which liberalizers have otherwise shied away. The SEZ policy is a convenient means of overcoming the huge obstacles (bureaucratic and legal, but ultimately political) to urban redevelopment' (Jenkins 2007b: 6). While Ong thus writes of the withdrawal of the state, Jenkins offers us a 'hybrid' model in which the state cedes partial control while retaining some level of influence. In the Indian case, this mixed approach ostensibly provides an alternate channel around bureaucratic red tape and popular resistance. But, insofar as 'sovereignty consists both of states' ability to make decisions independently of external authorities and their capacity actually to govern' (Jenkins 2002: 486), the SEZ policy arguably entails a 'retreat' of the state.

While segregated economic enclaves such as SEZs are but one example of spatial exceptions that reconfigure space and sovereignty (Ong 2006: 92), it is in the context of precisely these spatial implications of corporate capital promotion through new forms of 'development' that notions of state accountability, and uncertainty over the applicability and rule of law in SEZs, have emerged among concerned citizens and fenceline communities. For example, the SEZ law is very vague regarding governance authority within the spatially differentiated zones. While provision 5f of the SEZ Act provides for the maintenance of sovereignty and integrity of India and the security of the state, it fails to specify how the SEZs will relate to or communicate with local or state law enforcement. Moreover, the shifting of territorial sovereignty for SEZs removes the powers conferred on local governance institutions in India through political decentralisation in the shape of the *panchayati raj* system.[1] *Panchayati raj* institutions were set up to make 'development more effective through local participation' (Jayal 2006: 6) on the assumption that localised decision-making would be a means to avoid the uniform application of centralised rules, which may not suit the local needs of a plural, diverse, and multilingual India. The obvious question thus arises of who has governance authority at a particular local site, thus generating ambiguity regarding operating and governing norms. This is not to suggest that SEZs will uniformly be perceived as 'zones of exception'. Indeed, based on prolonged ethnographic fieldwork at a diamond polishing SEZ in India, Cross (2010) has critically questioned Ong's conceptualisation of SEZs as exceptional spaces. To Cross, SEZs are spaces where citizenship claims are made; and, by tracing the flow of workers and informal exchanges within and outside of the zone, he argues that the kind of 'informality' we usually associate with neoliberalisation and SEZs is actually a reflection of practices *outside* the SEZ. Cross's intervention is undoubtedly an important one, but his empirical foci are in fundamental ways different from those that concern us here. First, he is predominantly interested in labour relations within the zone, and not in perceived governance changes outside the zones. And second, he focuses on an industry that requires a range of informal, non-skilled workers – in contrast, the SEZs proposed in Goa required workers with specialised training and skills, and would thus likely have an altogether different impact on the area in terms of migration and formality/informality.[2] As I show in the following, among fence-line communities involved in the struggle against SEZs, the zones did indeed appear as exceptional when seen through the prism of land governance and sovereignty.

The anti-SEZ movement: land and visions of the Goan state

The fate of the SEZ policy in Goa remains unique in India: Goa is the only state to first adopt, and then later reject the SEZ policy after widespread citizen protests. Following the national SEZ legislation, the then-incumbent Congress-led government of Goa adopted a state SEZ policy – adapted to local conditions – on 5 June 2006. The state government forwarded seven SEZ applications to the central government, which approved three of them. After that, two major social movements formed to oppose the SEZs. Led by the late tourism minister, Mathany Saldanha, the Goa Movement against SEZs (GMAS) included a coalition of political parties then in the opposition. A second social movement, the SVM, refused to link up with political parties and instead drew together an unusual coalition of SEZ affected villagers, architects, Catholic Church leaders, former government officials, and activists (for further discussion on movement identities and modes of organising, see Da Silva (2014) and Bedi (2013, 2015)).

One of the most important struggles that paved the way for the SEZ resistance was the agitation – from the mid-2000s – against the flawed planning process surrounding the Regional Plan (RP) 2011. The RP is a government document that frames the state's land-use plans for a specific period of time, as stipulated under Section 11 of the Goa Town and Country Planning Act, 1974. Section 13 of this act requires that the draft RPs should be submitted to the public for review. Initial efforts by the government to pass the 2011 RP without transparency and public review were met with resistance from a wide range of actors, including people who had never engaged in activism. The RP came to exemplify and solidify the concerns of many Goans that the small state was increasingly being carved up and parcelled out for real estate development, new airports, industrialisation, and coastal regulations. Many social movement organisers noted in interviews that the agitation against the RP led to the SEZ struggle, and informed protest ideas regarding the state and governance.

In addition, Goa is exceptional given the small size of the state. Goan citizens have expectations that various elected representatives of the state – from Members of Parliament to *panchayat* officials – will be responsive to the will of the majority (Bedi 2013). Constituencies are small, as is often the distance between politicians; and the electorate and many citizens expect the state to be accessible, and to listen and act on their behalf. As one informant put it, 'if the people rise the politicians are quick to respond because they are bothered about [those who will constitute] their constituency in the future' (quoted in Bedi 2013: 45).[3] In concert with their visions of an accessible and responsive state, SVM members articulated a desire for an active state presence at various levels, including active local governing institutions. In particular, they wanted the state to be empowered to govern land and development decisions, and not to cede ground to SEZ developers because of the inbuilt legal ambiguity and governance uncertainties associated with the SEZ model. The state government made matters worse by emphasising that the zones would operate as 'self-governing, autonomous municipal bodies' (Government of Goa 2006). The unknown nature of SEZs created a sense of 'fear of the unknown' on the ground and gave rise to local resistance narratives around governance themes, which gained traction among a larger Goan public.

Affected villagers, including those active in SVM, demonstrated clear ideas regarding what the zones would mean for their everyday lives, and in particular for their relation with the local state/*panchayat* as well as for their ability to access formerly communally or government owned lands. The SEZ developers and the state sited the three approved SEZs within or next to villages. While part of one of the villages bordered an already existing industrial estate, all three locales were rural and dependent on watershed and other services from the land zoned for the SEZs. The case of the Meditab SEZ on the Bhutkhamb plateau in Keri village provides a suitable illustration of some of the consequences of setting up SEZs adjacent to existing villages. The Meditab SEZ was geographically isolated from the rest of the village by a large 15-ft barbed wire fence encircling the zone. SVM argued that a number of families around the Keri SEZ were dependent on grazing and herding their cattle and goats on the plateau (SEZ Virodhi Manch 2007: 18–19) and that by creating an exclusive space out of what had hitherto been common grazing land, herders suddenly no longer had access to these important grazing lands. Tellingly, once the SEZ was stalled a large hole was cut in the fence to allow villagers' animals to return to their fields.

As geographically separated areas, SEZs came to resemble foreign entities in the minds and imaginations of villagers, organisers, and the political opposition, prompting fenceline communities to evoke ideas that a visa or passport would be required to enter; or that the SEZs would operate under a different set of rules and legal regime. One female villager explained that the SEZ was:

> Like a different state in our village. Where our government [does not] have any rights, [no] rights to go inside, no rights to ask what you are doing inside, afterwards. It is a huge compound, and afterward they will build a wall and to enter inside you will need to use a visa.
>
> (Interview, 30 August 2008)

Another seasoned social movement activist explained:

> SEZs [are] going to become a government in a territory. You will have another government [that] is not accountable to people. What happened to the voter rights? Do they have their own prime ministers? In Keri most of them are tribal communities. It is a mockery, it does not exist.
>
> (Interview, 2 September 2008)

Another SEZ critic similarly stated that 'the basic objection is to the creation of a state within a state or an authority which is different within a state' (interview, 8 May 2009). Evidently, SEZs were envisioned as separate geographical entities that were territorially distinct from all levels of state governance – as one female villager aptly summarised, an SEZ was 'a separate village in itself wherein the villagers themselves do not have an entry or the Goa government won't have rights over it' (interview, 7 December 2008).[4] In this way, fenceline communities expressed their concerns regarding the potentially diminished powers of local and state level government administrators. This is not to suggest that Goans are not sometimes discontent with the quality of local level governance. Indeed, it is actively critiqued by citizens. However, the pre-existing perception of a significant measure of state responsiveness to popular demands legitimised a more general authority of the state to govern in the name of societal order and rationality (Hansen 2001b: 130), and to be present in people's everyday lives. When the authority of the local state to govern was threatened or circumscribed by the arrival of SEZs, Goans reacted. And, many concerns over local governance and sovereignty were heightened because the local *panchayats* were neither asked, nor informed about proposed SEZs, thus fuelling speculations that the zones would indeed operate outside of the purview of the *panchayats*. This was perceived as highly problematic insofar as the zones were very likely to lead to major changes to the local demography, the environment, land use, water availability, and infrastructure. Put simply, the *panchayat* and the fenceline communities would have to deal with significant social and environmental challenges without having had any say in the process of deliberation, planning, and implementation, and without having the authority to influence operations in the zones in the future. As a Catholic priest explained, the zones would, in effect, create a non-democratic space within the nation state: 'Within a village there would be people who would not be responsible to the *panchayat*. They [have] no obligations to go for a vote or participate in the election process' (interview, 6 January 2009).

In addition, legal governance ambiguities and the suspected capability of the SEZs to operate in blatant disregard of the wishes of the local *panchayat* prompted additional fear that the SEZs would be allowed to function in an extra-legal manner more generally. For example, once the three zones were notified, corporate developers soon proceeded to dig borewells and construct buildings without having the necessary permissions. Such actions confirmed fears on the part of local villagers and activists that the businesses indeed had a kind of carte blanche to act however they pleased behind the safety of their fences. Such fears were also echoed in the apprehension regarding what would happen if crimes were committed within the zone. A young female activist who resided in an SEZ affected village explained her personal fears that in the SEZ:

> There will be foreign rules. There will be a different *nagar* [village]. They don't have any rules. If any crime takes place, for example if someone is raped, there cannot be a police complaint, no MLA can interfere in the case.
>
> (Interview, 12 October 2008)

Another village level organiser voiced similar concerns that the zones were perceived to not fall under the government's jurisdiction: 'It is going to make its own rules! Hence if there is any problem, we won't have any authority to take our complaints to. That is why we are opposing the SEZ' (interview, 12 October 2008), he explained. In this way, governance concerns also became a question of law and order, something that intensified the SVM's protests against the zones.

In the face of these threats of a potential state retreat that may culminate in an 'absent state' – at least within the zones themselves, but with severe negative spill-over effects – fenceline communities and social movement organisers rallied around a demand for governance by state rather than market actors. They envisioned existing state structures of governance as entities that protected village justice and safeguarded it from the potentially adverse impacts associated with the zones. As part of their efforts, social movement organisers devoted resources to ensure that *panchayats* were aware of the SEZ issue, leading to *gram sabhas* passing resolutions against SEZs. In fact, the grassroots call for the abolishment of SEZs eventually came from a majority of the *gram sabhas* in the state (Saldanha 2008). While mostly symbolic in nature, these resolutions were a way for the fenceline communities to reaffirm the power of the *panchayat*, and to reclaim the space for local participation and voice that had been taken away through the implementation of the notified SEZs. And, it reflected a genuine preference for decentralised decision-making. As was expressed during a village meeting in Keri organised by the SVM:

> Traditionally, to protect the village, the decisions of the village have been taken by the villagers together. That is why we have taken a decision that whatever good or bad is going to happen, it will be decided by the village people.
>
> (SVM Keri Village Meeting, 15 November 2008)

The importance of the *panchayat* in articulating local governance concerns in the context of the resistance to SEZs was, it must be noted, in many ways an adaptation of the format adopted during the campaign against the flawed Goan RP, where *panchayats* were – and continue to be – important venues to discuss and pass resolutions contesting land uses that are deemed to be incongruent with local preferences.

While it was thus feared that the *panchayats* may lose power with the introduction of SEZs, select politicians were believed to benefit. A narrative based on mistrust of Members of the Legislative Assembly (MLAs) circulated as people suspected that these elected representatives would gain disproportionally from the setting up of new SEZs. In particular, some felt that the anticipated influx of SEZ workers would allow MLAs to build new vote banks of non-Goans, and that the MLAs would therefore no longer be compelled to represent the interests of the people living permanently in the villages. This apprehension grew out of the widely shared common sense that Goa's 40 MLAs – who are colloquially referred to as the '40 thieves' – run the state with little concern for their constituents' needs, coupled with a genuine concern about the tiny state becoming the destination for an ever growing number of labour migrants from other states. As one retired Goan civil servant who lived outside of the state for most of his career explained: 'Goa is not run by a political party, but ... by an association of MLAs. Today they have institutionalised it to such an extent that you cannot move or do anything without them' (interview, 21 April 2009). Another villager based in an SEZ affected area further explained that they cannot:

> Rely on these ... MLAs because they can change, they have vote banks and [get] elected ... We cannot now change MLA state level politics because [of the] money and muscle power they are using to elect [politicians]. They are bribing the people.
>
> (Interview, 2 August 2008)

Such concerns that elected state leaders at the higher levels were somehow involved in the active promotion of SEZs were not unfounded. Right to Information requests for the SEZ applications in Goa revealed politically facilitated fraudulent land transfers, and ultimately led various members of SVM to file Public Interest Litigation court cases in the Bombay High Court (which has jurisdiction over Goa) in 2007 and 2008. The legal documentation of land irregularities galvanised the general public, already widely critical of the fact that land in Goa is becoming increasingly unaffordable for the common man, while questionable and even outright illegal land transactions proceed apace (Bedi 2015). When the High Court eventually ruled in November 2010 that the allocation of land to SEZ developers was done in a fraudulent manner, the ruling confirmed the suspicion that SEZ corporate developers had been treated exceptionally by representatives at the higher levels of the state. Fenceline community members also argued that these illegal land transfers could point towards a more general disregard for state and national laws in the future. While the state was thus the preferred avenue for fenceline communities and movement activists to reassert authority in Goa, they remained acutely aware of state imperfections at multiple levels. In this sense, their perceptions and actions mirror those captured by Hansen's (2000) idea of the simultaneity of the sublime and profane dimensions of the state: Goan citizens are highly critical of the state's role in facilitating illegal land transactions for the SEZs, and yet they prefer the evil they know to the unknown governance potentials of corporate capital as embodied in SEZs.

Conclusion: state of exceptionality?

As shown above, the introduction of SEZs created a new context for how citizens in Goa envision, engage, and contest the imperfect and multi-faceted state. Although similar in basic ways to existing industrial enclaves, the scale, pace, tax exemptions, and perceived sovereign exceptions associated with the SEZ model became emblematic of new and emergent concerns and issues facing the Indian state, a state perceived as central to the promotion of economic liberalisation and the implementation of rapid industrialisation through the SEZ model. In prioritising this model over other alternatives, the state in effect became a promoter of corporate capital interests, something that, as shown in this chapter, had significant implications for the use, control, and governance of land. The fact that the state soon faced civil society tumult demonstrates how social movements contest the changing roles and powers of the close nexus between the state and corporate capital. The outcome of the resistance in Goa was, as mentioned, the unprecedented scrapping of the zones by the then-chief minister, a victory that may, however, turn out to be pyrrhic insofar as the status of the land allocated for the SEZs remains disputed.

The perceptions of the fenceline communities of SEZs as exceptional spaces with the potential to act outside of the purview of the *panchayat* echo Ong's (2006: 84) arguments regarding the sovereignty implications of SEZs and the fragmentation of citizenship. The local awareness among fenceline communities of the governance transformations inherent in the SEZ model indexes an acute and nuanced understanding of the potential magnitude of the spatial changes associated with the zones, as well as the agency of citizens in making demands on the state. Indeed, social movement members and organisers drew on these latent and manifest governance concerns to question how SEZs would alter their experience with, and access to, local governance for the worse. In contrast to Cross's argument about the unexceptional and structurally embedded (2010: 370) nature of SEZs, I have thus argued here that in Goa they were seen as fundamentally separated from people's everyday economic, social, and environmental lives. This territorial exceptionality of the zones in turn framed how people experienced and responded to the potential or actual governance structures of the enclaves. This was coupled with a very real fear that the zones were in fact serving as a vehicle for the promotion of real estate development and other similar initiatives, which would not have been possible without the special status granted to the zones. In this way, the anti-SEZ movements can be seen as an attempt at deepening democracy (Jenkins 2007a) by reaffirming the centrality of the state – and perhaps especially the *panchayat* – in representing citizens and ensuring accountability. This particular manifestation of governance preferences reflects the importance of the *panchayat* in people's everyday visions of the Indian state. The commonly repeated claim that 'we will need a passport to enter the site' thus became a way for fenceline communities to actively demand and assert their rights in the face of unknown, but presumably negative, governance changes to their lands.

Notes

1 Constitutional Amendments detailing the *Panchayati Raj* system (the seventy-third and seventy-fourth amendments) were passed in December 1992. The amendments empower village *panchayats* to serve as self-governing institutions; to elect local representatives, including those allocated seats via reservations (women, scheduled tribes, and scheduled castes); to prepare and implement economic development plans, social justice, and development schemes; and to receive state authorisation to assign or appropriate relevant taxes or duties. Decentralisation was encouraged as an 'alternative system of governance where a "people-centred" approach to resolving local problems is followed to ensure economic and social justice' (Kothari 2005: 48).

2 Cross's claim about 'unexceptionality' may reflect specialised forms of SEZs that are reliant on local labour, whether unskilled or skilled. In addition, arguments about the unexceptionality of informal labour practices do not address the experience of contestation prior to SEZ approval and implementation, or protests by affected communities after SEZs are built.

3 While this expectation of government responsiveness is prevalent, it is noteworthy that caste and class shape the relative political accessibility of individuals or groups. The political and social clout of some members of SVM allowed them to protest without fear of arrest. For example, they illegally staged protests within the SEZ sites, but never faced arrest. This is in stark contrast to the anti-mining movement in the state, which is predominantly organised by people officially categorised as 'scheduled tribes' or 'scheduled castes'. At the height of the SEZ protests several mining activists were arrested or roughed up following public demonstrations similar to those orchestrated by SVM.

4 Another activist similarly asked: 'How do you have two authorities within the state? The SEZ is considered a boundary where the state government does not have a role. Even the administration, like police, can ... [take] place only after the SEZ authority permits' (interview, 8 May 2009).

References

Bedi, Heather P. (2013). 'Special Economic Zones: National Land Challenges, Localized Protest'. *Contemporary South Asia* 21(1): 38–51.

Bedi, Heather P. (2015). 'Judicial Justice for Special Economic Zone Land Resistance'. *Journal of Contemporary Asia* 45(4): 596–617.

Bedi, Heather P. and Louise Tillin (2015). 'Inter-state Competition, Land Conflicts and Resistance in India'. *Oxford Development Studies* 43(2): 194–211.

Chatterjee, Partha (2011). 'Democracy and Economic Transformation in India'. In: Sanjay Ruparelia, Sanjay Reddy, John Harriss, and Stuart Corbridge (eds). *Understanding India's New Political Economy: a Great Transformation?* London: Routledge, pp. 17–34.

Corbridge, Stuart, Glyn Williams, Manoj Srivastava, and Rene Veron (2005). *Seeing the State: Governance and Governmentality in India.* Cambridge: Cambridge University Press.

Cross, Jaime (2010). 'Neoliberalism as Unexceptional: Economic Zones and the Everyday Precariousness of Working Life in South India'. *Critique of Anthropology* 30(4): 355–373.

Da Silva, Solano J.S. (2014). 'Goa: The Dynamics of Reversal'. In: Rob Jenkins, Loraine Kennedy, and Partha Mukhopadhyay (eds). *Power, Policy, and Protest: The Politics of India's Special Economic Zones,* Oxford: Oxford University Press, pp. 108–136.

Fuller, Chris J. and John Harriss (2001). 'For an Anthropology of the Modern Indian State'. In: Chris J. Fuller and Veronique Benei (eds). *The Everyday State and Society in Modern India,* London: C. Hurst & Co, pp. 1–30.

Government of Goa (2006). 'Government of Goa's Policy on Special Economic Zones'. Porvorim, Goa: Industries Trade and Commerce Department, Government of Goa.

Guha, Ramachandra (2011). 'A Nation Consumed by the State'. *Outlook,* 31 January. Online, available at: www.outlookindia.com/magazine/story/a-nation-consumed-by-the-state/270136 (accessed 12 March 2016).

Gupta, Akhil, and K. Sivaramakrishnan (eds) (2011). *The State in India after Liberalization.* London: Routledge.

Hansen, Thomas Blom (2001a). 'Governance and State Mythologies in Mumbai'. In: Thomas Blom Hansen and Finn Stepputat (eds). *States of Imagination: Ethnographic Explorations of the Postcolonial State,* Durham: Duke University Press, pp. 221–252.

Hansen, Thomas Blom. (2001b). *Wages of Violence: Naming and Identity in Postcolonial Bombay.* Princeton: Princeton University Press.

Jayal, Niraja G. (2006). *Representing India: Ethnic Diversity and the Governance of Public Institutions.* New York: Palgrave Macmillan.

Jenkins, Rob (2002). 'The Emergence of the Governance Agenda: Sovereignty, Neo-liberal Bias and the Politics of International Development'. In: Robert Potter and Vandana Desai (eds). *The Companion to Development Studies,* London: Hodder, pp. 516–519.

Jenkins, Rob (2007a). 'Civil Society Versus Corruption'. *Journal of Democracy* 18(2): 55–69.

Jenkins, Rob (2007b). The Politics of India's Special Economic Zones. Paper presented at the research colloquium on 'India's Great Transformation?' at Columbia University, 14–16 September.

Kothari, Smitu (2005). 'Women Displaced: Democracy, Development, and Identity in India'. In: Wendy Harcourt and Arturo Escobar (eds). *Women and the Politics of Place,* Bloomfield, CT: Kumarian Press, pp. 115–129.

Ong, Aihwa (2006). *Neoliberalism as Exception: Mutations in Citizenship and Sovereignty.* Durham: Duke University Press.

Planning Commission (2011). 'Faster, Sustainable and More Inclusive Growth'. New Delhi: Government of India.

Posco Pratirodh Solidarity (2011). 'Central Government: Stop Playing Games with People's Lives'. Petition. 8 February.

Saldanha, M. (2008). 'Why Goa Does Not Need SEZs'. *The Hindu.* 23 January.

Sampat, Preeti (2015). 'The "Goan Impasse": Land Rights and Resistance to SEZs in Goa, India'. *Journal of Peasant Studies* 42(3/4): 1–26.

SEZ Virodhi Manch. (2007). 'SEZ Location Considerations: SEZ Virodhi Manch'. Internal Paper.

Index

Page numbers in *italics* denote tables, those in **bold** denote figures.